Strategies for Writers

Level **D**

Authors

Leslie W. Crawford, Ed.D.
Georgia College & State University

Rebecca Bowers Sipe, Ed.D.
Eastern Michigan University

Zaner-Bloser

Table of Contents

NARRATIVE writing

DESCRIPTIVE writing

Table of Contents

EXPOSITORY writing

PERSUASIVE writing

NARRATIVE writing tells a story about real or imaginary events.

Hi, my name is Jack. I'm learning all about narrative writing. I love telling stories to my friends! I also like listening to my grandfather tell me stories about when he was growing up. Now, I'm going to learn strategies for turning stories into good pieces of writing.

IN THIS UNIT

1. **Personal Narrative**
2. **Biographic Sketch**
3. **Adventure Story**
4. **Writing for a Test**

Name: Jack

Home: Washington

Favorite Sports: soccer and hockey

Favorite Book: *S.O.R. Losers* by Avi

What's a Personal Narrative?

It's a story I write about me!

What's in a Personal Narrative?

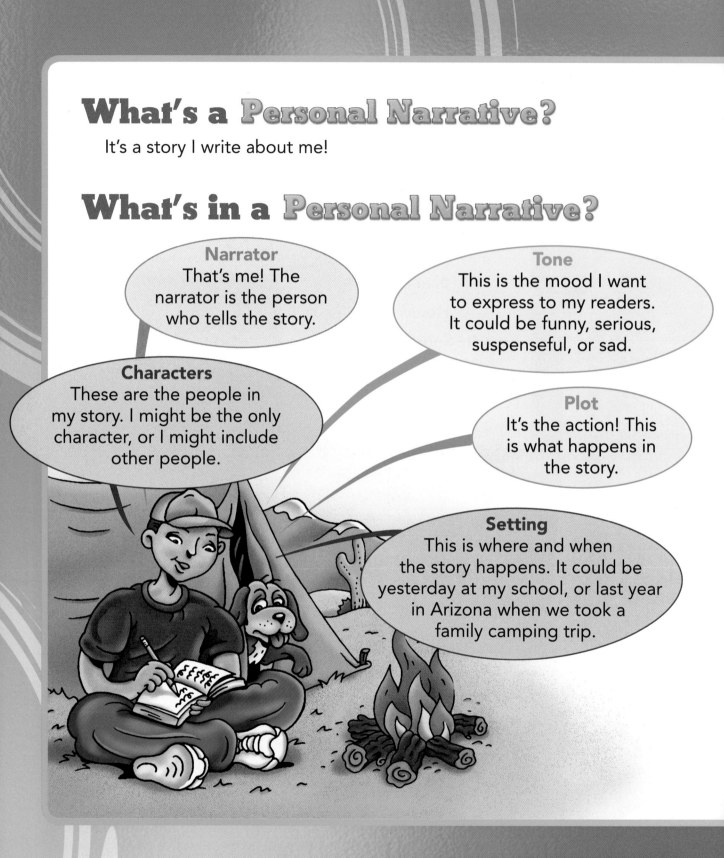

Narrator
That's me! The narrator is the person who tells the story.

Tone
This is the mood I want to express to my readers. It could be funny, serious, suspenseful, or sad.

Characters
These are the people in my story. I might be the only character, or I might include other people.

Plot
It's the action! This is what happens in the story.

Setting
This is where and when the story happens. It could be yesterday at my school, or last year in Arizona when we took a family camping trip.

Why write a Personal Narrative?

There are plenty of reasons for writing a personal narrative. Here are some that I thought of.

Entertainment
Sometimes, something happens that is so exciting that I just have to share it with someone else. It's such a good story that my reader will be really entertained.

Personal Reflection
Sometimes, writing a personal narrative can help me think about things in my life from a different perspective.

Information
Some events can be really informative. I can write a personal narrative about something that happened to me. I can share the information about what I've learned.

Personal Narrative
Writing Traits

What makes a good personal narrative? A personal narrative should always have a clear beginning, middle, and end. You should use the words **I** or **we** to tell the story. Here are some traits to use when you write your own personal narrative.

Information/ Organization	The story focuses on one interesting event. Events follow each other in order.
Voice/ Audience	The writer's voice connects with the audience.
Content/ Ideas	Details make the story interesting.
Word Choice/ Clarity	The language is clear and specific.
Sentence Fluency	Sentence variety makes the story flow.
Grammar/ Mechanics	Spelling, punctuation, and capitalization are correct. There are no sentence fragments.

Let's read Stephen Jensen's personal narrative on the next page. Did he follow all of the writing traits?

MY LEAP FOR LOONS

by Stephen Jensen

first person narrator

I'm not the outdoors type. Every time my sister Jennifer invited me to go on a canoe trip, I tried my best to get out of it. "I'm busy that weekend," I would say. Jennifer didn't give up, though. One day, I just gave in.

beginning

A few weeks later, Jennifer and I were floating on a lake in northern Minnesota. As our paddles cut through clean waters, we pushed past green wooded land. We never saw other people. Jennifer went wild every time she saw deer or moose drinking at the shore. One day, we heard a *whoosh* and saw an eagle swoop down to grab a fish. My sister got so excited, I thought she was going to fall out of the boat.

characters

setting

middle

"Wow," I'd say, but I didn't really care. I was counting the hours until we'd pack up the car and drive home. While Jennifer went on and on about moose, I thought about a hot shower followed by a movie.

plot

On our last day, however, even I got excited. We heard a high-pitched wailing sound. Jennifer said "ah" softly, smiled at me, and pointed across the lake. I saw the shadow of a bird gliding slowly over the water. Then we heard a reply. It was coming from right next to our campsite.

tone

In the fading light of day, I spotted my first loon. I couldn't take my eyes off this beautiful creature, whose wail and laugh I would hear in my mind ever after. Before nightfall, we saw many loons. Their backs were delicately etched with a checkered pattern, but their bills were shaped like daggers. Their eyes glowed a spooky red.

These amazing birds dive deep, and they can swim long distances under water. Just when I thought one had disappeared forever, it popped up halfway across the lake!

end

I can't say I went totally loony for loons. However, when we were driving home, I found myself thinking more about those loons than about a shower or a movie.

Personal Narrative Rubric

The traits of a good personal narrative from page 10 were used to make the rubric below. By assigning 1, 2, 3, or 4 stars to each trait, you can decide how well any personal narrative was written.

	Excelling	Achieving	Developing	Beginning
Information/ Organization	The story focuses on one event. Events follow each other in order.	The story focuses on one event most of the time. Most events are in order.	The story sometimes goes off focus. Some events are in order.	The story does not focus on one event. The events are not in order.
Voice/ Audience	The writer's voice always connects with the audience.	The writer's voice connects with the audience most of the time.	The writer's voice sometimes connects with the audience.	The writer's voice almost never connects with the audience.
Content/ Ideas	The story has many interesting details.	There are enough interesting details to keep the reader engaged.	There are some interesting details in the story.	There are very few interesting details.
Word Choice/ Clarity	There are many clear and specific words.	There are some clear and specific words.	There are a few clear and specific words.	Clear and specific words are needed.
Sentence Fluency	A great variety of sentences makes the whole story flow well.	A variety of sentences makes most of the story flow.	A variety of sentences makes some of the story flow.	A variety of sentences is needed to make the story flow.
Grammar/ Mechanics	There are no spelling and grammar errors, and no sentence fragments.	There are almost no spelling and grammar errors or sentence fragments.	There are a few spelling and grammar errors and a few sentence fragments.	There are many spelling and grammar errors and sentence fragments.

Using the Rubric to Study the Model

Personal Narrative

Now, let's use the rubric to check Stephen Jensen's personal narrative, "My Leap for Loons." What score would you give Stephen for each category in the rubric?

Information/ Organization

- **The story focuses on one interesting event.**
- **Events follow each other in order.**

I didn't know anything about loons before I read this story, so I found his trip really interesting! He also tells everything in order, starting with his sister's invitation and going through the last day, so it's really easy to follow the story. Read what he wrote about the last day.

On our last day, however, even I got excited. We heard a high-pitched wailing sound. Jennifer said "ah" softly, smiled at me and pointed across the lake.

Voice/ Audience

- **The writer's voice connects with the audience.**

Reading the story, I felt as if the writer were talking directly to me. He sounds a lot like my best friend—it often takes a lot of persuading to get him to try new things, too! The author drew me into the story and made me want to keep reading to find out what would happen next. Read the beginning of his narrative.

I'm not the outdoors type. Every time my sister Jennifer invited me to go on a canoe trip, I tried my best to get out of it.

Content/Ideas

• Details make the story interesting.

All of the interesting details helped me picture the writer's canoe trip. He painted a vivid picture of his experience by describing how he **cut through clean waters** and **pushed past green wooded land**.

As our paddles cut through clean waters, we pushed past green wooded land. We never saw other people. Jennifer went wild every time she saw a deer or moose drinking at the shore.

Word Choice/Clarity

• The language is clear and specific.

When Stephen described the loons, he used very clear and specific words. Even though I'd never seen a loon before, I was able to picture one. Phrases such as **checkered pattern** and **shaped like daggers** gave me a clear picture.

Their backs were delicately etched with a checkered pattern, but their bills were shaped like daggers.

Using the Rubric to Study the Model

Personal Narrative

Sentence Fluency

• Sentence variety makes the story flow.

Stephen used a lot of different kinds of sentences in his personal narrative. For example, some sentences are longer and some are shorter. This helps the story flow smoothly.

In the fading light of day, I spotted my first loon. I couldn't take my eyes off this beautiful creature, whose wail and laugh I would hear in my mind ever after. Before nightfall, we saw many loons.

Grammar/ Mechanics

• Spelling, punctuation, and capitalization are correct. There are no sentence fragments.

I looked through the whole story, and every word is spelled correctly. All the sentences are capitalized and punctuated correctly. Every sentence is complete, and there are no sentence fragments.

These amazing birds dive deep, and they can swim long distances under water. Just when I thought one had disappeared forever, it popped up halfway across the lake!

Now it's my turn to write a personal narrative! I'll use the rubric and good writing strategies to help me. Follow along to see how I do it.

Prewriting Gather Information

Information/Organization

The story focuses on one interesting event.

Writing Strategy Make notes about an interesting personal experience.

My teacher said we could write about any experience that we think the rest of the class will find interesting.

I think I'll write about the day the Saddok family moved in next door to us. Many of my classmates live in big apartment buildings like mine. I'm sure they have neighbors from other countries, too. They'll probably be interested in my experience. First, I'll jot down some notes on what I remember about that day.

My Notes

✔ Mrs. Saddok did not want to shake Dad's hand.

✔ Mr. Saddok put his right hand over his heart.

✔ No one said anything.

✔ We helped pick up everything.

✔ It all started with a big noise.

Practice!

Think about interesting events in your life. Brainstorm some ideas and pick one event you think will be the most interesting. Jot down some notes about the event.

Prewriting Organize Ideas

Information/Organization
Events follow each other in order.

Writing Strategy Make a Sequence Chain to organize my notes.

The rubric says the events in my story need to follow each other in order. I'll use a graphic organizer to put my notes in order. I've used graphic organizers before, and I think a Sequence Chain would be the best one for ordering my notes this time. A Sequence Chain helps me to place the events first, second, third, and so on.

Writer's Term

Sequence Chain
A **Sequence Chain** organizes events in the order in which they happen.

Sequence Chain

The Day We Met Our New Neighbors

First Event	There was a loud noise outside our door.
Second Event	We said hello and offered to help. Nobody said a word to us.
Third Event	Dad told his name and wanted to shake hands with the new neighbors.
Fourth Event	We started picking up all the things. We helped a lot.

Practice!
Look at the notes you took. Choose notes that tell about the events. Make a Sequence Chain to organize the events.

Think About It
Look at my notes and my Sequence Chain. Will they help me write a good story?

Drafting **Write a Draft**

The writer's voice connects with the audience.

Writing Strategy Use the first person point of view to connect with my audience.

Writer's Term

First Person Point of View

Point of view tells the reader who is telling the story. In a personal narrative, the point of view is **first person** because the writer is telling his or her own story. Writers using the **first person point of view** use words such as **I, me, my, mine, we, us, our,** and **ours** to tell their story.

Now it's time to start writing. I'll use my Sequence Chain to write a draft. I have to remember that a personal narrative is my own story. My audience needs to know that I'm actually in the story. This means I will use the words **I** and **we** as I tell the story.

According to the rubric, I also need to remember to use voice to connect with my audience. I need to write in a way that will help my readers relate to my story. I love listening to my grandpa's stories. I always feel as if I am right there as the story is happening. I will try to make my readers feel the same way as they read my story.

As I write, I'll do my best with grammar and spelling, but I won't worry about mistakes. I'll have a chance to fix them later.

[DRAFT]

The Day We Met Our New Neighbors

Noise outside our door. My dad ran out, and I

followed him.

> first person point of view

In the hallway were for strangers. The woman

wore cloths I'd never seen before. The rest of the

family wore unusual cloths too.

Dad said, "Hi, do you need help?" Not a word!

They just looked at us

Dad held out his hand to the man Dad said, "Hi, I'm

Ken Washington, and I live here." The man took Dad's

hand. He shook it a little. Didn't say a word. My dad

held out his hand to the woman. Turned away.

We could see that a big wooden box had split

open. We helped pick up everything.

Practice!

Use your Sequence Chain to write your own draft. Don't forget to use the first person point of view as you write.

Think About It

Read my draft. Did I use the first person point of view?

Revising Extend Writing

Content/Ideas

Details make the story interesting.

Writing Strategy Add interesting details.

After I finished my draft, I looked back at the rubric. It says that a writer should use details to make the story interesting. Which parts of my story could be improved if I added details? I think I'll add details about the noise I heard. I will also describe Mrs. Saddok's clothes.

Writer's Term

Details

Details are words or phrases that give more information about a person or event. Details make writing more interesting.

[DRAFT]

A loud crashing

Noise outside our door. My dad ran out, and I

followed him.

In the hallway were for strangers. The woman

She was covered from head to toe in brightly colored cloth.

wore cloths I'd never seen before. The rest of the

added interesting details

family wore unusual cloths too.

Practice!

Read your draft. Look for places to add details that will interest your reader. Add these details to your draft.

Revising Clarify Writing

Word Choice/ Clarity
The language is clear and specific.

Writing Strategy Use clear and specific words to tell the story.

The rubric says to use clear and specific language to tell my story. I'll read through my draft again. Then I'll add more specific words if something is unclear. Look at the section below to see how I fixed one part of my story.

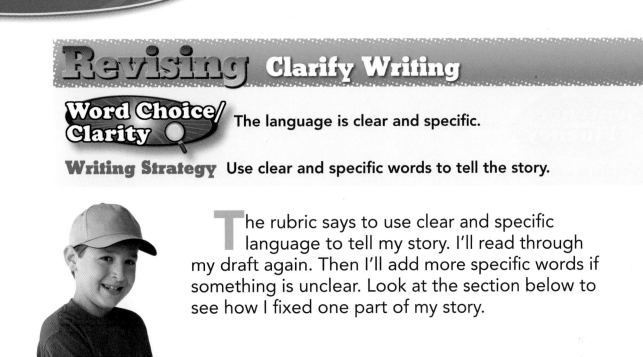

[DRAFT]

specific words

trunk

We could see that a big wooden ~~box~~ had split

That was the loud crashing noise we heard.   the books

open. We helped pick up ~~everything~~ that had spilled out.

clear words

Practice!
Read your draft again. Look for parts that aren't clear. Use clear and specific words to make your writing clearer.

Think About It
Look at my revisions. Did I add interesting details and use clear and specific words?

Editing Check Sentences

Sentence Fluency Sentence variety makes the writing flow.

Writing Strategy Use different types of sentences to help the writing flow.

Now I have to edit my writing. The rubric says that I should use a variety of sentences to help my writing flow. I read through my draft and saw that I used too many simple sentences. Look at how I fixed the problem.

Writer's Term

Sentence Types

Simple sentences have a **subject** and a **predicate**.
Example: He lifted the box.

Compound sentences have **two independent clauses,** which are connected with a **punctuation mark** and a **conjunction,** or a **semicolon**.
Example: Ella was a new student, but she quickly made friends.

added punctuation mark

added conjunction

[DRAFT]

simple sentence

Ken Washington, and I live here." The man took Dad's

, but

hand. He shook it a little. Didn't say a word. My dad

shook the man's hand, and then he

held out his hand to the woman.

made a compound sentence

Practice!

Look for simple and compound sentences in your draft. Make sure your draft has a variety of sentence types.

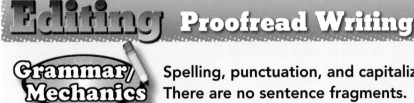

Grammar/ Mechanics Spelling, punctuation, and capitalization are correct. There are no sentence fragments.

Writing Strategy Make sure there are no sentence fragments.

Next I'll check my spelling, punctuation, and capitalization. Also, the rubric reminds me to check for sentence fragments. A sentence fragment is an incomplete thought. A subject or a predicate is missing. I'll fix any sentence fragments I find.

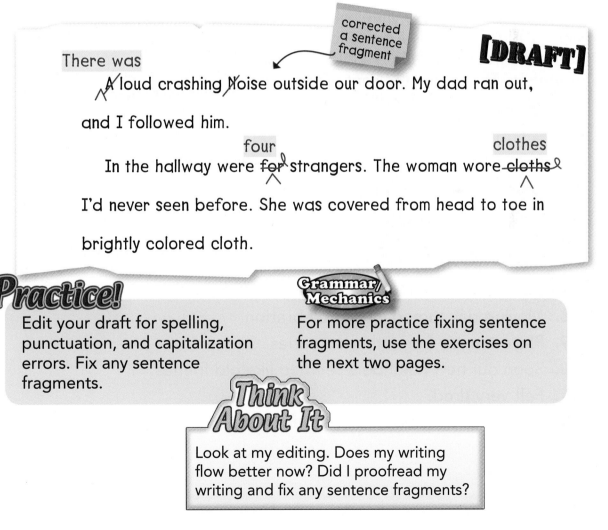

corrected a sentence fragment

[DRAFT]

There was
~~A~~ loud crashing ~~Noise~~ noise outside our door. My dad ran out,

and I followed him.

four   clothes
In the hallway were ~~for~~ strangers. The woman wore ~~cloths~~

I'd never seen before. She was covered from head to toe in

brightly colored cloth.

Practice!

Edit your draft for spelling, punctuation, and capitalization errors. Fix any sentence fragments.

Grammar/ Mechanics

For more practice fixing sentence fragments, use the exercises on the next two pages.

Think About It

Look at my editing. Does my writing flow better now? Did I proofread my writing and fix any sentence fragments?

Sentence Fragments

Know the Rule

A sentence tells a complete thought. A sentence needs a subject (what the sentence is about) and a predicate (what the subject does).
Example: I love living in the new apartment.
A **sentence fragment** is a group of words that is missing a subject, a predicate, or both.
Example: Living in the new apartment.

Practice the Rule

Number a separate sheet of paper 1.–12. Read each group of words. If the group is a sentence, write **Correct**. If the group is a sentence fragment, add a subject or a predicate to make it a sentence. Then write the sentence correctly.

1. My new neighbors in the next apartment.
2. A huge truck began to unload boxes.
3. Looked out the window at the people outside.
4. Several men carried tables and chairs up the stairs.
5. Rested and ate their lunch under a tree.
6. Everyone came out and welcomed them to the neighborhood.
7. Cookies and lemonade.
8. Moving day turned into a celebration.
9. Played music from other countries.
10. Soon our new neighbors seemed like old friends.
11. Felt very tired.
12. Moving days can be very busy for the people moving in.

Apply the Rule

Read the following paragraphs. Find any sentence fragments and rewrite the paragraphs.

Saturday was a day I'll never forget, but I wish I could. The hottest day of the year. I wanted to go the park. Play with my friends. The swings. Swim in the pool. But our neighbors needed my help.

I had to help our neighbors pack and move, or they would never get the job done. Leaving for California tomorrow. The house was filled with boxes and packing tape. Big job! I thought the work could take all day. Never go to the pool.

I started work in the playroom. There were books and toys everywhere. Sweat poured down my face, but I kept working. Books in boxes. Toys in boxes. I was careful to put things away carefully. I didn't want anything to break. Wrapped up dolls.

Publishing Share Writing

Publish on a class bulletin board.

My personal narrative is done! Now, it's time to publish it. There are all kinds of ways to publish a story. I could turn my story into a book, send it to the school newspaper, or read it aloud to my class. I think I'll post my story on the class bulletin board. That way, anyone in my class who is interested in my story will have a chance to read it. Before posting my story on the bulletin board, I read through it one last time. Here's my final checklist.

My Checklist

✔ The title of my story and my name are at the top of the page.

✔ All events are in the correct order.

✔ There are lots of interesting details.

✔ Everything is described clearly. Nothing important is left out.

✔ Spelling, grammar, and punctuation are all correct. There are no sentence fragments.

✔ My handwriting is neat.

Practice!

Make your own checklist. Then, make a final draft to post on your class bulletin board. You can make a colorful border for your story from construction paper.

The Day We Met Our New Neighbors
by Jack

There was a loud crashing noise outside our door. My dad ran out, and I followed him.

In the hallway were four strangers. The woman wore clothes I'd never seen before. She was covered from head to toe in brightly colored cloth. The rest of the family wore unusual clothes, too.

Dad said, "Hi, do you need help?" Nobody said a word! They just looked at us as if we were from another planet! Dad held out his hand to the man. Dad said, "Hi, I'm Ken Washington, and I live here." The man took Dad's hand. He shook it a little but didn't say a word. My dad shook the man's hand, and then he held out his hand to the woman. She turned away.

We could see that a big wooden trunk had split open. That was the loud crashing noise we had heard. We helped pick up the books that had spilled out. Then Dad and I helped the family with the rest of the suitcases and trunks. Soon we knew they didn't speak English.

At the end of the day, Mr. Saddok put his right hand over his heart, and then he nodded to us all. Later, we learned that the Saddoks were from Algeria. That was their Algerian way to say a sincere thank you.

Think About It

Use the rubric to check my story. Are all the traits of a good personal narrative there? Don't forget to check your own story against the rubric.

Ways to Publish a Personal Narrative

As you decide how to publish your work, make sure you think about who will be reading it. Then pick the best way to share it. Here are some ideas for publishing your personal narrative.

✓ **Read your personal narrative to a younger student. Then have the student tell you what the story was about.**

✓ **Post your story in the school library.**

✓ **Send your personal narrative to a magazine that publishes student work.**

✓ **Videotape yourself reading the story and take the video home to share with your family.**

✓ **Add your story to the class or school Web site.**

Writing Across the Content Areas
Personal Narrative

The subjects you study in school can give you many ideas to write stories about. Just pick a subject, and before you know it, you'll think of a topic that relates to it. Here are some examples.

Math

- Write about the first time you ever got money for doing a job or chore.
- Write about a day when you learned how to do a math problem.

Language Arts

- Tell about a game you played or would like to play.
- Write about a place in the city or country that you like to visit.

Art and/or Music

- Tell about a time you made a picture or greeting card for someone.
- Write about a music class you enjoyed.

What's a Biographic Sketch?

It's a story written in third person that tells something important about someone else.

What's in a Biographic Sketch?

Basic Facts
Facts are important pieces of information, such as the person's first and last name, where he or she lives, and specific events that helped the person to become who he or she is.

Characteristics
These are the special qualities that the person has, such as courage, determination, concern for others, or talents.

Accomplishments
This is what the person has achieved. It could be winning at sports, finding success as an artist, helping others, or discovering something new.

Interesting Details
These are interesting facts about the person, such as favorite activities, how the person feels about what he or she does, and any challenges the person has faced.

Why write a Biographic Sketch?

People write biographic sketches for a lot of different reasons. Here are just three that I thought of.

Inspiration
Some people do really cool things that I might like to do, too. It's interesting to learn how they got started, who helped them, and how they got to be successful.

Admiration
I may not want to do what other people have done, but I can look up to them. I might want to do a biographic sketch of a person who I think is special in some way.

Information
I can learn all kinds of things by finding out about another person. I might find out what it feels like to come here from another country or how someone makes music with a computer. Finding out about other people can lead to fascinating discoveries.

Biographic Sketch
Writing Traits

What makes a good biographic sketch? A biographic sketch should always tell important events in a person's life and when they happened. Include information that shows that the person is special in some way. Here are traits of a good biographic sketch.

Information/ Organization	The sketch tells important events in a person's life. It tells when these events happened and shows why they are important.
Voice/ Audience	The sketch convinces the audience that this person is special in some way.
Content/ Ideas	The sketch includes interesting information about the person, such as characteristics, talents, challenges, and accomplishments.
Word Choice/ Clarity	The sketch has time-order words that make the order of events clear.
Sentence Fluency	Sentences vary in length, giving flow to the writing.
Grammar/ Mechanics	Spelling, punctuation, and capitalization are correct. Subjects and verbs agree.

Let's read Bob Gadski's biographic sketch about a man whose job is listening. Did Bob follow all the writing traits?

Listening for a Living

by Bob Gadski

third person point of view

Tim Farley should be called Ears Farley. That's because he listens all day long. In fact, he listens for a living.

Mr. Farley works in a city called Sprintfield. Like many cities, Sprintfield has a lot of noise. Several years ago, in 2003, Mr. Farley saw an ad for a job as a "noise detective." Right away, he decided it was the job for him.

basic facts

the important event

First, he went for an interview. He learned the purpose of the job. It was to measure and record exactly how much noise was coming from different places in the city. He would go all around Sprintfield with a sound meter, a little machine that measured decibel levels. Decibels are units that measure sound.

Mr. Farley got the job. During the spring of 2004, he worked along the freeway and on other roads. First, he gathered information. Later, he focused on sounds above 60 decibels. These sounds are really loud! In fact, they are louder than in most places in the United States.

time-order words

an accomplishment

After Mr. Farley had been working for a few months, he had a lot of information. By fall of 2004, he knew the city's major sources of noise. The worst source was the sound of car and truck traffic. The second major source was the sound of trains. The third major source was the sound of commercial and industrial activities. Soon, Mr. Farley's job included finding out how to solve the noise problems.

Mr. Farley loved to solve problems. But he learned that some problems were not so easy to solve. In 2005, he recommended that the city put up walls to help block noise. The high walls were ugly. In 2006, he recommended that the city also plant trees and shrubs. These were attractive, but they did not block noise very well.

accomplishments

challenges

Mr. Farley keeps listening and looking for the answers to the city's noise problems. When it comes to his job, he is definitely "all ears."

characteristics

talent

Biographic Sketch Rubric

The rubric below was made from the traits of a good biographic sketch from page 32. Using a rubric can help you figure out how successful a piece of writing is. Use this rubric to decide if a biographic sketch gets 1, 2, 3, or 4 stars for each of the traits.

	Excelling	Achieving	Developing	Beginning
Information/ Organization	The sketch tells important events in the person's life, when they happened, and why they are important.	The sketch focuses on important events most of the time. It usually tells when they happened and why they are important.	The sketch tells a few important events and when they happened. It tells when they happened or why they are important sometimes.	The sketch does not tell important events or when they happened.
Voice/ Audience	The sketch convinces the audience that this person is very special.	Most of the sketch shows how the person is special.	Some of the sketch shows how the person is special.	The sketch begins to show how the person is special.
Content/ Ideas	Information about the person is interesting and complete. It makes the person seem real.	Most of the information about the person is interesting. The sketch seems mostly complete.	Some of the information is interesting, but some important information is missing.	There is little interesting or important information about the person.
Word Choice/ Clarity	Time-order words make the order of all events in the person's life clear.	Time-order words are used most of the time to make the order of events clear.	Time-order words are used some of the time, but the order of other events is unclear.	Time-order words are rarely used. The order in which events took place is confusing.
Sentence Fluency	Sentences vary in length. The writing flows well.	Sentences vary. The writing flows well most of the time.	The writing flows well sometimes.	The writing needs variety in sentence length to keep it flowing.
Grammar/ Mechanics	Spelling, punctuation, and capitalization are correct. All subjects and verbs agree.	Spelling, punctuation, and capitalization are mostly correct. Most subjects and verbs agree.	There are some spelling, punctuation, or capitalization errors. Some subjects and verbs agree.	There are many spelling, punctuation, or capitalization errors. Few subjects and verbs agree.

Using the Rubric to Study the Model

Biographic Sketch

Now, let's use the rubric to check Bob Gadski's biographic sketch, "Listening for a Living." What score would you give Bob for each category in the rubric?

Information/Organization

- **The sketch tells important events in the person's life.**
- **It tells when they happened and why they are important.**

The writer tells all about the important events and when they happened. He begins by telling about an interesting person, Mr. Tim Farley, and his job. Then he tells the first important event and the time it happened.

Several years ago, in 2003, Mr. Farley saw an ad for a job as a "noise detective." Right away, he decided it was the job for him.

First, he went for an interview.

Voice/Audience

- **The sketch convinces the audience that this person is special in some way.**

Right away, the writer makes the audience see how Tim Farley is special. In his opening paragraph, he entertains the reader while he gives information about Tim Farley.

Tim Farley should be called Ears Farley. That's because he listens all day long. In fact, he listens for a living.

Content/Ideas

- The sketch includes interesting information about the person, such as characteristics, challenges, and accomplishments.

The writer tells many things about Mr. Farley. He makes Mr. Farley's job sound exciting and interesting. I can imagine Mr. Farley doing his work. I get to know what Mr. Farley is like.

Mr. Farley loved to solve problems. But he learned that some problems were not so easy to solve. In 2005, he recommended that the city put up walls to help block noise. The high walls were ugly. In 2006, he recommended that the city also plant trees and shrubs.

Word Choice/Clarity

- The sketch has time-order words that make the order of events clear.

The writer uses time-order words to signal when things happen. I noticed the time-order words **during, first,** and **later** in this example.

During the spring of 2004, he worked along the freeway and on other roads. First, he gathered information. Later, he focused on sounds above 60 decibels.

Using the Rubric to Study the Model

Biographic Sketch

Sentence Fluency

• Sentences vary in length, giving flow to the writing.

Bob used lots of different kinds of sentences in his biographic sketch. For example, some sentences are longer and some are shorter. Usually, long and short sentences follow each other. This helps the story flow smoothly. It makes the biographic sketch easy to read, too.

First, he went for an interview. He learned the purpose of the job. It was to measure and record exactly how much noise was coming from different places in the city.

Grammar/Mechanics

• Spelling, punctuation, and capitalization are correct. Subjects and verbs agree.

All the subjects and verbs agree in number. Singular subjects have singular verbs, and plural subjects have plural verbs. In these sentences, the subject, **source,** is singular, so the verb, **was,** is also singular.

The worst source was the sound of car and truck traffic. The second major source was the sound of trains. The third major source was the sound of the commercial and industrial activities.

My Turn!

Now it's my turn to write a biographic sketch! I'll use the rubric and good writing strategies to help me. Read along to see how I do it.

Prewriting Gather Information

Information/Organization

The sketch tells important events in the person's life.

Writing Strategy Make a list of interesting questions for an interview.

My mom has a little stone bear carved by an Inuit artist. I have always wondered about the person who made it.

When my teacher asked us to write a biographic sketch, I decided to write about the Inuit artist who made that stone bear. I knew I had to gather information, so I sent the artist an e-mail with interview questions. This will help me get information about his work and give me more than just simple details like his name.

Writer's Term

Interview

An **interview** is the process of asking questions of another person and listening to and recording that person's answers.

Questions for My Interview

✔ What kinds of objects do you make?

✔ Why do you like to carve?

✔ When did you first start to carve in stone?

✔ How did you learn to carve?

✔ What skills do you need to be a stone carver?

Practice!

Think about a person you would like to write about. List interesting questions you could ask. Then, interview the person.

Prewriting Organize Ideas

Information/Organization The sketch tells when events happened and shows why they are important.

Writing Strategy Make a Timeline to organize the important events.

I know from the rubric that organization is important. I want to find a good order for my biographic sketch. During the interview, Mr. Aniksak, the artist, told me when the main events of his life happened and why they are important. If I put the events in the order in which he experienced them, my paper will make sense to the reader. I can put these events on a Timeline to help me stay organized.

> ✏️ **Writer's Term**
> ## Timeline
> A **Timeline** is a graph that shows events in the order in which they happened. A Timeline also shows dates.

Timeline

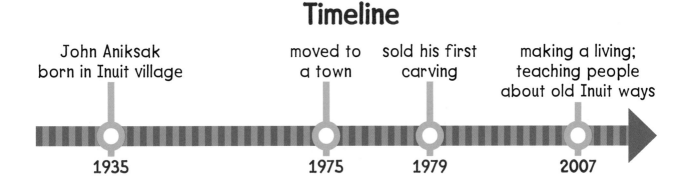

John Aniksak born in Inuit village — 1935

moved to a town — 1975

sold his first carving — 1979

making a living; teaching people about old Inuit ways — 2007

Practice!

Look at the notes from the interview you did. Identify the important events. Put the events on a Timeline to organize your biographic sketch.

Think About It

Look at my questions and Timeline. Do I have enough information? Do I need to ask some more interview questions?

Drafting Write a Draft

Voice/Audience The sketch convinces the audience that this person is special in some way.

Writing Strategy Use the third person point of view to set the tone.

Writer's Term

Third Person Point of View

Writers use **third person point of view** to tell about the experiences of others and to show that they are not part of the story. For **third person,** we use the person's name and words such as **he, she, him, her, his, hers, they,** and **theirs**.

Now it's time to tell the whole story. I will use the answers that Mr. Aniksak e-mailed back and my Timeline to write a draft. I am going to use my Timeline to make sure I include all the important events and when they happened. The rubric says I need to convince my readers that my subject is special. So, I will use events from Mr. Aniksak's life to show why he is a special artist. My writing will be in third person so I will refer to the artist by his name and with the words **he, his,** and **him**.

Right now, I'm not going to worry about writing in complete sentences or whether everything I write is spelled perfectly. I know I'll have a chance to fix grammar and spelling mistakes later.

Carving Art from Stone

third person point of view

John Aniksak carves stone bears, dear, seals, and other animals. He was not always a stone carver, though. Mr. Aniksak was born in an Inuit village in 1935. A very different kind of life. You would be surprised. He lived very far from roads, stores, and factorys. In 1975, Mr. Aniksak moved to a town. He had to get use to a new way of life. He need a new way to earn a living. He took up carving. He found and chose stone. He learn about carving tools. He is also able to use many skills from his days in the wilderness. His knowledge of artic animals were especially importent. Mr. Aniksak learn his new skill well. In 1979, he sold his first carving, a seal. likes his animals. He sell many pieces. People all over the country buy his carvings now.

Today, he still loves his work. He makes his living by it and he also uses his carved animals to teach people about the old Inuit way of life.

Practice!

Use your interview notes and Timeline to write your own draft. Remember to write in third person.

Think About It

Are the events in my draft clear? Did I use third person point of view to set the tone?

Revising Extend Writing

Content/Ideas The sketch includes interesting information about the person, such as characteristics, talents, challenges, and accomplishments.

Writing Strategy Add interesting information about the person.

After I finished my draft, I looked back at the rubric for writing a biographic sketch. The rubric says that I should include interesting information about the person. I should make sure my sketch tells about the person's talents and accomplishments. So I am wondering where I could add more interesting information about Mr. Aniksak. I know! I can tell more about his culture. Mr. Aniksak told me about how he and his family lived. I'll include this information to make my biographic sketch more interesting.

[DRAFT]

added interesting information

His family hunted walrus and seal. They fished for salmon. They gathered roots and berrys. lived very far from roads, stores, and factorys.

Read your draft. Find other interesting information in your interview notes you can add to your biographic sketch.

Revising Clarify Writing

Word Choice/ Clarity
The sketch has time-order words that make the order of events clear.

Writing Strategy
Use time-order words to make the order of events clear.

This morning, I read my paper to my friend Ramon. He said that some parts were hard to follow.

I remembered that the rubric said that I should use time-order words to make the order of events clear. They will show when the events happened. I looked for places where I could add time-order words to make my writing clear.

Writer's Term
Time-order Words

Time-order words help tie ideas together. They show that the writing is moving from one idea to another. All time-order words tell **when** something happened.

Here are some time-order words:

**after   during   finally   first   later
soon   then   until   now**

[DRAFT]

added time-order words

lived very far from roads, stores, and factorys. In 1975, Mr. Aniksak

First,

moved to a town. He had to get use to a new way of life. He need a new

Soon

Then

way to earn a living. He took up carving. He found and chose stone. He

learn about carving tools.

Practice!

Read your draft again. Look for places where you can add time-order words to make your writing even clearer.

Think About It
Look at the time-order words I added. Did they make it easier to follow the events I described in my writing?

Editing   Check Sentences

Sentence Fluency   Sentences vary in length, giving flow to the writing.

Writing Strategy   Rewrite long, confusing sentences.

The next thing I need to do is edit my writing. The rubric says I shouldn't use all short or all long sentences. So, I need to go back to be sure there is variety in my sentences. Also, I'll check that my sentences are complete thoughts and that there are no sentence fragments in my writing.

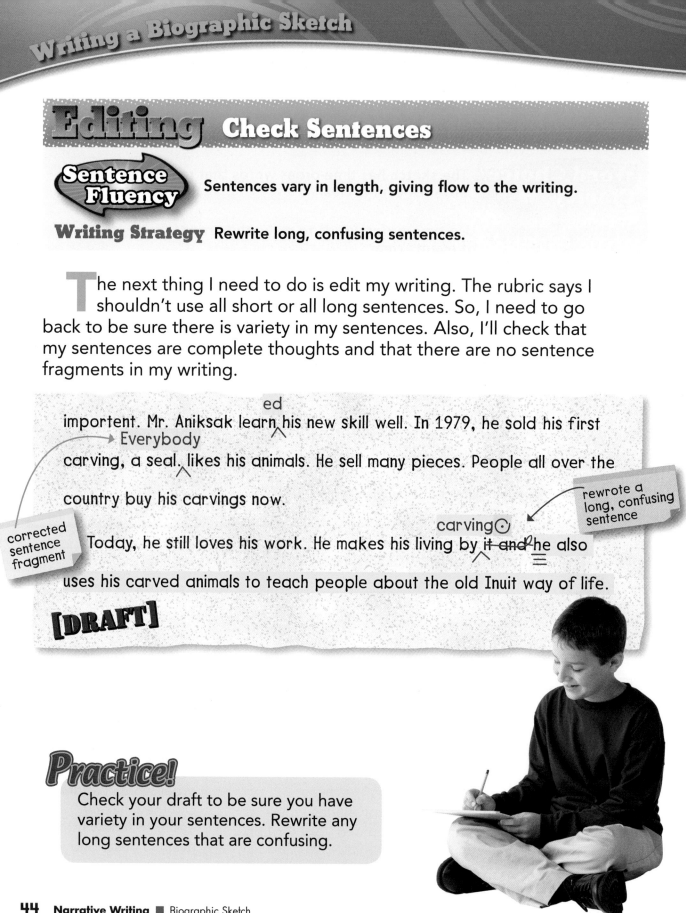

ed

important. Mr. Aniksak learn his new skill well. In 1979, he sold his first

→ Everybody

carving, a seal. likes his animals. He sell many pieces. People all over the

country buy his carvings now.

corrected sentence fragment

rewrote a long, confusing sentence

carving⊙

Today, he still loves his work. He makes his living by it and he also

uses his carved animals to teach people about the old Inuit way of life.

[DRAFT]

Practice!

Check your draft to be sure you have variety in your sentences. Rewrite any long sentences that are confusing.

Editing Proofread Writing

Grammar/Mechanics Spelling, punctuation, and capitalization are correct. Subjects and verbs agree.

Writing Strategy Make sure all subjects and verbs agree.

Now I need to check for errors. I know from the rubric that I always need to check spelling, capitalization, and punctuation. I'll also make sure that all my subjects and verbs agree.

Writer's Term

Subject-Verb Agreement

Subject-Verb Agreement means that subjects and verbs must agree in number. Singular nouns or pronouns take singular verbs, and plural nouns or pronouns take plural verbs. In the present tense, singular verbs often end in **-s** or **-es**.

corrected subject-verb agreement error

[DRAFT]

Everybody

carving, a seal. likes his animals. He ~~self~~ has sold many pieces. People all over the

Practice!

Reread your work to make sure that subjects and verbs agree.

Grammar/Mechanics

For more practice on subject-verb agreement, use the exercises on the next two pages.

Think About It

Look at the editing I did. What changes did I make? Why did I make them?

Subject-Verb Agreement

 Add **-s** or **-es** to a regular verb in the present tense when the subject is a singular noun or **he, she,** or **it**.
Examples: John throws the ball. She catches the ball.
Do not add **-s** or **-es** to a regular verb in the present tense when the subject is a plural noun or **I, you, we,** or **they**.
Examples: We watch the game. They take pictures.

Practice the Rule

Number a separate sheet of paper from 1.–12. Decide which verb in parentheses agrees with the subject. Then write the correct verb.

1. Historians (feel/feels) that art is an important part of history.
2. Civilizations (use/uses) art in many ways.
3. Early art forms (tell/tells) us much about the people who created them.
4. Art (remain/remains) an important part of any culture.
5. Artists sometimes (carve/carves) on cave walls and rocks.
6. They (learn/learns) to use certain tools.
7. Carvers must (know/knows) the final form they wish to create.
8. Carvers cannot (correct/corrects) a mistake.
9. Therefore, they always (make/makes) a small clay model first.
10. Some artists (do/does) all the stone cutting.
11. Many carvers (give/gives) the simple cutting jobs to an assistant.
12. The style of carving (change/changes) over time.

Apply the Rule

Read the following paragraphs. Find any errors in subject-verb agreement. Rewrite the paragraphs correctly on a separate piece of paper.

Wood furniture often contains carved designs. They appear on the arms and legs of chairs. Some craftspeople uses modern tools to carve these designs. Others relies on simple tools and their skills. Furniture makers may decorate a piece with materials such as shells or mother-of-pearl. Brightly colored paint cover the carvings in some early furniture. The style of carving change over time. Animal and plant carvings make furniture interesting. A table's legs sometimes look like a bird's feet. A carefully carved leaf appear on each corner. Plain furniture often needs colorful cushions to brighten a room. Carved furniture and colorful fabrics brightens a dull room.

Furniture makers often covers a common wood with a better wood. Oak tabletops may hides a pine board. Furniture makers calls this a veneer. Cabinetmakers uses this method frequently. This way, they makes more use of their best woods. Look closely at most modern furniture, and you will see a veneer. Some tables has a veneer of plastic that looks like wood.

Publishing Share Writing

Share your final paper in an author's circle.

I have finished my biographic sketch. Now I will publish it by sharing it with my class. My classmates will be interested in hearing the story of the artist. The author's circle will be a good way to publish this piece. Before I read my sketch to my classmates, I want to check it one more time against my checklist.

My Checklist

✔ The title of the sketch and my name are at the top of the paper.

✔ The important events of Mr. Aniksak's life are in time order.

✔ There are details that will interest my audience.

✔ A variety of sentences makes my writing flow.

✔ Spelling, grammar, and punctuation are correct. All subjects and verbs agree.

✔ My handwriting is easy to read.

Practice!

Make a checklist to check your biographic sketch. Then make a final draft to share in an author's circle.

Carving Art from Stone
by Jack

John Aniksak carves stone bears, deer, seals, and other animals. He was not always a stone carver, though.

Mr. Aniksak was born in an Inuit village in 1935. He and his family are from Canada. The Inuit people have lived in Canada for a very long time. It was a very different kind of life. You would be surprised. He lived very far from roads, stores, and factories. His family hunted walrus and seals. They fished for salmon. They gathered roots and berries.

In 1975, Mr. Aniksak moved to a town. He had to get used to a new way of life. First, he needed a new way to earn a living. Soon, he took up carving. He found and chose stone. Then, he learned about carving tools. Now he was also able to use many skills from his days in the wilderness. His knowledge of Arctic animals was especially important.

Mr. Aniksak learned his new skill well. In 1979, he sold his first carving, a seal. Everybody likes his animals. He has sold many pieces. People all over the country buy his carvings.

Today, he still loves his work. He makes his living by carving. He also uses his carved animals to teach people about the old Inuit way of life.

Think About It

Use the rubric to be sure I included all the traits of a good biographic sketch. Then use the rubric to check the sketch you wrote.

Ways to Publish a
Biographic Sketch

✓ Make a computer slide presentation with text and pictures. Illustrate your work with clip art or scanned photos. Give your presentation to a group of parents.

✓ Present a puppet show for younger children. Make a puppet that represents the person you wrote about.

✓ Start a book about local heroes with another classmate. Bind your sketches together with a cover. Take your book to a group of elderly citizens in an assisted-living home.

✓ Share your work in an author's circle. Show your enthusiasm by reading with expression in your voice and face.

CARVING ART FROM STONE by Jack

Writing Across the Content Areas
Biographic Sketch

The subjects we study in school are filled with many interesting people to write about. Here are some examples.

Science

- Write about someone you know who works in a science-related field such as medicine, gardening, or astronomy.
- Interview someone who loves to fix cars or lawn mowers. Find out what interests them about machines.

Social Studies

- Interview a grandparent—yours or someone else's—who has an interesting job or hobby, or who has traveled to faraway places.
- Choose a person from history that you admire. Write about people and events in his or her childhood that influenced who that person became.

Language Arts

- Write a letter to your favorite author. Ask him or her for an interview to help you write your biographic sketch.
- Interview a local storyteller. Find out how he or she became good at telling stories.

What's an Adventure Story?

It's a tale about a character who does something exciting. It can be something that really happened to someone, or it can be made up. Most adventure stories are fiction—invented by the author.

What's in an Adventure Story?

A Problem
The story is built around a problem or challenge that has to be faced. What happens around the problem is called the **plot**.

Setting
This is when and where the story happens. It could be last week at the soccer field or the other day at the park.

A Lead Character
This is the main person in the story. She or he must face dangers or take risks in order to solve the problem. The lead character may not look like a hero at first.

Dialogue
These are the conversations that characters in the story have. Dialogue should sound like how people talk in real life.

I'LL SAVE YOU!

Why write an Adventure Story?

People write adventure stories for different reasons. Here are some reasons that I thought of.

Entertainment
Adventure stories get you excited and involved. You can imagine yourself as the brave and daring hero. Both the author and the reader can enjoy solving difficult problems in an invented world. Sometimes heroes do things we would never do. This can make it fun and exciting to write about.

Understanding
Stories about heroes can help us understand others. We can learn how different people solve problems and how they find the courage to face danger.

Adventure Story
Writing Traits

What makes a good adventure story? An adventure story has a lead character who solves a problem or tries something new. The story tells about risks, excitement, and courage. Here are some traits of a good adventure story.

Information/ Organization	The story has a lead character who solves a problem. The story has a setting, action, and an ending.
Voice/ Audience	The story builds to a climax and makes the audience curious to find out what happens.
Content/ Ideas	The story has dialogue that makes the characters seem real.
Word Choice/ Clarity	The story is filled with suspense and excitement.
Sentence Fluency	The story has different kinds of sentences to add drama and keep the story moving.
Grammar/ Mechanics	Spelling, punctuation, and capitalization are correct. Direct quotations are punctuated correctly.

Let's read Becky Silver's adventure story on the next page. Then, we can check to see if she followed all the traits of a good adventure story.

The Unexpected Voyage

by Becky Silver

lead characters

"We never should have gone by ourselves," said Jeremy. "I'll bet we're lost."

"Don't worry," answered Samantha. "Our stop is probably next."

setting

The subway train stopped again. The doors opened. Passengers got off. New people came on. The train started up again.

dialogue

problem

"But it shouldn't take so long to get to the nature museum," said Jeremy. "When we go with Mom and Dad, it doesn't take long at all. If we don't get there soon, we're going to miss Dr. Forrest and his amazing change-of-seasons machine."

action

Jeremy looked out the window. By twisting a little, he could see where the train was headed. It seemed about to leave the dark underground. In a split second, the train broke into bright daylight. Two things happened at once. Samantha and Jeremy couldn't see for a few seconds because of the blinding sunlight, and the train conductor announced, "We will arrive in Brighton at 11 o'clock. No stops between here and Brighton."

climax

Brighton! Samantha and Jeremy looked at each other in disbelief. Brighton was miles and miles from where they lived. The nature museum was just a few city subway stops from home.

"I know!" yelled Jeremy. "We must have gotten on the train in the wrong direction! We should have been traveling south, and instead we've been going north!"

Jeremy thought he should be upset, but instead he felt like laughing. The train was speeding toward Brighton. He and Samantha looked out the window. They were going so fast that the sunny world seemed to change color as they moved. Trees that had been green now flamed red and gold. Acorns fell from branches and thudded against the train. Fluffy white clouds danced in an endless, brilliant blue sky.

end

"We can take the train back once we get to Brighton," said Jeremy.

"Meanwhile, we can watch the real change-of-seasons show from right here!" exclaimed Samantha.

Adventure Story Rubric

The rubric below was made using the traits of a good adventure story on page 54. Read your own adventure story or someone else's. Then, assign stars for each of the traits. Give a trait four stars if you think that trait is excellent! Give one or two stars if the trait still needs a lot of work.

	Excelling	Achieving	Developing	Beginning
Information/ Organization	The story has a setting, action, ending, and a lead character who solves a problem.	The story has a setting, action, ending, and a lead character.	The story is missing an element, such as a setting, action, ending, or lead character.	The story is missing many elements, such as a setting, action, ending, or lead character.
Voice/ Audience	The story keeps the reader curious to see what happens next, as it builds to a climax.	The reader stays curious most of the time, as the story builds to a climax.	The reader stays curious some of the time. The story needs to build to a climax more effectively.	The reader is rarely curious, and the story does not build to a climax.
Content/ Ideas	The story has convincing dialogue that makes the characters seem real.	The story has some dialogue that makes the characters seem real.	The story has a little dialogue to make the characters seem real.	The story needs dialogue to make the characters seem real.
Word Choice/ Clarity	The story is filled with suspense and excitement.	The story has some suspense and excitement.	The story has a little suspense and excitement.	The story needs suspense and excitement.
Sentence Fluency	Sentence variety adds drama and keeps the story moving.	Some sentence variety adds drama and helps move the story.	A little sentence variety moves the story along, but doesn't add drama.	The story lacks sentence variety to add drama and help the flow of the story.
Grammar/ Mechanics	There are no spelling or grammar errors. All direct quotations are punctuated correctly.	There are few spelling or grammar errors. Most direct quotations are punctuated correctly.	There are some spelling and grammar errors. Several direct quotations are not punctuated correctly.	There are many spelling and grammar errors. Many direct quotations are not punctuated correctly.

Using the Rubric to Study the Model

Adventure Story

We can use the rubric to check Becky Silver's adventure story, "The Unexpected Voyage." What score would you give Becky for each category in the rubric?

- **The story has a lead character who solves a problem.**
- **The story has a setting, action, and an ending.**

The beginning of the story sets up everything. I find out that the story has two main characters, Jeremy and Samantha, and that the setting is a subway train. Later on, I find out the problem. The subway train is not taking Jeremy and Samantha to the nature museum. The action of the story shows the train taking Jeremy and Samantha farther and farther away.

The subway train stopped again. The doors opened. Passengers got off. New people came on. The train started up again.

- **The story builds to a climax and makes the audience curious to find out what happens.**

I know right away that Jeremy and Samantha are worried that something is wrong. They will have to solve the problem by themselves. Their worry builds until they find out just how far from the museum they are. I wonder what I would do if I was alone on a train going the wrong way.

Brighton! Samantha and Jeremy looked at each other in disbelief. Brighton was miles and miles from where they lived. The nature museum was just a few city subway stops from home.

Content/ Ideas

- The story has dialogue that makes the characters seem real.

I can tell that Jeremy and Samantha are about my age. They are trying to get to the museum by themselves. Jeremy reacts the way that I might react if I were lost. His words show that he is upset at first. Samantha's words show that she is trying to stay calm.

"We never should have gone by ourselves," said Jeremy. "I'll bet we're lost."

"Don't worry," answered Samantha. "Our stop is probably next."

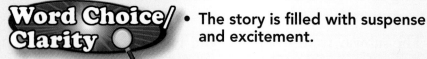

Word Choice/ Clarity

- The story is filled with suspense and excitement.

The writer uses several words and phrases to build suspense and excitement. Phrases like **broke into bright daylight** and **two things happened at once** make me want to read more.

It seemed about to leave the dark underground. In a split second, the train broke into bright daylight. Two things happened at once. Samantha and Jeremy couldn't see for a few seconds because of the blinding sunlight, and the train conductor announced, "We will arrive in Brighton at 11 o'clock. No stops between here and Brighton."

Using the Rubric to Study the Model

Adventure Story

Sentence Fluency

- The story has different kinds of sentences to add drama and keep the story moving.

Once Samantha and Jeremy discover where the train is going, they can relax. Becky uses long, flowing sentences to keep the story moving, even when Samantha and Jeremy are just looking out the window.

They were going so fast that the sunny world seemed to change color as they moved. Trees that had been green now flamed red and gold. Acorns fell from branches and thudded against the train. Fluffy white clouds danced in an endless, brilliant blue sky.

Grammar/ Mechanics

- Spelling, punctuation, and capitalization are correct.
- Direct quotations are punctuated correctly.

I've checked the whole story and can't find any spelling or punctuation errors. All the direct quotations are punctuated correctly. They begin and end with quotation marks. A new paragraph shows that another person is speaking.

"We can take the train back once we get to Brighton," said Jeremy.

"Meanwhile, we can watch the real change-of-seasons show from right here!" exclaimed Samantha.

My Turn!

Now it's my turn to write an adventure story! I will use the rubric and good writing strategies to help me. Read along to see how I do it.

Prewriting Gather Information

Information/Organization The story has a lead character who solves a problem.

Writing Strategy Choose a lead character and a problem.

I know that an adventure story can be about something that really happened to someone, or it can be made up. I can even make myself the lead character.

I'd like to show myself doing something brave. I know! My problem can be when a little girl in our neighborhood is surrounded by bees. I can make myself the hero of a story about rescuing her! I'll start by writing down the problem I plan to solve in my story.

The Problem
A little girl is surrounded by bees. She is so scared she cannot move.

Have you ever solved a problem that would make a good adventure story? Clearly write out your problem and include a lead character. Then, brainstorm about how you solved it.

Prewriting Organize Ideas

Information/ Organization The story has a setting, action, and an ending.

Writing Strategy Make a Story Map to organize the events.

I have written down a problem for my adventure story. The rubric reminds me that I also need a setting, action, and an ending for my story. A graphic organizer can help me plan out my adventure. I think I'll make a Story Map to help me organize my story from start to finish.

Story Map

Setting: Where: a road near my house
When: an August day

Characters: Amy Sisson, Mom, Michael, and me

Problem: Amy Sisson is scared by bees.

Action: Michael and I hear Amy screaming.
We run to help her.
I am scared, but I act like Superkid.
I help Amy get away from the bees.

Ending: Amy gets home safely.

Writer's Term

Story Map
A Story Map organizes the setting, characters, problems, events, and ending of a story.

Look at the brainstorming you did about a problem. Pick out ideas that show the setting, characters, action, and ending to your problem. Make a Story Map to organize these ideas into a story.

Think About It
Look at my notes and my Story Map. Will they help me write a good story?

Drafting Write a Draft

Voice/ Audience The story builds to a climax and makes the audience curious to find out what happens.

Writing Strategy Build the story to a climax to make it exciting for the reader.

I'm ready to start writing my adventure story. I'll use my Story Map to make sure my story has a clear problem, setting, action, and ending.

The rubric reminds me that a good adventure story builds to a climax. I need to make the story exciting for my readers, so they will want to read to the end. I love watching adventure movies. The movie keeps me guessing what will happen to the lead character. Will the character escape from danger? Will he or she find the treasure? I always want to find out the ending. In my story, I want readers to wonder how I will save Amy from the bees.

I'll do my best with grammar and spelling as I write, but I won't worry about mistakes right now. I know I'll have a chance to fix them later.

Writer's Term

Climax

The **climax** is the most exciting or important moment in the story. The climax leads to the solution of the problem.

Just Call Me Superkid

It was a long, hot August day. I was playing superhero with my little brother. I was dressed up as Superkid. I was pretending to take on the bad guy when Michael herd something.

I listened, too. Sure enough, I herd someone. Then I saw little Amy Sisson standing in the road. Michael and I flew down the street to her find out what was wrong.

> event building to a climax

As we got closer, I saw what was making Amy scream. A beehive had fallen about five feet from her. Bees were everywhere. Amy was frozen with fear. I knew she wouldn't be able to move by herself. I had to help her.

> event building to a climax

I was plenty scared of those bees, too, but I was five years older than Amy. More important, I felt like Superkid. I didn't get any closer to the bees, but I did tell Amy quietly in my most soothing voice that I could help her. I tells her not to be afraid. Superkid was there.

Practice!

Use your Story Map to write your own draft. Don't forget to build the action to a climax as you write.

Think About It

Read my draft. Did I make you want to keep reading to find out how the story ends?

Revising Extend Writing

Content/Ideas The story has dialogue that makes the characters seem real.

Writing Strategy Add dialogue to make the story more interesting.

I read my draft. I noticed that I didn't have any sentence fragments in it. I'm glad I'm getting better at those.

Writer's Term

Dialogue
Dialogue means "conversation." In a story, the dialogue is the conversation between the characters.

Then I looked at the rubric. It reminded me to add dialogue to my story. Adding some dialogue when Michael hears Amy would help make the story more exciting.

[DRAFT]

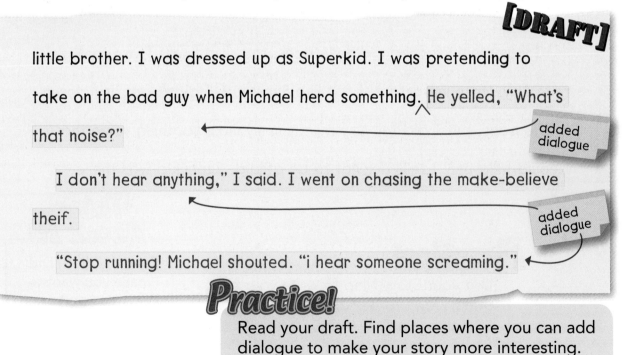

little brother. I was dressed up as Superkid. I was pretending to take on the bad guy when Michael herd something. He yelled, "What's that noise?"

added dialogue

I don't hear anything," I said. I went on chasing the make-believe theif.

added dialogue

"Stop running! Michael shouted. "i hear someone screaming."

Practice!

Read your draft. Find places where you can add dialogue to make your story more interesting.

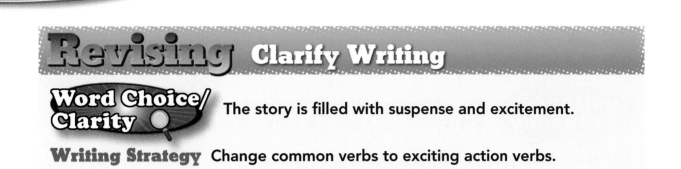

Revising Clarify Writing

Word Choice/Clarity The story is filled with suspense and excitement.

Writing Strategy Change common verbs to exciting action verbs.

When I read the rubric again, I saw that I need to think about building suspense. I'll go through my draft and pick out plain verbs, and I'll change them to more exciting verbs. For example, I can write "yelled" instead of "said." See how much more interesting my story becomes when I use action verbs? Now, I just have to make sure that my verbs agree with their subjects.

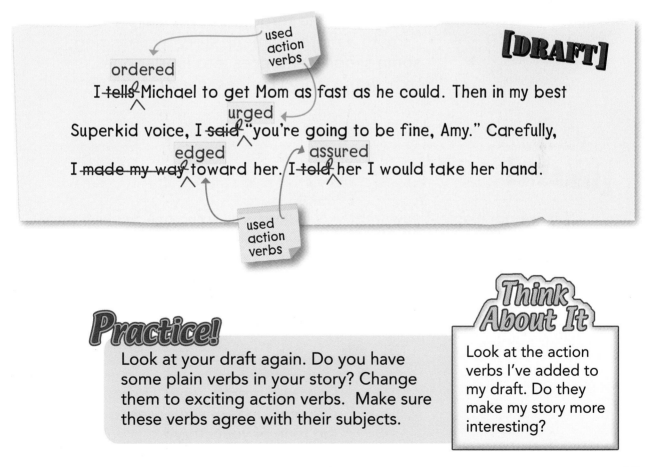

[DRAFT]

used action verbs

ordered

I ~~tells~~ Michael to get Mom as fast as he could. Then in my best

urged

Superkid voice, I ~~said~~ "you're going to be fine, Amy." Carefully,

edged   assured

I ~~made my way~~ toward her. I ~~told~~ her I would take her hand.

used action verbs

Practice!

Look at your draft again. Do you have some plain verbs in your story? Change them to exciting action verbs. Make sure these verbs agree with their subjects.

Think About It

Look at the action verbs I've added to my draft. Do they make my story more interesting?

Editing Check Sentences

Sentence Fluency The writer uses different kinds of sentences to add drama and keep the story moving.

Writing Strategy Vary sentences to add drama.

Now it's time to edit my draft. The rubric says that I need to use different kinds of sentences to vary the tone throughout my story. I can create a more dramatic story by changing some simple sentences into longer ones. See how the story changes when I do this?

Writer's Term

Tone

Tone is how the story sounds. The tone can be serious, funny, sarcastic, objective, and so on.

[DRAFT]

changed sentence to add drama

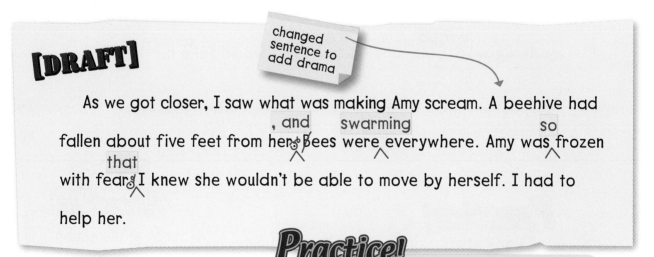

As we got closer, I saw what was making Amy scream. A beehive had fallen about five feet from her. Bees were everywhere. Amy was frozen with fear. I knew she wouldn't be able to move by herself. I had to help her.

(editing marks added: ", and" and "swarming" and "so" and "that")

Practice!

Check your draft again. Do you use different kinds of sentences to vary the tone of your story?

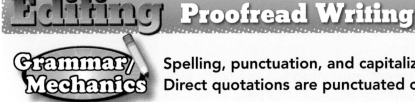

Editing Proofread Writing

Grammar/Mechanics
Spelling, punctuation, and capitalization are correct.
Direct quotations are punctuated correctly.

Writing Strategy Be sure direct quotations are punctuated correctly.

I'm ready to check my spelling, punctuation, and capitalization. I also need to check all the dialogue in my story. Each direct quotation should begin and end with quotation marks. A new paragraph shows that a new speaker is talking.

Writer's Term

Direct Quotations
Direct quotations give the exact words of someone speaking. Put quotation marks around a direct quotation.

[DRAFT]

"I don't hear anything" I said. I went on chasing the make-believe
thief
~~theif~~.

new speaker

"Stop running! Michael shouted. "i hear someone screaming."

Practice!
Edit your draft for spelling, punctuation, and capitalization. Correct any mistakes in direct quotations.

Grammar/Mechanics
For more practice punctuating direct quotations, use the exercises on the next two pages.

Think About It
Look at my edits. Did I punctuate direct quotations correctly? Did I vary the tone to add drama?

Direct Quotations

A **direct quotation** is a speaker's exact words. Use quotation marks at the beginning and end of the speaker's exact words. Use a comma to separate the speaker's exact words from the rest of the sentence. Begin a direct quotation with a capital letter, and add end punctuation before the last quotation mark.

Examples: The child shouted, **"W**ow**!"**

"I'm not surprised**,"** the man replied.

Practice the Rule

Read each sentence. If the sentence uses a direct quote correctly, write **Correct**. If the sentence has errors in punctuation, rewrite the sentence correctly on a separate sheet of paper.

1. Our teacher said, "Kids, we're going to visit an apiary."

2. What's an apiary, asked Gina.

3. "An apiary is a place where a beekeeper keeps hives of bees" explained Mr. Frantz.

4. Mr. Frantz continued, "The beekeeper takes care of the bees and then harvests honey from each hive."

5. Ryan asked, But aren't bees dangerous? Won't we get stung?"

6. Mr. Frantz said, "No, we won't be touching any hives, and the bees are peaceful if we leave them alone.

7. "Beekeepers wear protective clothes when it's time to harvest the honey," Mr. Frantz said.

8. "Oh, I see" exclaimed Gina.

9. "That way the beekeeper can't get stung," she added.

10. "You'll find the beekeeper's work very interesting said Mr. Frantz.

Apply the Rule

Read the following paragraphs. Find any errors in the use of direct quotes. Rewrite the paragraphs correctly on a separate piece of paper.

"Sure is hot out here. We need to get a drink out of the water fountain Tony said. We got in line behind the other kids.

Suddenly one kid yelled, Look out! It's a bee!" All the kids scattered, but Tony just stood here.

Come on, Tony, I called. "Let's get away from the bee!"

Tony grinned. "It's okay" he said. "The bee is hot, too. It wants to get a drink, just like we do." We watched as the bee perched, wings still buzzing, on the edge of the fountain. We couldn't see how, but the bee got a drink. It flew off happily.

"Wow, Tony!" I said. You really know a lot about bees! You knew just what to do.

Yeah—we just had to wait our turn for a drink, Tony said.

Publishing Share Writing

Publish my story as a big book to read to younger students.

My adventure story is done! Now, it's time to publish it. There are many ways to publish a story. I think that younger students would really enjoy my story, so I think I'll publish it in a big book. I can read the big book to younger students at my school. A big book has the story's words printed very large. Each page has a picture that shows what is happening in the story. Before I draw the pictures and make the big book, I want to check my story one last time. Here's the checklist I used.

My Checklist

✔ The title of the story and my name are at the top of the page.

✔ A sense of adventure keeps the reader interested as the story builds to a climax.

✔ The story has interesting dialogue that sounds like real people talking.

✔ The story is full of suspense and excitement.

✔ Spelling, grammar, and punctuation are correct. Direct quotations are correct.

✔ My handwriting is easy to read.

Practice!

Make a checklist to check your adventure story. Then make a final copy.

Just Call Me Superkid
by Jack

It was a long, hot August day. I was playing superhero with my little brother. I was dressed up as Superkid, and I was pretending to take on the bad guy when Michael heard something. He yelled, "What's that noise?"

"I don't hear anything," I said. I went on chasing the make-believe thief.

"Stop running!" Michael shouted. "I hear someone screaming."

I listened, too. Sure enough, I heard someone. Then I saw little Amy Sisson standing in the road. Michael and I flew down the street to her to find out what was wrong.

As we got closer, I saw what was making Amy scream. A beehive had fallen about five feet from her, and bees were swarming everywhere. Amy was so frozen with fear that I knew she wouldn't be able to move by herself. I had to help her.

I was plenty scared of those bees, too, but I was five years older than Amy. More important, I felt like Superkid. I didn't get any closer to the bees, but I did tell Amy quietly in my most soothing voice that I could help her. I told her not to be afraid. Superkid was there.

I ordered Michael to get Mom as fast as he could. Then in my best Superkid voice, I urged, "You're going to be fine, Amy." Carefully I edged toward her. I assured her that I would take her hand. I said that we would walk slowly backward from the hive. I don't know how I made myself go to Amy, but I did. The first step was the hardest. Soon Mom was there, taking steps backward with us. Only five minutes later, we were far away from the buzzing bees, walking Amy to her front door.

As soon as Amy got inside, she cried, "Daddy! Daddy! Superkid saved me!" Well, I guess Amy was right.

Use the rubric to check my story. Did I include all the traits of a good adventure story? Be sure to use the rubric to check your own story.

Ways to Publish an Adventure Story

As you choose how to publish your work, think about who will be reading it. Then pick the best way to share it. Here are some ideas for publishing your adventure story.

✓ **Make a recording of the story, reading with excitement and suspense in your voice. Put the recording in the reading center.**

✓ **Combine your story with other student adventure stories in a book called *Adventurers!* Create a cover illustration and table of contents. Then, add your book to the class library.**

✓ **Write your adventure story as a short skit, with roles for each character. Help classmates learn the lines and perform your story for the class.**

✓ **Turn your story into a comic strip. Draw a frame for each event, and add dialogue to tell the story.**

Writing Across the Content Areas
Adventure Story

You can find ideas for stories of adventure and adventurous people in many subjects that you study in school. Here are a few places to look for ideas:

Math

- Write about an adventurer who is stuck in a tough situation and uses math knowledge to save the day.
- Write about a student who tries to get out of a math test—and then does just fine.

Art and/or Music

- Write a theme song for your favorite superhero.
- Design and write the text for a poster to advertise an adventure story. Then, write the story!

Social Studies

- Find out about a great adventurer from the past. Read about his or her life. Then, write an adventure story from this adventurer's point of view.
- Read about an interesting time in history. Imagine that you live during that time. Write an adventure story that could happen to you during that time.

NARRATIVE test writing

Read the Writing Prompt

Every writing test starts with a writing prompt. Most writing prompts have three parts:

Setup This part of the writing prompt gives you the background information you need to get ready for writing.

Task This part of the writing prompt tells you exactly what you're supposed to write: a story about what happened in the castle.

Scoring Guide This section tells how your writing will be scored. You should include everything on the list to do well on the test.

Remember the rubrics you've been using in this book? When you take a writing test, you don't always have all the information that's on a rubric. But, the scoring guide is a lot like a rubric. It lists everything you need to think about to write a good paper. Many scoring guides will include the six important traits of writing that are in all of the rubrics we've looked at:

Information/Organization Content/Ideas Sentence Fluency

Voice/Audience Word Choice/Clarity Grammar/Mechanics

Suppose your family told you that you were moving to a new place. When you pulled up to your new home, this is what you saw.

Write a story about what happened over the next few months after you moved in.

Be sure your story

- tells who or what the story is about and when and where it takes place.
- gets the audience's attention at the beginning.
- includes details to make the events and the characters more real.
- clearly describes each event.
- has questions to get the reader thinking about what might happen.
- has correct grammar, spelling, and punctuation.

Writing Traits

in the Scoring Guide

The scoring guide in the prompt on page 77 has been made into this chart. How does it relate to the writing traits in the rubrics you've been using? Test prompts won't always include all of the six writing traits, but this one does!

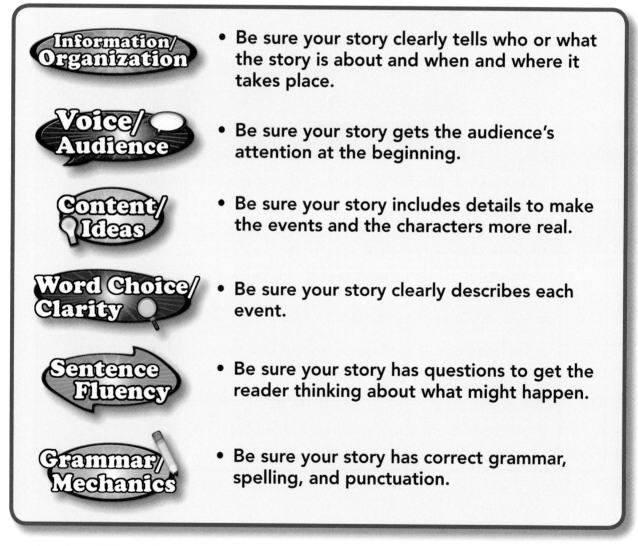

Information/Organization
- Be sure your story clearly tells who or what the story is about and when and where it takes place.

Voice/Audience
- Be sure your story gets the audience's attention at the beginning.

Content/Ideas
- Be sure your story includes details to make the events and the characters more real.

Word Choice/Clarity
- Be sure your story clearly describes each event.

Sentence Fluency
- Be sure your story has questions to get the reader thinking about what might happen.

Grammar/Mechanics
- Be sure your story has correct grammar, spelling, and punctuation.

Look at Marta Simmons' story on the next page. Did she follow the scoring guide?

My New HOME

by Marta Simmons

Do you ever imagine yourself living like royalty? I used to dream I was a princess in a castle. Life would be so perfect.

Then one day last year, it happened. We were moving, but I hadn't seen our new house yet. I just knew it would be bigger than our old apartment. Mom and Dad piled us all in the car and we headed off. After we had been driving for a while, Mom turned and said, "Close your eyes. It's just around the next corner." Then when she said to open our eyes, I couldn't believe what I saw.

It was a castle, like the kind you see in movies or read about in fairy tales with knights and princesses living in it. It had tall towers, a drawbridge, and a moat with alligators!

My family moved into the castle that day. We didn't need any of our stuff from our old house, since we started wearing clothes from long ago when the castle was built. Instead of going to school, we had a tutor to teach us in the castle.

After a few weeks, I began to get kind of bored. There were servants to do all the chores, and there were no kids my age.

Each day seemed to pass more and more slowly. Sometimes I spent hours counting the stones that made up the turret where I'm sure they used to keep misbehaving princesses. I'd pile old rugs on the floor trying to get a glimpse of what was over the wall that separated the courtyard from the rest of the neighborhood.

Our new home was so big that a game of hide-and-seek with my sisters lasted all day. I missed my friends and I missed my old room in my old apartment, even though I had shared it with my sisters.

Then one day, my parents called us all together. They said, "We decided we're not really castle people. We're moving back."

Well, you never saw a group of kids get ready so fast in your life. In minutes Jessie, Anna, Katie, and I were packed and ready to go. We drove back to our old building. It was just like when we left it.

Now, I can't wait to go back to school tomorrow. And I can't wait to sleep in my old room—sisters and all. Sometimes you really just need to get away from home to appreciate it.

Using the Scoring Guide to Study the Model

Now, let's use the scoring guide to check Marta's writing test, "My New Home." See if you can find examples from her writing to show how well she did on each part of the scoring guide.

- **The story clearly tells who or what the story is about and when and where it takes place.**

Who, what, when, and where are pieces of information you need to make a story clear. Marta told the audience where the story took place: at a castle. She made sure she told who was in the story: her family. Even though the story is made up, she wrote when it could take place. Read what she wrote.

Then one day last year, it happened.

My family moved into the castle that day.

- **The story gets the audience's attention at the beginning.**

The scoring guide reminds you to keep the audience in mind as you write and be sure to get its attention. Marta starts her story with a question to get our attention.

Do you ever imagine yourself living like royalty? I used to dream I was a princess in a castle. Life would be so perfect.

Content/ Ideas
- The story includes details to make the events and the characters more real.

The scoring guide tells you to add details. Details make everything in the story seem more real. Here are some of the details Marta included in her story.

We didn't need any of our stuff from our old house, since we started wearing clothes from long ago when the castle was built. Instead of going to school, we had a tutor to teach us in the castle.

Word Choice/ Clarity
- The story clearly describes each event.

Marta describes events in her story so the reader knows exactly what's going on. Read what she wrote:

After a few weeks, I began to get kind of bored. There were servants to do all the chores, and there were no kids my age.

Well, you never saw a group of kids get ready so fast in your life. In minutes Jessie, Anna, Katie, and I were packed and ready to go.

Using the Scoring Guide to Study the Model

• The story has questions to get the reader thinking about what might happen.

The scoring guide reminds you to use questions to get the reader thinking about what might happen in your story. Marta starts her story with a question to get the reader thinking about what it might be like to live in a castle.

Do you ever imagine yourself living like royalty? I used to dream I was a princess living in a castle. Life would be so perfect.

• The story has correct grammar, spelling, and punctuation.

Looking back at the scoring guide, you can see the reminder to check grammar and spelling. You should look for any mistakes that you often make, such as problems with commas. Marta seems to have caught all of the grammar and spelling mistakes. Her final draft doesn't have any errors.

Planning My Time

Before giving us a writing test prompt, my teacher tells us how much time we'll have to complete the test. I'll think about how much time I have. Then I'll divide the time up into the different parts of the writing process. I'll also make sure I give myself some time to study the writing prompt. Look at how I've divided my time into four steps.

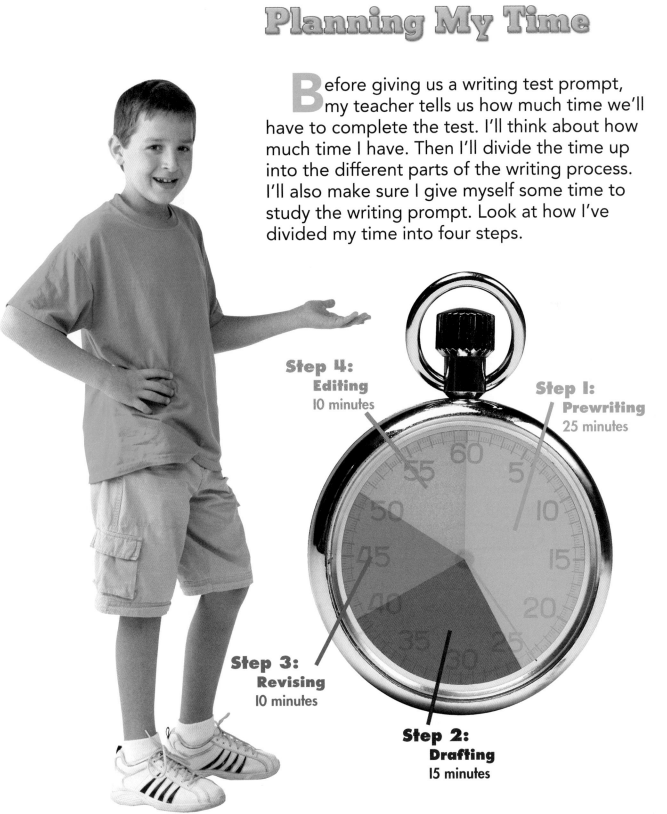

Step 4:
Editing
10 minutes

Step 1:
Prewriting
25 minutes

Step 3:
Revising
10 minutes

Step 2:
Drafting
15 minutes

Prewriting Study the Writing Prompt

Information/Organization

Writing Strategy Study the writing prompt to be sure I know what to do.

Once I have my writing prompt, I study it and make sure I know exactly what I'm supposed to do. Usually a writing prompt has three parts. You should find and label the setup, task, and scoring guide on your prompt, just like I did below! Then, you can circle key words that tell what kind of writing you need to do. I circled the picture of the clown. This is who I will be writing about. I also circled **Write a story** because it tells what kind of writing I'll be doing. Finally, I circled **what happened** because I need to tell what the clown did.

My Writing Test Prompt

Setup — Suppose you arrived at school to find that your teacher wasn't there. Instead you saw this person in your classroom.

Task — (Write a story) about (what happened) at school during the next week with this person in your classroom.

Scoring Guide — Be sure your story
- tells who or what the story is about and when and where it takes place.
- gets the audience's attention at the beginning.
- includes details to make the events and the characters more real.
- clearly describes each event.
- has questions to get the reader thinking about what might happen.
- has correct grammar, spelling, and punctuation.

Next I'll think about how the scoring guide relates to the six writing traits I've studied in the rubrics. All of the traits might not be included in every scoring guide, but I need to remember them all to write a good essay.

 • Be sure your story tells who or what the story is about and when and where it takes place.

 • Be sure your story gets the audience's attention at the beginning.

I have to make a good first impression. I don't want the reader to think my story is boring!

 • Be sure your story includes details to make the events and the characters more real.

When I describe my events and characters, I have to remember to include plenty of details.

 • Be sure your story clearly describes each event.

My descriptions need to be clear so I don't confuse my reader.

 • Be sure your story has questions to get the reader thinking about what might happen.

Asking questions in my story gets the reader involved. A question makes the reader wonder what might happen next. And hopefully she will keep reading to find out.

 • Be sure your story has correct grammar, spelling, and punctuation.

Whenever I write anything, I need to check grammar, spelling, and punctuation!

Prewriting   Gather Information

Information/ Organization   **Writing Strategy**   Respond to the task.

I've learned that writers always gather information before they begin writing. When you write to take a test, you can gather information from the writing prompt. Let's take another look at the task in the writing prompt, since this is the part of the prompt that explains what I'm supposed to write. Remember, you won't have much time when writing for a test! That's why it's really important to think about how you'll respond before you begin to write.

I know that I have to write a story. I need to tell what happened at school when a clown was in my classroom. I think jotting down some notes will help, but I have to do it quickly because the clock is ticking!

Task — Write a story about what happened at school during the next week with this person in your classroom.

Notes
• The clown trips people with his big feet.
• The clown takes over the class.
• The clown gets us in trouble.

Remember! Make sure you think about how you'll respond to the task in your writing prompt before you write. Then you can jot down some notes to help you gather information.

Prewriting **Organize Ideas**

Information/Organization **Writing Strategy** Choose a graphic organizer.

I don't have a lot of time, so I need to start organizing my ideas. First, I need to pick the right organizer for my writing. I'm writing a story, so a Story Map is a good prewriting tool. The Story Map will help me get the basics of my story down, like when and where it takes place, and what happens. Some of the information comes right out of the setup and task in my writing prompt.

Setting: **Where:** in school
When: last week

Characters: circus clown, my class

Problem: A circus clown takes over the class.

Plot Events: The circus clown keeps getting us in trouble.
People trip on his big feet.
We have to show him how to act in school.
He honks his nose when we get the right answers.

Ending: The circus clown learned how to behave in school.

Think About It

Look at my Story Map. Does it have the details I'll need to write a good story?

Remember! Choose the best graphic organizer for the assignment. Include important details, such as the characters, setting, and plot, in the organizer.

Prewriting Check the Scoring Guide

Information/Organization

Writing Strategy Check my graphic organizer against the scoring guide.

In a test, you don't always get much time to revise. Prewriting is more important than ever! So before I write, I'll check my Story Map against the scoring guide in the writing prompt.

Setting: **Where:** in school
When: last week

Characters: circus clown, my class

Problem: A circus clown takes over the class.

Plot Events: The circus clown keeps getting us in trouble.
People trip on his big feet.
We have to show him how to act in school.
He honks his nose when we get the right answers.

Ending: The circus clown learned how to behave in school.

Information/ Organization

- tells who or what the story is about and when and where it takes place.

That's in the Characters and Setting parts of my Story Map.

Voice/ Audience

- gets the audience's attention at the beginning.

This isn't in my Story Map, but that's okay. I just need to remember to do this when I start writing.

Content/ Ideas

- includes details to make the events and the characters more real.

I don't have many details in my Story Map, but I'll add more when I write my draft.

Word Choice/ Clarity

- clearly describes each event.

I've listed all of the events in my Story Map. I need to make sure I describe each one clearly in my draft.

Sentence Fluency

- has questions to get the reader thinking about what might happen.

There are no questions in my Story Map, but I can think of a whole bunch of questions about having a circus clown in class!

Grammar/ Mechanics

- has correct grammar, spelling, and punctuation.

I need to check grammar, spelling, and punctuation when I edit my draft.

Think About It

Does my Story Map cover all the points in the scoring guide? What else do I need to include?

Remember! Before you begin writing, look back at the scoring guide in the writing prompt to make sure you know everything you need to do.

Drafting Write a Draft

 **Voice/Audience**

Writing Strategy Get the reader's attention at the beginning.

Every story needs a good beginning, middle, and end. I can use the information from my Story Map to write all three sections. Looking at the scoring guide, I see that it's also important to get the audience's attention at the beginning. I thought about all of this as I wrote my draft.

[DRAFT]

The Substitute
by Jack

Did you ever wish something really amazing would happen? A big surprise was waiting for us last Monday morning. Our teacher had told us she would be out all week, so we weren't surprised to find a substitute teacher when we got to school. We were surprised at the kind of sub we had, though.

Mr. Foot introduced himself to the class. We couldn't believe it he was a clown! He was bald on top. He wore baggy pants.

 got reader's attention

Proofreading Marks

⅂ Indent	ℓ Take out something
≡ Make a capital	⊙ Add a period
/ Make a small letter	⌗ New paragraph
∧ Add something	ⓢⓟ Spelling error

[DRAFT]

We started doing math. Each time one kid answered a math problem right, Mr. Foot honked his nose. It made a beep sound. We didn't know what to make of Mr. Foot. At first we tried to act cool, like nothing special was going on. But then Mr. Foot looked sad, so we started giggling at the funny things he did. Once, as we were walking down the hall, he stuck out his big shoes and tripped the librarian. (she didn't get hurt.) We all started laughing and she told the principal that our class was out of control.

We had a class meeting at resess. We decided that we would teach Mr. Foot how to act in school. When he pulled out a frog, we ignored it and handed him a piece of chalk.

We stopped laughing at his nose honking, so he stopped doing it. And we told him that the librarian did not like his joke. By the end of the week Mr. Foot had learned his lesson. And we couldn't wait for things to get back to normal when our teacher came back.

Remember! Every story needs a clear beginning, middle, and end. The beginning should get the reader's attention, the middle should include most of your plot points, and the end should sum everything up.

Think About It

Read my draft. Does the beginning get the reader's attention?

Revising Extend Writing

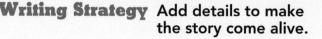

Content/Ideas

Writing Strategy Add details to make the story come alive.

Now that I've written a draft, I'll look back at the scoring guide and make sure I've included all the points I'll be graded on. I'll reread my draft to myself to see what's missing.

I have the **who, when,** and **where**— a clown, last Monday, in school. I remember from the rubrics in this unit that adding details always makes a story better. I should add more details to improve my description of Mr. Foot.

[DRAFT]

added details

Mr. Foot introduced himself to the class. We couldn't believe it he

with orange hair that stuck out over his ears

with purple and green polka dots

was a clown! He was bald on top. He wore baggy pants.

He kept pulling handkerchiefs and flowers out of his pockets.

Remember! Read your draft. Add details to make your descriptions come alive.

Word Choice/Clarity

Writing Strategy Replace vague words with exact words.

Okay, I'll read my paper again. Is there anything I need to make clearer? The rubrics in this unit had a lot of tips on making my writing clear, so I know several strategies I could use. The scoring guide says to clearly describe each event. If I replace vague words with exact words, my audience will have a clearer picture of the events.

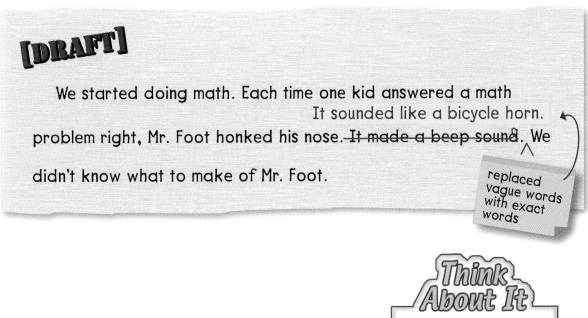

[DRAFT]

We started doing math. Each time one kid answered a math problem right, Mr. Foot honked his nose. ~~It made a beep sound~~. It sounded like a bicycle horn. We didn't know what to make of Mr. Foot.

replaced vague words with exact words

Remember! Make sure everything in your story is clear. Replace any vague words with exact words.

Think About It
Look at my revisions. Did I include interesting details and use exact words?

Editing Check Sentences

Sentence Fluency

Writing Strategy Include questions that get the reader thinking about what might happen.

The scoring guide tells me to include questions to get the reader thinking about what might happen. I started my story with a question to draw in the reader. I should add another question in the middle to keep the reader interested in what happens next.

we started giggling at the funny things he did. Once, as we were walking down the hall, he stuck out his big shoes and tripped the librarian. (she didn't get hurt.) We all started laughing and she told the principal that our class was out of control. Would we all get in trouble?

added question to get reader thinking

[DRAFT]

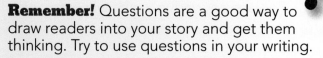

Remember! Questions are a good way to draw readers into your story and get them thinking. Try to use questions in your writing.

Editing Proofread Writing

Grammar/ Mechanics

Writing Strategy Check the grammar, spelling, capitalization, and punctuation.

The scoring guide says to use correct grammar and spelling. I also need to check my capitalization and punctuation. When I planned my time, I left plenty of time to check for these kinds of errors.

[FINAL DRAFT]

The Substitute
by Jack

Did you ever wish something really amazing would happen? A big surprise was waiting for us last Monday morning. Our teacher had told us she would be out all week, so we weren't surprised to find a substitute teacher when we got to school. We were surprised at the kind of sub we had, though.

Mr. Foot introduced himself to the class. We couldn't believe it with orange hair that stuck out over his ears with purple and green polka dots he was a clown! He was bald on top. He wore baggy pants. He kept pulling handkerchiefs and flowers out of his pockets.

Remember! Every time you write for a test, you need to check your grammar, spelling, capitalization, and punctuation.

That morning

We started doing math. Each time one kid answered a math

It sounded like a bicycle horn.
problem right, Mr. Foot honked his nose. ~~It made a beep sound.~~ We

didn't know what to make of Mr. Foot. At first we tried to act cool,

like nothing special was going on. But then Mr. Foot looked sad, so

we started giggling at the funny things he did. Once, as we were

walking down the hall, he stuck out his big shoes and tripped the

librarian. (she didn't get hurt.) We all started laughing'and she told

Would we all get in trouble?
the principal that our class was out of control.

We had a class meeting at re§ess. We decided that we would

teach Mr. Foot how to act in school. When he pulled out a frog, we

ignored it and handed him a piece of chalk.

We stopped laughing at his nose honking, so he stopped doing

it. And we told him that the librarian did not like his joke. By the end

of the week' Mr. Foot had learned his lesson. And we couldn't wait

for things to get back to

normal when our teacher

came back.

Think About It

Check my story against the scoring guide. Did I include everything I will be graded on?

We're finished! That wasn't so bad! Remember these important tips when you write for a test.

TEST TIPS

1. **Study the writing prompt before you start to write.** Most writing prompts have three parts: the setup, the task, and the scoring guide. The parts probably won't be labeled. You have to figure them out for yourself!

2. **Make sure you understand the task before you start to write.**
   - Read all three parts of the writing prompt carefully.
   - Circle key words in the task part of the writing prompt that tell what kind of writing you need to do. The task might also identify your audience.
   - Make sure you know how you'll be graded.
   - Say the assignment in your own words to yourself.

3. **Keep an eye on the clock.** Decide how much time you will spend on each part of the writing process and try to stick to your schedule. Don't spend so much time on prewriting that you don't have enough time left to write.

4. **Reread your writing. Compare it to the scoring guide at least twice.** Remember the rubrics you have used all year? A scoring guide on a writing test is like a rubric. It can help you keep what's important in mind.

5. **Plan, plan, plan!** You don't get much time to revise during a test, so planning is more important than ever.

6. **Write neatly.** Remember, if the people who score your test can't read your writing, it doesn't matter how good your essay is!

DESCRIPTIVE writing
uses words to give a clear picture of objects, people, places, or events.

Hi, my name is Marta. I am studying descriptive writing. I'm learning to use my five senses in writing to describe how things look, sound, feel, smell, and taste. Every summer my family and I take long drives up the coast. I like to send postcards about my trips to friends in faraway places. By learning to become a better writer, I'll be able to really describe the sights, sounds, and feel of the California coast.

IN THIS UNIT

1. **Descriptive Paragraph**
2. **Character Sketch**
3. **Poetry Review: Response to Literature**
4. **Writing for a Test**

Name: Marta

Home: California

Favorite Activities: sailing, reading, and writing poetry

Pets: angelfish

Favorite Book: *Emily's Runaway Imagination* by Beverly Cleary

What's a Descriptive Paragraph?

It's a clear, detailed picture in words of a specific person, place, or thing.

What's in a Descriptive Paragraph?

Sensory Details

I can bring my paragraph to life with details related to the five senses. I can tell how something looks, sounds, smells, feels, or tastes when I create word pictures.

A Main Idea

This is what my paragraph is all about. It could be the day I spent at the beach with my family or a biking trip with my friends. The details I write will support the main idea.

Tone

This is the mood I want to set. It creates feelings in the reader. The tone could be one of sadness or a feeling of excitement.

Why write a Descriptive Paragraph?

Describing is important for all writers. I can think of a lot of reasons for writing a descriptive paragraph. Here are a few.

Entertainment

Writers of stories use descriptive paragraphs to make the characters, setting, and action seem real. Good descriptions help the readers picture the story in their minds. The reader can enjoy an amazing imaginary world.

Information

Describing is one way to give people information. Describing what you observe is an important activity of scientists. The observations that they write are detailed descriptions of what they see or hear. I can write about something I've seen or heard to share with others.

Opinion

How a writer describes something can influence a reader's opinion about it. That's why historians try hard to describe without giving an opinion.

Fiction writers have a different goal. They often use opinion words like **beautiful, scary, awful,** and **delicious** to bring emotion to a story. They want to affect how the reader thinks and feels about a character, setting, or events.

Descriptive Paragraph
Writing Traits

What makes a good descriptive paragraph? A descriptive paragraph should have vivid sensory details that create word pictures. Here are some traits of a good descriptive paragraph.

Information/ Organization	The paragraph describes a subject. Descriptions are organized around a main idea.
Voice/ Audience	A topic sentence invites the reader to visualize the subject.
Content/ Ideas	Word pictures help the reader to imagine the real subject.
Word Choice/ Clarity	Personal language makes the paragraph more interesting.
Sentence Fluency	Questions and exclamations vary the tone.
Grammar/ Mechanics	Spelling, punctuation, and capitalization are correct. Plural nouns are formed correctly.

Let's read Andrea Baum's descriptive paragraph on the next page. Did she follow all of the writing traits?

OUR SECRET HIDING PLACE

by Andrea Baum

main idea

For a quiet, happy afternoon, away from my little brothers, there is nothing like the special place that Sarah and I found. It is in the woods, not far from my house. To get there, we walk a half-mile down a dirt path, turn off just before a wooden walkway, and go down another short trail. Suddenly, there it is! With a few more steps, we reach a quiet, open place about eight feet by ten feet. In that one place, there are no trees, but the sunlight cuts through the leaves of the surrounding trees with bright knives of light. It is an ideal hideaway! Sarah and I spend hours there playing. We talk, plan, listen, and sit quietly together. We hear the *rat-a-tat-tat* of woodpeckers and the soft whistles of nuthatches. We listen as the breeze whispers in the leaves of the maple trees. We watch orange and black butterflies flutter nearby. The soft pine needles make a scented cushion. Sometimes, we sit and imagine the country when the pioneers came here, and we pretend we are explorers. All friends should have a secret place as special as ours.

tone

sensory details

Descriptive Paragraph Rubric

The rubric below was made using the traits of a good descriptive paragraph on page 102. Assign one to four stars for each trait. Four stars mean that trait is excellent! Three stars mean it is very good. One or two stars mean that trait needs more work.

	Excelling ⭐⭐⭐⭐	Achieving ⭐⭐⭐	Developing ⭐⭐	Beginning ⭐
Information/ Organization	The paragraph describes a subject. Descriptions are organized around a main idea.	The paragraph mostly describes a subject. Most descriptions are organized around a main idea.	The paragraph sometimes describes a subject. Some descriptions are organized around a main idea.	The paragraph may not describe a subject. Descriptions need to be organized around a main idea.
Voice/ Audience	A topic sentence invites the reader to visualize the subject and makes the reader curious about it.	A topic sentence invites the reader to visualize the subject.	The topic sentence is unclear.	The paragraph needs a topic sentence.
Content/ Ideas	All word pictures are vivid and help the reader to imagine the real subject.	Many word pictures help the reader to imagine the real subject.	There are a few word pictures that help the reader to imagine the real subject.	The paragraph needs word pictures that help the reader to imagine the real subject.
Word Choice/ Clarity	Personal language makes the paragraph very interesting and convincing.	Personal language makes the paragraph interesting.	Some of the personal language makes the paragraph interesting.	Personal language is missing or does not make the paragraph more interesting.
Sentence Fluency	Questions and exclamations are used effectively to vary the tone.	There are many questions and exclamations to vary the tone.	There are some questions and exclamations to vary the tone.	Questions and exclamations are needed to vary the tone.
Grammar/ Mechanics	There are no spelling or grammar errors. Plural nouns are correct.	There are few spelling or grammar errors. Plural nouns are correct.	There are some errors in spelling, grammar, and/or plural nouns.	There are many errors in spelling, grammar, and/or plural nouns.

Descriptive Paragraph

Using the Rubric to Study the Model

Now, let's use the rubric to check Andrea Baum's descriptive paragraph, "Our Secret Hiding Place." What score would you give Andrea for each category in the rubric?

 **Information/Organization**

- **The paragraph describes a subject.**
- **Descriptions are organized around a main idea.**

I think the writer creates a place that seems very real. The words are just right, and the descriptions are well organized. In this example, you can imagine the quiet and the rays of sunlight streaming in. Her description puts you there.

> With a few more steps, we reach a quiet, open place about eight feet by ten feet. In that one place, there are no trees, but the sunlight cuts through the leaves of the surrounding trees with bright knives of light.

 **Voice/Audience**

- **A topic sentence invites the reader to visualize the subject.**

Andrea starts with a clear topic sentence. It gives the main idea of the paragraph, and it creates a lot of interest in the place. All the other sentences give details that explain the topic sentence.

> For a quiet, happy afternoon, away from my little brothers, there is nothing like the special place that Sarah and I found.

Content/ Ideas

- **Word pictures help the reader to imagine the real subject.**

The writer creates word pictures by describing what she sees and hears in her secret hiding place. You can picture what she's writing about. She uses interesting descriptive words all through the paragraphs.

> We listen as the breeze whispers in the leaves of the maple trees. We watch orange and black butterflies flutter nearby. The soft pine needles make a scented cushion.

Word Choice/ Clarity

- **Personal language makes the paragraph more interesting.**

Andrea uses a lot of personal language in her paragraph. You know how she sees her secret place and what she likes about it. You see her secret place from her point of view.

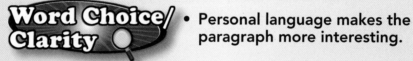

> It is an ideal hideaway! Sarah and I spend hours there playing. We talk, plan, listen, and sit quietly together.

Using the Rubric to Study the Model

Sentence Fluency

- **Questions and exclamations vary the tone.**

The writer uses exclamations to add excitement to the paragraph. When she describes the way to her secret place, she uses an exclamation to show that finding the place is an exciting moment.

> Suddenly, there it is! With a few more steps, we reach a quiet, open place about eight feet by ten feet.

Grammar/Mechanics

- **Spelling, punctuation, and capitalization are correct.**
- **Plural nouns are formed correctly.**

I read the description very carefully. Every word is spelled correctly. There are no errors in capitalization or punctuation either. The writer has formed every plural noun correctly. Look at this example. It has six plural nouns. Can you find them?

> We hear the *rat-a-tat-tat* of woodpeckers and the soft whistles of nuthatches. We listen as the breeze whispers in the leaves of the maple trees. We watch orange and black butterflies flutter nearby.

My Turn!

Now it's my turn to write a descriptive paragraph! I'll use the rubric and good writing strategies to help me. Follow along to see how I do it.

Prewriting Gather Information

Information/Organization The paragraph describes a subject.

Writing Strategy Make some notes about an interesting place I know.

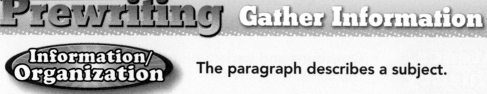

I love visiting Splash Zone at the Monterey Bay Aquarium. I can see and even touch a lot of sea creatures there. My teacher asked us to think of a place we had visited and liked. Right away, I thought of Splash Zone. My strategy will be to jot down notes from my memory.

Notes For My Paragraph

- Splash Zone—best part of the aquarium
- a place for families
- different species of fish
- salty smell of the sea
- can hold starfish
- a beautiful coral reef
- walls of bubbling water
- hear excited children
- a window that puts you next to penguins
- giant clam chair
- sounds of fish eating
- hear "talking" penguins
- walls that feel like coral
- smell of animals
- water play area

Practice!

Think about an interesting place you have been to. Jot down notes about it. What would a visitor want to know about it?

Prewriting Organize Ideas

Descriptions are organized around a main idea.

Writing Strategy Make a Web to organize my notes.

I know from the rubric that organization is important. To organize my notes, I'm going to make a Web. I'll put the main idea of my paragraph in the middle of my Web. Then I'll put the details in circles around my topic. I can use my five senses to organize my descriptions.

Writer's Term

Web
A **Web** organizes information about one main topic. The main topic goes in a center circle. Related details go in outside circles.

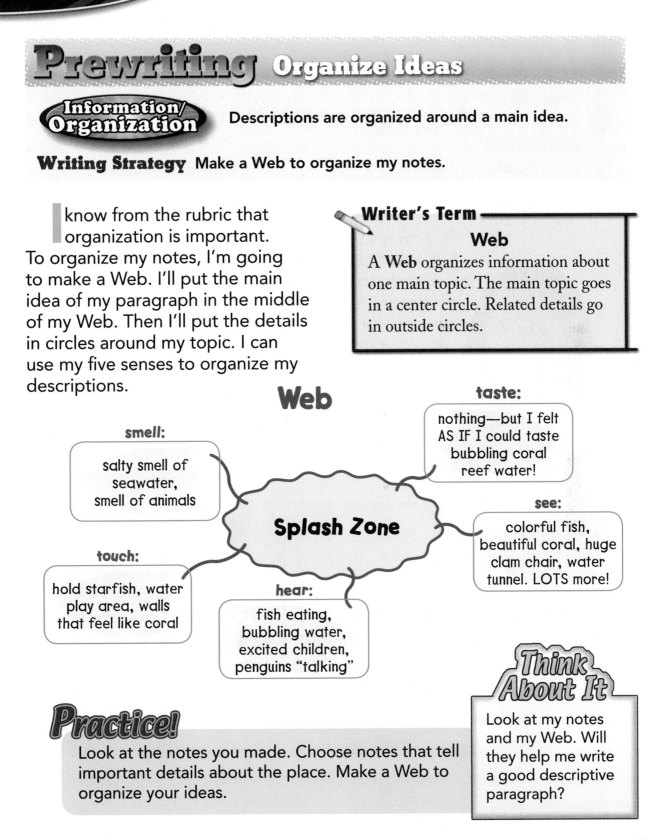

Web

smell: salty smell of seawater, smell of animals

taste: nothing—but I felt AS IF I could taste bubbling coral reef water!

touch: hold starfish, water play area, walls that feel like coral

Splash Zone

hear: fish eating, bubbling water, excited children, penguins "talking"

see: colorful fish, beautiful coral, huge clam chair, water tunnel. LOTS more!

Practice!

Look at the notes you made. Choose notes that tell important details about the place. Make a Web to organize your ideas.

Think About It
Look at my notes and my Web. Will they help me write a good descriptive paragraph?

Drafting Write a Draft

Voice/Audience A topic sentence invites the reader to visualize the subject.

Writing Strategy Begin with a topic sentence that helps the reader to "see" the place.

Now it's time to write my descriptive paragraph. I'll use the center of my Web to write my topic sentence. Then I'll choose information from the other circles to write detail sentences. I know from the rubric that my topic sentence needs to be so clear that my reader can almost "see" my subject.

I won't worry about checking grammar or spelling right now. I know I'll get a chance to fix any mistakes later.

Writer's Term

Topic Sentence and Detail Sentences

A **topic sentence** states the main idea of a whole paragraph.

Detail sentences go with, tell about, or give examples of the topic sentence.

[DRAFT]

Wet, Wild, and Wonderful

detail sentence →

topic sentence →

No one should miss Splash Zone at the Monterey Bay Aquarium. It is the best place to learn about the lifes of sea animals. Where else can kids sit in a giant clam chair or hear fish eating? Where else is there a coral reef with bubbling walls of water There is a tunnel to crawl throuh and touch walls that feel like rough and soft coral. In the tunnel I saw sea horses, eeles, reef sharks, and all kinds of brightly colored fish. I smelled the salty sea air, and I could allmost taste the bubbling cold water. At the touch pool, there are model starfish and other creatures. In the water play area, kids can make waves and tide pooles. At the end of Splash Zone, are the blackfooted penguins. They hop and swim around there home with rocks by the water. They talk like donkys. A neat special window makes it seem as if I suddenly popped up next to them. We even stood behind a big wall where we put your heads inside that has cutout faces

detail sentence →

detail sentence →

detail sentences →

Practice!

Use your notes and Web to write your own draft. Remember to write a clear topic sentence that invites the reader to visualize the subject you are describing.

Think About It

Read my draft. Does my topic sentence describe a real place that the reader would like to visit?

Revising Extend Writing

Content/Ideas Word pictures help the reader to imagine the real subject.

Writing Strategy Include word pictures to improve my description.

After I wrote my draft, I decided to write a word picture to support my topic. At Splash Zone, we had a picture taken of us behind the painted penguins with cutout faces. I'll write a word picture to describe that photograph. That way, my audience will be able to "see" how much fun Splash Zone is.

Writer's Term
Word Picture
A **word picture** is a vivid description of something in words. By painting pictures with words, you help the reader imagine the place you are describing.

[DRAFT]

word picture

My parents and I looked like a family of chubby birds wearing tuxedos in the picture we took there. I remember Splash Zone and laugh whenever I look at the photograph of my family as penguins!

Practice!
Read your draft. Find places where you can include word pictures to help the reader imagine what you are describing.

Revising Clarify Writing

Word Choice/Clarity Personal language makes the paragraph more interesting.

Writing Strategy Replace all dull language with more personal language.

The rubric says that personal language would make my description more interesting for the reader.

I found a way to add personal language. I decided to make my paragraph like a conversation with the reader. Then the reader would be more interested in what I was describing.

used personal language

[DRAFT]

the best place to learn about the lifes of sea animals. Where else can

I
~~kids~~ sit in a giant clam chair or hear fish eating? Where else ~~is there~~ a
could I visit

coral reef with bubbling walls of water ~~There is a tunnel to~~ crawl
I can
a tunnel above
throuh and touch walls that feel like rough and soft coral.

used personal language

Practice!

Read your draft again. Look for places where you can add personal language that will make your description more interesting for the reader.

Think About It

Look at the words I changed. Did I add personal language and word pictures to make my paragraph more interesting?

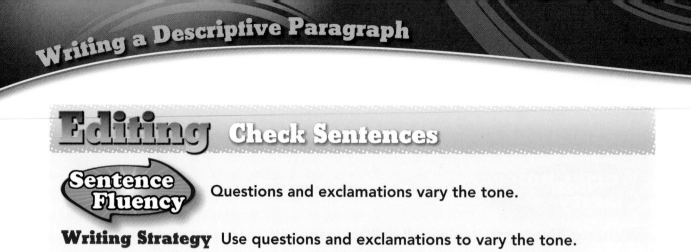

Editing   Check Sentences

Sentence Fluency Questions and exclamations vary the tone.

Writing Strategy Use questions and exclamations to vary the tone.

Now I need to edit my writing. The rubric says I should use questions and exclamations to vary the tone of my paragraph. I read through my draft and found that I had put in some questions. That's good. Then I found a sentence that I could turn into an exclamation. Look how I made it more exciting.

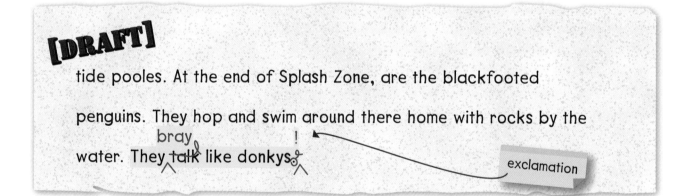

[DRAFT]

tide pooles. At the end of Splash Zone, are the blackfooted

penguins. They hop and swim around there home with rocks by the

water. They talk like donkys. _bray_ ! exclamation

Practice!

Check your draft for questions and exclamations. These will help vary the tone of your paragraph.

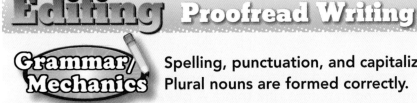
Grammar/ Mechanics Spelling, punctuation, and capitalization are correct. Plural nouns are formed correctly.

Writing Strategy Make sure plural nouns are formed correctly.

Next I'll check my spelling, capitalization, and punctuation. Also, the rubric reminds me to make sure that all my plural nouns are formed correctly.

Writer's Term

Plural Nouns

A **plural noun** names more than one thing. Add **-s** to most singular nouns to form the plural. Add **-es** to singular nouns that end in **s, x, ch,** or **sh.** Some nouns form the plural in other ways.

[DRAFT]

No one should miss Splash Zone at the Monterey Bay Aquarium. It is

lives

the best place to learn about the lifes of sea animals.

corrected plural noun

Practice!

Edit your draft for spelling, capitalization, and punctuation. Make sure all your plural nouns are correct.

Grammar/ Mechanics

For more practice with plural nouns, use the exercises on the next two pages.

Think About It

Look at my editing. Did I use questions and exclamations to vary the tone? Are my plural nouns correct?

Plural Nouns

Know the Rule

A **noun** is a word that names a person, place, or thing. A singular noun names one thing. A plural noun names more than one thing. Most singular nouns become plural when you add **-s**.
   Example: dog/dogs
If a singular noun ends in **s, x, ch,** or **sh,** add **-es** to make it a plural noun.
   Example: tax/taxes
If a singular noun ends in **y,** change the **y** to **i** before adding **-es**.
   Example: daisy/daisies
Many singular nouns that end in **f** change the **f** to **v** to form the plural.
   Example: shelf/shelves, hoof/hooves
However, not all singular nouns that end in **f** do this.
   Example: roof/roofs, chief/chiefs, cliff/cliffs

Practice the Rule

Read these sentences and decide how to form the plural of the nouns in parentheses. Write the nouns using the plural form on a separate piece of paper.

1. We spent two (week) at a national park.
2. The (beach) had soft white sand.
3. We ate many picnic (lunch) there.
4. One beach was divided into two (half).
5. People could swim and have (party) on one side.
6. Birds raised their (baby) on the other side.
7. Sometimes (fox) would raid a nest.
8. Some people pitched (tent) at a nearby campground.
9. Campers were careful not to leave any (mess) behind.
10. People always carried their trash and (dish) away.

Apply the Rule

Read this description of a campsite. Check to see that plural nouns have been formed correctly. On a separate piece of paper, rewrite the paragraphs with correct plural nouns.

Our campsite was perfect because it was near pine trees. The ground was covered with soft pine needlees, so we did not need air mattresss. Instead, we put our sleeping bags right on the ground. Many dead pine branchs lay near our tent. We used our axs to cut them into neat logs. These gave us all the firewood we needed. The trees also provided homes for many kinds of birds. Bird watching is one of my hobbyes.

While we were setting up camp I saw many different kinds of birdz. The prettiest were the blue jayes and the cardinals. I was pounding tent stakes when two hawkes flew overhead. Their winges were long and beautiful. My dad thought they were eaglies, but I think they were hawkes. At night we went for a short walk in the woods. We spotted three owles sitting high in the trees.

Publishing Share Writing

Publish my description as part of a brochure.

My descriptive paragraph is done! My next step is to publish it. I think I should publish my description as part of a brochure. I know my classmates will love Splash Zone since I have already talked to a few of my friends about it online. In a brochure, I can describe what it's like to be there and invite others to visit, too! Then my classmates will see why they should go! I used this checklist to check my descriptive paragraph one more time.

My Checklist

✔ The title of my descriptive paragraph and my name are at the top of the paper.

✔ My descriptions are organized around a main idea.

✔ Personal language makes the description more interesting.

✔ Questions and exclamations vary the tone.

✔ Spelling, grammar, and punctuation are all correct. Plural nouns are formed correctly.

✔ My handwriting is neat and easy to read.

Practice!

Make a checklist to check your own descriptive paragraph. Then, make a final draft and publish it as part of a brochure. Make copies of your brochure to share with your classmates.

Wet, Wild, and Wonderful
by Marta

No one should miss Splash Zone at the Monterey Bay Aquarium. It is the best place to learn about the lives of sea animals. Where else could I sit in a giant clam chair or hear fish eating? Where else could I visit a coral reef with bubbling walls of water? I can crawl through a tunnel above and touch walls that feel like rough and soft coral. As I crawl, I see sea horses, eels, reef sharks, and all kinds of brightly colored fish. I smell the salty sea air, and I can almost taste the bubbling cold water. At the touch pool, I can pick up live and model starfish and other creatures. In the water play area, I can make waves and tide pools. At the end of Splash Zone, are the blackfooted penguins. They hop and swim around their rocky home. They bray like donkeys! A special window makes it seem as if I suddenly pop up next to them. I can even stand behind a big wall that has cutout faces on top of painted penguin bodies. My parents and I looked like a family of chubby birds wearing tuxedos in the picture we took there. I remember Splash Zone and laugh whenever I look at the photograph of my family as penguins!

Think About It

Use the rubric to check my paragraph. Are all the traits of a good descriptive paragraph there? How does your paragraph compare against the rubric?

Ways to Publish a
Descriptive Paragraph

There are many ways to publish your work. Think about who will enjoy reading about your topic. Then pick the best way to share it. Here are some ideas for publishing your descriptive paragraph.

✓ Submit your descriptive paragraph to the school newspaper.

✓ Send your descriptive paragraph to a magazine that publishes student work.

✓ **Work with classmates to compile a book of descriptive paragraphs from your class.**

✓ **Videotape yourself reading your paragraph. Create a backdrop that illustrates your paragraph.**

✓ Create a computer presentation that includes photographs or drawings of your descriptive paragraph.

SCHOOL NEWS
WET, WILD, & WONDERFUL
By Marta

Writing Across the Content Areas
Descriptive Paragraph

You've learned that a descriptive paragraph is a clear, detailed picture in words of a specific person, place, or thing. Subjects in school can give you many topics to write about. Let's look at some examples.

Social Studies

- Describe a historical event or a day in the life of a historical figure.
- Write a description of a famous city or landmark you have visited.

Science

- Write a description of a classroom experiment that you observed.
- Describe a place on Earth or an object in space that scientists are studying.

Art and/or Music

- Write a description of a piece of artwork that you like.
- Describe going to a music concert or a dance performance.

What's a Character Sketch?

It's a description of a real person or a character in a book.

What's in a Character Sketch?

Thoughts
That's what my character thinks. Describing what my character thinks will make the person more interesting.

Appearance
That's what my character looks like. Describing my character will help the reader "see" the person.

Talk
That's what my character says. Describing what a character says makes the person seem real.

Actions
That's what my character does. My character's actions will tell a lot about his or her personality. The actions could be adventuresome like an astronaut in space or thoughtful like an author.

Why write a Character Sketch?

Describing a person can be fun, but it's also helpful. Here are some good reasons for writing a character sketch.

Entertainment

People are so interesting! Characters can be quiet or adventuresome, heroes or villains. They make good decisions or bad ones. Exploring the world of people—real and imaginary—is fascinating!

Information

Biographers write character sketches to help us get to know the people they are writing about. Reporters may write character sketches of people in the community. I can write a character sketch about an interesting person to share with others.

Understanding

No two people are exactly the same. Writing about real people and characters in books can help us understand others. We can recognize what we have in common. We can learn to appreciate our differences.

Writing Traits

What makes a good character sketch? A good character sketch makes the person seem real to the reader. Here are the writing traits of a good character sketch.

Information/ Organization	The sketch focuses on one character. It is well organized according to the character's looks, actions, words, and thoughts.
Voice/ Audience	The sketch contains word pictures to help the reader "see" the character.
Content/ Ideas	The sketch includes specific details about the character.
Word Choice/ Clarity	Ideas are expressed with interesting phrases.
Sentence Fluency	The sketch has a repeated sentence pattern to emphasize a point.
Grammar/ Mechanics	Spelling, punctuation, and capitalization are correct. There are no run-on sentences.

Let's read Ed Lee's character sketch on the next page. Did he follow all of the writing traits?

JOHNNY APPLESEED

Character MODEL Sketch

by Ed Lee

Johnny Appleseed is the title of a book by Reeve Lindbergh. It is also the name of the folk hero who is the main character in the book. Johnny Appleseed was a real person, but Appleseed wasn't his real last name. The name given to him at birth was John Chapman. He was later called Johnny Appleseed because he traveled around the country planting apple trees.

appearance → Johnny Appleseed was a thin man with a lean face. He traveled barefoot, sometimes in rain and snow. His clothes were old and worn, but he did not care about how he looked. He cared about what he did with his life.

actions → The life he chose was to spread apples across the country. He knew that apples were a very important crop in early America, and they could be grown easily. However, pioneers did not have room to carry small trees with them. Johnny Appleseed carried young, healthy apple trees to families who were settling the western frontier. Sometimes he shared a meal and talked with the families, but he never stayed long in any one place. *actions* Wherever he went next, he scattered his precious apple seeds.

Johnny Appleseed was a very gentle man. He walked alone through unsettled territory filled with wild animals, but he never carried anything to protect himself. He told people that *talk* he would never harm a living creature. He was also a very grateful person, and he appreciated the beauty around him. He spoke about his love for the grand green forests, the vast prairies, and the wide rivers. He spoke about his respect for the rich and fertile land he traveled.

thoughts → Johnny Appleseed gave a lot to people. The wilderness blossomed with his apple trees. Even so he did not believe that anyone owed him any special thanks. In our day, people express their thanks by writing books about him. The next time you take a bite of fresh-baked apple pie, think of Johnny Appleseed!

Character Sketch Rubric

The rubric below was made using the traits of a good character sketch on page 124. Assign one to four stars for each trait. Four stars mean that trait is excellent! Three stars mean it is very good. One or two stars mean that trait needs more work.

	Excelling ⭐⭐⭐	Achieving ⭐⭐	Developing ⭐⭐	Beginning ⭐
Information/ Organization	The sketch is about one character. It is well organized around the character's looks, actions, words, and thoughts.	The sketch is about one character. It is mostly organized around the character's looks, actions, words, and thoughts.	The sketch is about one character. It is sometimes organized around the character's looks, actions, words, and thoughts.	The sketch is about a character. It needs to be organized around the character's looks, acts, words, and thoughts.
Voice/ Audience	The sketch is full of vivid word pictures that help the reader "see" the character.	The sketch has many word pictures that help the reader "see" the character.	The sketch has some word pictures that help the reader "see" the character.	The sketch needs word pictures that help the reader "see" the character.
Content/ Ideas	The sketch includes many specific details that make the character seem real.	The sketch includes some specific details that make the character seem real.	The sketch includes a few specific details that make the character seem real.	The sketch needs specific details that make the character seem real.
Word Choice/ Clarity	Ideas are expressed with interesting and original phrases.	Ideas are expressed with interesting phrases most of the time.	Some ideas are expressed with interesting phrases.	Ideas with interesting phrases are needed.
Sentence Fluency	The sketch repeats a sentence pattern to emphasize a point.	The sketch sometimes repeats a sentence pattern to emphasize a point.	The sketch sometimes repeats sentence patterns for no reason.	The sketch often repeats sentence patterns for no reason.
Grammar/ Mechanics	There are no spelling or grammar errors. There are no run-on sentences.	There are few errors in spelling or grammar. There are no run-on sentences.	There are some spelling or grammar errors. There are run-on sentences.	There are many spelling and grammar errors. There are run-on sentences.

Character Sketch

Using the Rubric to Study the Model

Now, let's use the rubric to check Ed Lee's character sketch, "Johnny Appleseed." What score would you give Ed for each category in the rubric?

Information/Organization

- **The sketch focuses on one character.**
- **It is well organized according to the character's looks, actions, words, and thoughts.**

The first paragraph introduces Johnny Appleseed. There are many well-organized descriptions in this character sketch. In this paragraph, it tells me about the life he chose and his actions.

The life he chose was to spread apples across the country. He knew that apples were a very important crop in early America, and they could be grown easily. However, pioneers did not have room to carry small trees with them. Johnny Appleseed carried young, healthy apple trees to families who were settling the western frontier. Sometimes he shared a meal and talked with the families, but he never stayed long in any one place. Wherever he went next, he scattered his precious apple seeds.

Voice/Audience

- **The sketch contains word pictures to help the reader "see" the character.**

Ed uses a lot of descriptive words like **thin** and **worn** that help the reader picture Johnny Appleseed. Look at these sentences.

Johnny Appleseed was a thin man with a lean face. He traveled barefoot, sometimes in rain and snow. His clothes were old and worn, but he did not care about how he looked.

Content/Ideas
- The sketch includes specific details about the character.

The writer gives lots of specific details about Johnny Appleseed. This part tells me about his personality. I can really tell that he was a gentle person by the things he said and did.

Johnny Appleseed was a very gentle man. He walked alone through unsettled territory filled with wild animals, but he never carried anything to protect himself. He told people that he would never harm a living creature.

Word Choice/Clarity
- Ideas are expressed with interesting phrases.

The writer makes Johnny Appleseed's life sound exciting and special. All of the interesting phrases helped me picture what his life was like. This next part has one of my favorite phrases in it.

Johnny Appleseed gave a lot to people. The wilderness blossomed with his apple trees.

Using the Rubric to Study the Model

Sentence Fluency

- The sketch has a repeated sentence pattern to emphasize a point.

The writer says that Johnny Appleseed was a grateful person who appreciated the beauty around him. In the next two sentences Ed uses the same sentence pattern to make his point stronger. See how he repeats "He spoke about."

> He spoke about his love for the grand green forests, the vast prairies, and the wide rivers. He spoke about his respect for the rich and fertile land he roamed.

Grammar/Mechanics

- Spelling, punctuation, and capitalization are correct.
- There are no run-on sentences.

Every word is spelled correctly. The punctuation and capitalization are correct, too. I looked for run-on sentences, but couldn't find any.

> Johnny Appleseed was a real person, but Appleseed wasn't his real last name. The name given to him at birth was John Chapman. He was later called Johnny Appleseed because he traveled around the country planting apple trees.

My Turn!

Now it's my turn to write my own character sketch. Follow along to see how I'll use the rubric and good writing strategies.

Prewriting Gather Information

Information/Organization The sketch focuses on one character.

Writing Strategy Choose a character from a book and jot down some details about him or her.

When my teacher said we could write about a character from a book, I decided to write about Pecos Bill. He is a funny, wild character from a tall tale. Heroes in tall tales do things that regular people can't do. Everyone would probably enjoy reading about Pecos Bill's fantastic adventures.

First, I'll jot down a list of details about Pecos Bill.

The Book: Pecos Bill
        by Steven Kellogg

The Character: Pecos Bill

Details from the Book

- falls in a river
- grows up with coyotes
- feels like a member of the coyote pack
- always looks happy and smiling
- looks strong
- decides to become a Texan
- tells outlaws he'll turn them into cowboys
- chases and catches a horse named Lightning
- says Lightning can go free
- ropes a tornado
- sure of himself

Practice!

Think about an interesting character from a book that you would like to write about. Jot down details about your character.

Prewriting Organize Ideas

Information/Organization The sketch is well organized according to the character's looks, actions, words, and thoughts.

Writing Strategy Use a Spider Map to organize the character's looks, actions, words, and thoughts.

I know from the rubric that I need details about how my character acts, talks, thinks, and looks. I'm going to use my Spider Map to be sure I have those kinds of details. I'll also use the Spider Map to organize them.

Writer's Term

Spider Map

A **Spider Map** organizes information about a topic. The topic goes in the center, the categories go on the spider's "legs," and specific details about the categories are attached to the "legs."

Spider Map

Pecos Bill

Looks
- always looks happy and smiling
- strong

Actions
- falls in a river
- grows up with coyotes
- chases and catches Lightning
- ropes a tornado

Words
- says Lightning can go free
- tells outlaws he'll turn them into cowboys

Thoughts
- sure of himself
- feels like a member of the coyote pack
- decides to become a Texan

Practice!

Look at your list. Choose the details that describe how your character looks, acts, talks, and thinks. Organize these details using the Spider Map.

Think About It

Look at my notes and my Spider Map. Will they help me write a good character sketch?

Drafting **Write a Draft**

Voice/Audience   The sketch contains word pictures to help the reader "see" the character.

Writing Strategy   Include word pictures to help the reader "see" the character.

Now I'm ready to describe my character. I'll use my Spider Map to help me write a draft. I want my audience to know my character as well as I do. That means I have to make my character come alive by telling what he looks like and what he does, says, and thinks. My readers have to feel as if they have met Pecos Bill! I'll do my best with grammar and spelling, but I won't worry about mistakes. I'll get a chance to fix them later.

Writer's Term

Word Picture

A **word picture** uses descriptive words to help the readers "see" the character or event as they read. This makes the writing more interesting.

Boring: Bill liked living like a coyote.

Word Picture: Bill howled at the moon like his coyote brothers and sisters.

Proofreading Marks

⌐ Indent   ℓ Take out something

≡ Make a capital   ⊙ Add a period

/ Make a small letter   ¶ New paragraph

∧ Add something   SP Spelling error

Pecos Bill

In the book <u>Pecos Bill</u> by Steven Kellogg, the main character is an interesting person. He is called Pecos Bill because as a child he falls into the Pecos River. That action makes changes that make new actions happen in his whole life.

A coyote rescues baby Bill from the river in the nick of time. Bill grows up in a family of coyotes. He runs with the coyotes during starry nights. He howls with them at the full yellow moon. he believes he is a coyote

word pictures

One day Pecos Bill is taking a coyote nap a Texan on a horse discovers him. Bill becomes a Texan instead of a coyote. Always happy and smiling. he grows strong and sure of himself. He informs outlaws that he will turn them into honest cowboys they agree!

word pictures

Then Pecos Bill trys to catch a wild horse named Lightning. Bill chases Lightning from the Arctic Circle to the Grand Canyon. Finally, he leaps onto the silver stallion's back and sings to it in its own language. Then he offers the horse freedom Lightning decides to stay with Pecos Bill forever.

Practice!

Use your Spider Map to write your own draft. Remember to use word pictures to help your readers to "see" the character.

Think About It

Read my draft. Did I include word pictures to make my character come alive?

Revising Extend Writing

Content/Ideas The sketch includes specific details about the character.

Writing Strategy Add specific details about the character.

I know from the rubric that a character sketch needs specific details about the character. I have to think of details I can add about Pecos Bill.

I know! I can tell exactly what I mean when I say that Pecos Bill grows strong and sure of himself. I can also add specific details about how he turned the outlaws into honest cowboys.

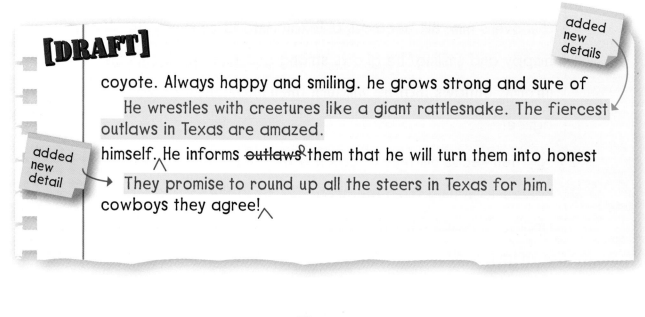

[DRAFT]

added new details

coyote. Always happy and smiling. he grows strong and sure of
He wrestles with creetures like a giant rattlesnake. The fiercest
outlaws in Texas are amazed.

added new detail

himself. He informs ~~outlaws~~ them that he will turn them into honest
They promise to round up all the steers in Texas for him.
cowboys they agree!

Practice!

Read your draft. Look for places to add details about your character. Add these details to your draft.

Revising **Clarify Writing**

Word Choice/Clarity Ideas are expressed with interesting phrases.

Writing Strategy Replace clichés with interesting phrases.

I read my paper to myself. I remembered from the rubric that I should use interesting phrases in my writing. I looked back and found a place in my draft where I had used a cliché. See what I did to fix it. I also noticed that I didn't use the correct form of a plural noun. I will fix that, too.

Writer's Term

Cliché

A **cliché** is an expression that has been overused. These expressions lose their meaning or freshness. For example, "flat as a pancake" and "good as gold" are clichés.

deleted cliché

added interesting phrase

just as he is sinking

[DRAFT]

A coyote rescues baby Bill from the river ~~in the nick of time~~. Bill grows up in a family of coyotes. He runs with the coyotes during starry nightes.

corrected plural noun

Think About It

Look at the changes I made. Have I added specific details about the character? Did I find and replace any clichés?

Practice!

Read your draft again. Look for places where you have used a cliché. Replace any clichés with interesting phrases.

Editing   Check Sentences

Sentence Fluency   The sketch has a repeated sentence pattern to emphasize a point.

Writing Strategy   Repeat a sentence pattern to emphasize a point.

Now I need to edit my writing. The rubric says that one way to emphasize a point is to repeat a sentence pattern. One sentence in my first paragraph was very long, and it didn't really emphasize the point I was trying to make. Here's how I fixed the problem.

an interesting person. He is called Pecos Bill because as a child he

repeated sentence pattern →

→ That accident changes more than Bill's name.

→ It changes his whole life.

falls into the Pecos River. ~~That action makes changes that make new actions happen in his whole life.~~

[DRAFT]

Look for places in your draft where repeating a sentence pattern will emphasize an important point. Be sure both sentences are clear and easy to read.

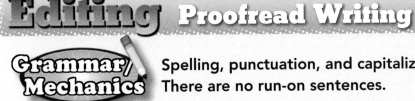

Editing Proofread Writing

Grammar/Mechanics Spelling, punctuation, and capitalization are correct. There are no run-on sentences.

Writing Strategy Make sure there are no run-on sentences.

Next I'll check spelling, capitalization, and punctuation. Also, the rubric reminds me to make sure that I don't have any run-on sentences.

Writer's Term

Run-On Sentences

A **run-on sentence** is made of two sentences that have been run together without a comma and a conjunction. To correct a run-on sentence, turn it into a **compound sentence** by adding a comma and a conjunction, such as **and, or,** or **but,** between the two complete thoughts.

[DRAFT]

corrected run-on sentence

, and

One day Pecos Bill is taking a coyote nap ∧ a Texan on a horse

discovers him. Bill becomes a Texan instead of a coyote. Always

Practice!

Edit your draft for spelling, punctuation, and capitalization. Fix any run-on sentences.

Grammar/Mechanics

For more practice fixing run-on sentences, use the exercises on the next two pages.

Think About It

Look at my editing. Did I use repeated sentence patterns, proofread my writing, and fix any run-on sentences?

Avoiding Run-on Sentences

Know the Rule

Begin every sentence with a capital letter and end with the correct punctuation mark. There should be no run-on sentences. A **run-on sentence** is two sentences that are run together without punctuation and a correct joining word.
  Example: Her story was long it was very interesting.
Use a comma followed by **and, but,** or **or** to join two sentences to make a compound sentence.
  Example: Her story was long, but it was very interesting.

Practice the Rule

Number a separate sheet of paper 1.–10. Read each sentence below. If the sentence is correct, write **Correct**. If there are errors in capitalization or punctuation, or if the sentence is a run-on sentence, write the sentence correctly.

1. On a hot June day in 1778, an important battle was fought.
2. One hero of the battle was Molly Hays most now call her Molly Pitcher.
3. Washington planned to attack the British and Molly knew there would be a terrible battle.
4. the sound of musket and cannon fire soon filled the air?
5. It was a hot summer day men began falling from the heat.
6. Molly saw the problem she heard the men cry for water.
7. Nearby, Molly spotted a cool stream she quickly filled a pitcher with water.
8. again and again, she brought pitchers of cool water to the thirsty soldiers.
9. Who was the woman who brought the water.
10. Her family called her Molly Hays the grateful soldiers called her Molly Pitcher.

Apply the Rule

Read the following paragraphs. Find any run-on sentences or errors in capitalization or punctuation. Then, on a separate piece of paper, rewrite the paragraphs correctly.

Annie Oakley is the most famous sharpshooter in american history. Annie could use a pistol, rifle, and shotgun with equal skill? For many years she was the star of Buffalo Bill's Wild West Show.

Phoebe ann oakley Mozee was born in Ohio in a log cabin in 1860. Her father died when she was 6 years old Annie began shooting game at age 9 to support her mother and seven siblings. She was only 16 when she entered a shooting contest against Frank Butler, an expert marksman. To everyone's amazement, she won the contest.

Later, Frank and Annie joined Buffalo Bill's wild west show. The public had never seen anything like annie's shooting ability. Toss up a dime she could shoot it in midair from 90 feet away! She could hit the thin edge of a playing card at 90 feet, then hit the card again and again as if fell to the ground. Annie starred in the Show for 17 years.

Annie oakley is remembered today in stories, poems, songs, and movies. One of the best celebrations of her life is a 1946 musical called "Annie get your Gun."

Publishing Share Writing

Create a portrait of my character to go with my character sketch. Display the illustrated character sketch on the classroom bulletin board.

I've finished my character sketch! Now, I have to decide how to publish it. I thought my classmates would want to "see" Pecos Bill in two ways. I decided to draw a picture of him to go along with my character sketch. They both went up on a class bulletin board that we call the Hall of Fame. It's filled with famous characters. Here's the checklist I used to check my sketch one more time.

My Checklist

✔ The title of the character sketch and my name are at the top of the paper.

✔ The sketch includes the character's looks, actions, words, and thoughts.

✔ There are many specific details.

✔ Interesting phrases express ideas. There are no clichés.

✔ Spelling, grammar, and punctuation are all correct. There are no run-on sentences.

✔ My handwriting is neat.

Practice!

Make a checklist to check your own character sketch. Then, make a final draft to post on your class bulletin board. You may want to draw a portrait of your character, too.

Pecos Bill
by Marta

In the book by Steven Kellogg, the main character is a funny, fantastic hero named Bill. He has wild, exciting adventures. He is called Pecos Bill because as a child he falls into the Pecos River. That accident changes more than Bill's name. It changes his whole life.

A coyote rescues baby Bill from the river just as he is sinking, and Bill grows up in a family of coyotes. He runs with the coyotes during starry nights. He howls with them at the full yellow moon. He believes he is a coyote.

One day Pecos Bill is taking a coyote nap, and a Texan on a horse discovers him. Bill becomes a Texan instead of a coyote. He is always happy and smiling, and he grows strong and sure of himself. He wrestles with creatures like a giant rattlesnake. The fiercest outlaws in Texas are amazed. He informs them that he will turn them into honest cowboys, and they agree! They promise to round up all the steers in Texas for him.

Then Pecos Bill tries to catch a wild horse named Lightning. Bill chases Lightning from the Arctic Circle to the Grand Canyon. Finally, he leaps onto the silver stallion's back and sings to it in its own language. Then he offers the horse freedom, but Lightning decides to stay with Pecos Bill forever.

Pecos Bill saves his bride, Slewfoot Sue, by roping a tornado in outer space! He and Sue are blown down to Earth, and they land on his family's wagon in California. What other character in a book has ever had adventures like that?

Think About It

Use the rubric to check my story. Are the traits of a good character sketch there? Don't forget to check your own sketch against the rubric.

Ways to Publish a
Character Sketch

As you decide how to publish your work, think about who will be reading it. Pick the best way to share your writing. Here are some ideas.

✔ **Illustrate your character sketch. Make front and back covers, staple the pages inside, and place your book in the class library.**

✔ **Hold a story exchange reading session with your classmates. Exchange character sketches to read about other people.**

✔ **Read your story to a younger student. Then, ask the student what they liked best about the character.**

✔ **Make your sketch into a play by adding dialogue.**

✔ **Create a "Classic Characters" radio series with classmates. Record your sketches, and play one sketch each week for a class of first graders.**

Writing Across the Content Areas
Character Sketch

You can get many writing ideas from the subjects you study in school. Let's look at some possibilities.

Math

- Write a character sketch about a famous mathematician.
- Read about a character in a book who enjoys math or uses math to solve a mystery. Use that character as the subject of your sketch.

Language Arts

- Write a character sketch of a writer or poet whose work you enjoy.
- Write a character sketch of a character from your favorite book.

Social Studies

- Choose a historical figure to be the subject of your character sketch.
- Create a fictional character from a period in history that interests you. For example, write about how a child living in Colonial America would look, act, talk, and think.

What's a Poetry Review?

It's an essay that describes the writer's experience of reading a poem.

What's in a Poetry Review?

Evidence of Careful Reading

The writer's ideas come from reading the poem carefully. A poetry review focuses on the feelings and images that the poem evokes. Reading a poem about the beauty of nature would make me want to spend time in a garden or at a lake.

Examples and Details

The writer supports his or her central idea with examples and details from the poem.

A Central Idea

The writer expresses a central idea about the poem. The central idea may be whether or not the writer liked the poem, or how the writer felt after reading the poem.

Why write a Poetry Review?

There are different reasons for writing a poetry review. Here are a few.

Personal Reflection
Poems can touch me in different ways. Writing about my response to a poem helps me put my feelings into words.

Entertainment
If I really love a poem, I enjoy sharing my response to it with others. My readers may find it interesting to compare my response with theirs.

Lessons
Sometimes a poem can teach a lesson. By giving the poem a closer look and writing about it, I can learn something of value.

Writing Traits

What makes a good poetry review? A poetry review should stay close to the poem. Here are some traits of a good poetry review.

Information/ Organization	The essay is about a poem. The writer's thoughts are well organized around a central idea.
Voice/ Audience	The first sentence sets a consistent tone for the audience.
Content/ Ideas	The essay includes details and examples from the poem.
Word Choice/ Clarity	The essay has comparisons to make descriptions clear.
Sentence Fluency	Different types of sentence beginnings help the writing flow.
Grammar/ Mechanics	Spelling, punctuation, and capitalization are correct. Comparative adjectives are used correctly.

Let's read Marcus West's poetry review on the next page. Did he follow the traits for a poetry review?

My Playful Friend, "The Wind"

by Marcus West

In his poem *The Wind,* Robert Louis Stevenson describes a child's joy experiencing the wind. In writing about the wind, he helps the reader feel what it is like to play outside and be a part of nature. A child who reads the poem might think, "Yes, I know that feeling." An older person reading the poem might feel like a child again.

Stevenson makes both the child speaker of the poem and the wind real characters. He makes the wind seem lively and real. He treats it like a person. The child always speaks to the wind directly. He says, "O wind," "O you," and "O blower." Maybe he is teasing the wind a little. In fact, the reader almost expects the wind to answer the child back.

In the first and second verses of the poem, the child explains how he knows the wind is there. He says that he saw the wind "toss the kites on high." He also heard it make sounds like the swish of "ladies' skirts across the grass." The child also shows how strong the wind is when he says, "I felt you push."

The child knows the wind is there and has seen the things it does. Yet everything the lively wind does is easier to see than the wind itself. Because of this, the child claims that the wind is hiding from him and tells it, "I could not see yourself at all." The child also is curious. He really wants to know who and what the wind is. In the last verse, the child asks whether the wind is "young or old," a "beast," or "just a stronger child than me."

The rhythm in this poem makes it seem playful. It is easy to imagine a little boy or girl outside, pretending the wind is a friend. The rhythm goes tah-DUM, tah-DUM, like a child skipping. Each two lines end with words that rhyme, like a child's song. The last two lines in each verse are the same. Children often say words over and over as they play. The poet uses rhythm, rhyme, and repeated words to make the reader feel as free as the wind and happy as a child.

(margin labels: central idea · detail · feelings · example · images · feeling *)*

Poetry Review Rubric

The rubric below was made using the traits of a good poetry review on page 146. To score a poetry review, assign one to four stars for each trait. Four stars means that trait is excellent! Three stars means it is very good. One or two stars means that trait needs more work.

	Excelling	Achieving	Developing	Beginning
Information/ Organization	The essay is about a poem. The writer's thoughts are well organized around a central idea.	The essay is about a poem. Most of the writer's thoughts are well organized around a central idea.	The essay is about a poem. Some of the writer's thoughts are organized around a central idea.	The essay needs to be about a poem. The writer's thoughts need to be organized around a central idea.
Voice/ Audience	The first sentence clearly sets a consistent tone for the audience.	The first sentence sets a consistent tone for the audience.	The first sentence sets a tone for the audience, but it is not maintained.	The first sentence needs to set a consistent tone for the audience.
Content/ Ideas	The essay always has relevant details and examples from the poem to support ideas.	The essay has relevant details and examples from the poem to support ideas most of the time.	The essay has relevant details and examples from the poem to support ideas sometimes.	The essay needs to have relevant details and examples from the poem to support ideas.
Word Choice/ Clarity	The essay has strong comparisons to make descriptions very clear.	The essay has comparisons to make descriptions clear.	The essay has comparisons, and they sometimes make descriptions clear.	The essay needs to have comparisons to make descriptions clear.
Sentence Fluency	Sentence variety keeps the writing flowing smoothly.	Sentence variety keeps the writing flowing smoothly most of the time.	Sentence variety keeps the writing flowing smoothly sometimes.	Sentence variety is needed to keep the writing flowing smoothly.
Grammar/ Mechanics	Spelling, punctuation, capitalization, and comparative adjectives are used correctly.	Spelling, punctuation, capitalization, and comparative adjectives are mostly correct.	There are some errors in spelling, punctuation, capitalization, and/or comparative adjectives.	There are many errors in spelling, punctuation, capitalization, and/or comparative adjectives.

Poetry Review
Using the Rubric to Study the Model

Now, let's use the rubric to check Marcus West's review, "My Playful Friend, 'The Wind.'" What score would you give Marcus for each category in the rubric?

Information/Organization

- The essay is about a poem.
- The writer's thoughts are well organized around a central idea.

I knew from the very first sentence that this essay is about a poem called "The Wind" by Robert Louis Stevenson. Marcus organizes his thoughts around a central idea. Each paragraph talks about a particular feeling or image that the poem brings to mind. In this example, he explains how Stevenson made the wind seem real.

Stevenson makes both the child speaker of the poem and the wind real characters. He makes the wind seem lively and real. He treats it like a person. The child always speaks to the wind directly. He says, "O wind," "O you," and "O blower." Maybe he is teasing the wind a little. In fact, the reader almost expects the wind to answer the child back.

Voice/Audience

- The first sentence sets a consistent tone for the audience.

In his first sentence, Marcus sets a tone that he holds consistently throughout the essay. Even though the poet never says that he is "describing a child's joy experiencing the wind," that is how Marcus responded to the poem. With his choice of the phrase **a child's joy,** he sets a tone of happy emotion.

In his poem *The Wind*, Robert Louis Stevenson describes a child's joy experiencing the wind.

Content/ Ideas

- The essay includes details and examples from the poem.

I really like the way Marcus uses details and examples to support his thoughts about the poem. Here's a good example. He believes that the child in the poem is curious about the wind. This is how Marcus supports this idea in his review.

> The child also is curious. He really wants to know who and what the wind is. In the last verse, the child asks whether the wind is "young or old," a "beast," or "just a stronger child than me."

Word Choice/ Clarity

- The essay has comparisons to make descriptions clear.

Sometimes the writer uses comparisons to make his descriptions clear. He compares something he is describing to something else that is familiar to the reader. In this example, he is describing the rhythm and rhyme of the poem. When he compares rhythm and rhyme to skipping and singing he makes his meaning clearer to me.

> The rhythm in this poem makes it seem playful. It is easy to imagine a little boy or girl outside, pretending the wind is a friend. The rhythm goes tah-DUM, tah-DUM, like a child skipping. Each two lines end with words that rhyme, like a child's song.

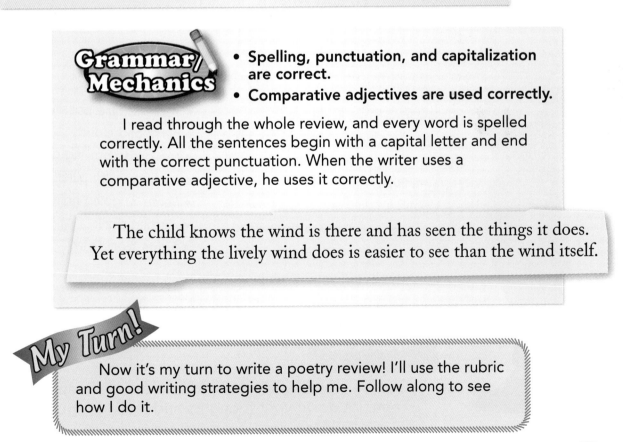

Sentence Fluency

• Different types of sentence beginnings help the writing flow.

The writer does a good job of varying the beginnings of his sentences. Almost every sentence begins differently from the one before it. This makes his writing easy to read and understand. It also makes it more interesting.

> In the first and second verses of the poem, the child explains how he knows the wind is there. He says that he saw the wind "toss the kites on high." He also heard it make sounds like the swish of "ladies' skirts across the grass." The child also shows how strong the wind is when he says, "I felt you push."

Grammar/ Mechanics

• Spelling, punctuation, and capitalization are correct.
• Comparative adjectives are used correctly.

I read through the whole review, and every word is spelled correctly. All the sentences begin with a capital letter and end with the correct punctuation. When the writer uses a comparative adjective, he uses it correctly.

> The child knows the wind is there and has seen the things it does. Yet everything the lively wind does is easier to see than the wind itself.

My Turn!

Now it's my turn to write a poetry review! I'll use the rubric and good writing strategies to help me. Follow along to see how I do it.

Prewriting Gather Information

Information/Organization The essay is about a poem.

Writing Strategy Jot down some ideas about a poem I find interesting.

Today, my teacher asked us to look through some poetry books and choose a poem that we find interesting. Whatever poem we choose will be the subject of an essay—a poetry review. I found a poem by Edna St. Vincent Millay that I really liked. It's called "Afternoon on a Hill."

I read the poem carefully and jotted down some notes. I included what I think the poem is about, how the poem makes me feel, and what it helps me to see.

My Notes

- painted pictures in my mind
- describes a happy day on the hill
- Verse 1: happy in the sun
- happy like a child
- a hundred flowers
- "gladdest"—a funny, happy word

- Verse 2: time passing
- cliffs and clouds
- the grass bowing and rising
- looking "with quiet eyes"
- Verse 3: going home
- getting dark
- lights from town

Choose a poem that you find interesting. Read it. Then, jot down your thoughts and feelings about it.

Information/Organization The writer's thoughts are well organized around a central idea.

Writing Strategy Make a Network Tree to organize details about my thoughts.

I know from the rubric that I need to organize my thoughts before I write. I'll use a Network Tree. The central idea goes at the top, verses go in the second level, and then the details that support level two.

Writer's Term

Network Tree

A **Network Tree** organizes information according to the level of ideas. At the top is the central idea. Key details that support the central idea go on the next level. Details that support these go on the bottom level.

Network Tree

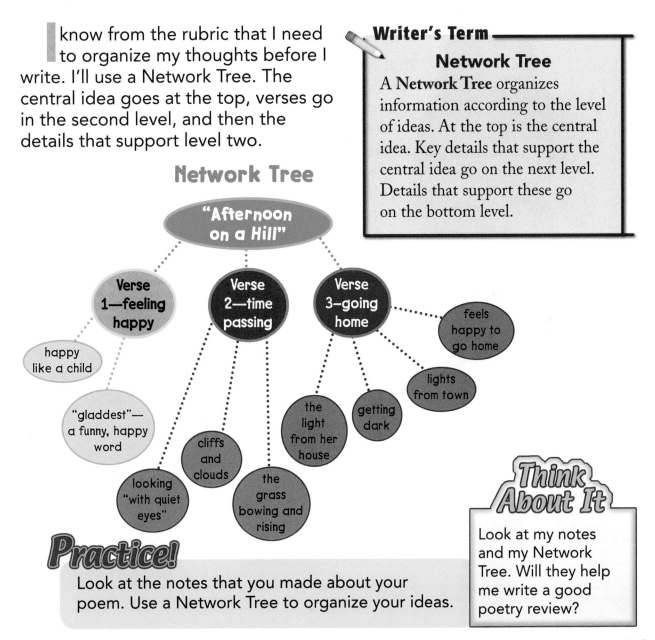

Practice!

Look at the notes that you made about your poem. Use a Network Tree to organize your ideas.

Think About It

Look at my notes and my Network Tree. Will they help me write a good poetry review?

Descriptive Writing ■ Poetry Review: Response to Literature   **153**

Drafting Write a Draft

Voice/Audience The first sentence sets a consistent tone for the audience.

Writing Strategy Sum up my thoughts in a topic sentence to set the tone.

Now it's time to write my draft. The rubric tells me that I need to sum up my thoughts about the poem in a topic sentence. This sentence will set the tone of my review. I liked the word pictures that this poem painted, so my topic sentence should talk about that. Then my readers will know what I'll be discussing in the essay and how I feel about my topic. You can read the first part of my draft on the next page.

"Afternoon on a Hill"
a poem by Edna St. Vincent Millay

topic sentence

The words of Edna St. Vincent Millay's poem "Afternoon on a Hill" seem to paint pictures in my mind. The words she chose help me see and feel the things that she imagined. I think this poem is about being happy wherever you are.

Millay tells a story in this poem. She goes out in the country during the day. She sits in the sunshine on top of a hill. She looks at flowers and clouds. At the end of the day, when it gets dark, she goes back home.

Practice!

Use your notes and Network Tree to write your own draft. Remember to write a topic sentence that sums up your thoughts and sets the tone for your essay.

Think About It

Read my draft. Did my topic sentence sum up my thoughts and set the tone for my essay?

Revising Extend Writing

Content/Ideas
The essay includes details and examples from the poem.

Writing Strategy Add any important details I left out.

I've finished my draft, so I'll now check to see if I included all the important details. The rubric tells me to add any important details that I left out of my essay. I'll add some details and an example from the poem to my draft. I will also check to see if all my plural nouns are formed correctly.

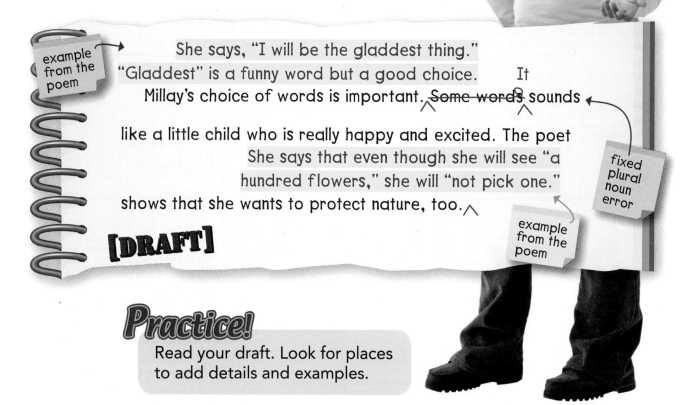

example from the poem

She says, "I will be the gladdest thing."
"Gladdest" is a funny word but a good choice.   It
Millay's choice of words is important. ~~Some words~~ sounds

like a little child who is really happy and excited. The poet
She says that even though she will see "a
hundred flowers," she will "not pick one."
shows that she wants to protect nature, too.

fixed plural noun error

example from the poem

[DRAFT]

Practice!
Read your draft. Look for places to add details and examples.

Revising Clarify Writing

Word Choice/ Clarity The essay has comparisons to make descriptions clear.

Writing Strategy Use comparisons to make my description clear.

The rubric tells me that using comparisons will help make my writing clearer. I read my draft again. My thoughts about the second verse are not very clear. I put in some comparisons that will help the reader understand just what I mean.

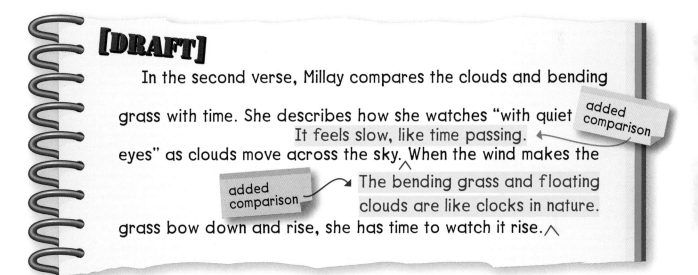

[DRAFT]

In the second verse, Millay compares the clouds and bending

grass with time. She describes how she watches "with quiet

added comparison

It feels slow, like time passing.

eyes" as clouds move across the sky. When the wind makes the

added comparison

The bending grass and floating clouds are like clocks in nature.

grass bow down and rise, she has time to watch it rise.∧

Practice!

Read your draft again. Look for descriptions that aren't clear. Add comparisons that will make them clearer.

Think About It

Look at my revisions. Did I add important details and use comparisons to make my descriptions clearer?

Editing Check Sentences

Sentence Fluency Different types of sentence beginnings help the writing flow.

Writing Strategy Use a variety of sentence beginnings.

It's time for me to edit my writing. According to the rubric, it's important to use different types of sentence beginnings. If I start every sentence the same way, my writing won't flow and will be hard to understand.

I looked over my essay and found a place where I used the same words over and over at the beginning. Look at how I fixed the problem.

[DRAFT]

> varied sentence beginnings

Millay tells a story in this poem. She goes out in the country
during the day. ~~She sits~~ *Sitting* in the sunshine on top of a hill,~~. She~~
looks at flowers and clouds. At the end of the day, when it
gets dark, she goes back home.

Practice!

Read through your draft. Make sure you have used different types of sentence beginnings. Don't forget to look for any run-on sentences.

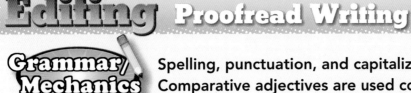

Editing Proofread Writing

Grammar/ Mechanics Spelling, punctuation, and capitalization are correct. Comparative adjectives are used correctly.

Writing Strategy Make sure that comparative adjectives are used correctly.

Now I'll proofread my essay for spelling, punctuation, and capitalization. The rubric says to make sure I've used comparative adjectives correctly. I'll look for places where I've compared two people, places, or things.

Writer's Term

Comparative Adjectives

Comparative adjectives describe the differences between two things. If an adjective has one syllable, the comparative is formed by adding **-er**. Adjectives with two syllables or more form the comparative by adding the word **more**. When a two syllable adjective ends in **-ly,** the **-y** is changed to **-ier**.

The poet can see her house from the hilltop. Maybe its light

seems ~~more bright~~ ^{brighter} than the others. When I come home after

dark, I feel ~~good~~ ^{better} if there are lights on.

corrected comparative adjectives

[DRAFT]

Practice!

Edit your draft for spelling, punctuation, and capitalization. Fix any comparative adjective that is incorrect.

Grammar/ Mechanics

For more practice using comparative adjectives, use the exercises on the next two pages.

Think About It

Look at my edits. Did I use different types of sentence beginnings, and use all of my comparative adjectives correctly?

Comparative Adjectives

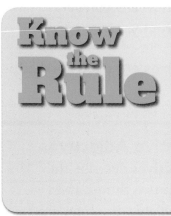

Adjectives are words that describe or modify nouns and pronouns. **Comparative adjectives** are used to describe the differences between two nouns or pronouns.
When an adjective has only one syllable, form the comparative adjectives by adding **-er**. **(bright/brighter)**
When an adjective has two syllables or more, form the comparative by using the word **more** before the adjective. **(important/more important)**
When a two syllable adjective ends in **-ly,** drop the **-y** and add **-ier**. **(early/earlier)**

Practice the Rule

Number a separate piece of paper 1.–8. Then read these sentences and decide how to form the comparative adjective from the adjective in parentheses. Write the correct form of the comparative adjective.

1. I used to think that poetry would be (difficult) to understand than prose.
2. I discovered that reading poems is (fun) than I expected.
3. Understanding poetry is a lot (easy) than I thought it would be, too.
4. There is one form of poetry that I think is (good) than other forms.
5. It is called haiku, and in my opinion, it is (beautiful) than other kinds of poetry.
6. With only three lines, a haiku is (short) than most other poems.
7. The way haiku uses language is (exciting) than other forms of poetry.
8. The poet must paint a mental picture in (few) words than most poetry forms allow.

Apply the Rule

Read this description of Edna St. Vincent Millay's poem "Ballad of the Harp-Weaver." Find any comparative adjectives that have been formed incorrectly. Rewrite the paragraphs with correct comparative adjectives.

My favorite poem by Edna St. Vincent Millay is "The Ballad of the Harp-Weaver." My mother first read it to me when I was much more young. It's about the love of a mother for her child.

The poem's tale begins in the fall. A mother and her little son are alone and very poor. The only thing she owns is "a harp with a woman's head nobody will buy."

As time passes, the mother sees her son grow more thin. His clothing becomes more shabby. Still he is more happy than many people with much more. His mother loves him.

The winter grows more fiercer. The mother and son are more cold and more hungry than ever. Then on Christmas night, the mother sits down with the harp. As her thin fingers move through the strings, beautiful clothes begin to appear. Morning finds her sitting with the harp against her shoulder, frozen by the cold. But she is smiling. Beside her, piled to the sky, are the most fine clothes—"the clothes of a king's son"—and they are just her son's size.

Publishing Share Writing

Read my response aloud to the class.

My poetry review is finished! Now I have to think about publishing it. I'd like to share the poem and my review with the rest of the class. I could hand out copies of the poem or read it aloud to the class, then follow up by reading my response to the poem. Here's the checklist I'll use.

My Checklist

✔ The title of my poetry review and my name are at the top of the page.

✔ There are lots of details and examples from the poem.

✔ The comparisons I used help to make my descriptions clear.

✔ A variety of sentence beginnings make the writing flow.

✔ Spelling, grammar, and punctuation are all correct. Comparative adjectives are used correctly.

✔ My handwriting is neat.

Practice!

Make a checklist to check your own poetry review. Then make a final draft. Practice reading the poem and your essay before reading them aloud to your class.

"Afternoon on a Hill"
a poem by Edna St. Vincent Millay

The words of Edna St. Vincent Millay's poem "Afternoon on a Hill" paint pictures in my mind. The words she chose help me see and feel the things that she imagined. I think this poem is about being happy wherever you are.

Millay tells a story in this poem. She goes out in the country during the day. Sitting in the sunshine on top of a hill, she looks at flowers and clouds. At the end of the day, when it gets dark, she goes back home.

In the first verse, Millay shows what it is like to feel happy. She says, "I will be the gladdest thing." At first I thought this might be a mistake in writing. I thought it was more correct to say, "I will be the most glad thing." Then I decided that "gladdest" makes the poet sound like a happy child. I think Millay is trying to show how a child feels. These words make me feel very happy, too. Poets often use words in surprising ways to express their feelings.

In the second verse, Millay compares the clouds and bending grass with time. She describes how she watches "with quiet eyes" as clouds move across the sky. It feels slow, like time is passing. When the wind makes the grass bow down and rise, she has time to watch it rise. The bending grass and floating clouds are like clocks in nature. They also make me think about how things change as time goes by. I think the second verse is a tiny bit sadder than the first verse.

In the third verse, Millay shows that a lot of time has gone by. The sky must be darker than it was earlier in the day. People in the town are starting to turn lights on in their houses. The poet can see her house from the hilltop. Maybe its light seems brighter than the others. When I come home after dark, I feel better if there are lights on. Lighted windows make a house feel welcoming. I think Millay feels good about going home.

Millay's choice of words is important. She says, "I will be the gladdest thing." "Gladdest" is a funny word but a good choice. It sounds like a little child who is really happy and excited. The poet shows that she wants to protect nature, too. She says that even though she will see "a hundred flowers," she will "not pick one."

The poet likes being alone on the hill, looking at the flowers and clouds as she sits in the sun. She also likes going back to her family. One place is not better than the other. They are both important, and you can be happy wherever you are.

Think About It

Use the rubric to check my poetry review. Are all the traits of a good poetry review there? Don't forget to use the rubric to check your own.

Ways to Publish a Poetry Review

As you decide how to publish your work, think about who will enjoy reading it. Then choose the best way to share it. Here are some ideas for publishing your poetry review.

✓ **Create an illustrated poster with a copy of the poem and a copy of your essay.**

✓ **Work with a classmate to compile a booklet of poems and reviews. Include illustrations.**

✓ **Have a class poetry festival. Include poetry readings by published poets and classmates.**

✓ **Find music that matches the tone of your poem. Play the music while you read your review to the class.**

✓ **Submit your essay and a copy of the poem to a magazine that publishes student reviews of literature.**

by Marta

POEM

Writing Across the Content Areas
Poetry Review

Did you know that different school subjects give you many chances to read poetry and write a poetry review? Here are some examples.

Social Studies

- Read a poem about a historic event and write a response to the poem.
- Learn about a poet whose work influenced history. Read one of the poet's poems and write a review.

Art and/or Music

- Read a poem that focuses on a work of art and write a response to the poem. Find a copy of the work of art to include with your essay.
- Find a selection of music that you feel matches the tone of a poem you enjoy. Write a review of the poem and include the music as part of your review.

Science

- Select a poem that relates to a topic you are studying in science (weather, the ocean, nature's cycles, insects, etc.). Write a response to the poem.
- Find a poem about a famous scientist or a poem that was written by a scientist. Write a review of the poem.

DESCRIPTIVE test writing

Read the Writing Prompt

Every writing test starts with a writing prompt. As you begin the test, look for three helpful parts in the writing prompt.

Setup This part of the writing prompt gives you the background information you need to get ready for writing.

Task This part of the writing prompt tells you exactly what you're supposed to write: a descriptive essay about what you saw.

Scoring Guide This section tells how your writing will be scored. You should include everything on the list to do well on the test.

T hink about the rubrics that you've been using in this book. When you take a writing test, you won't always have all the information that's on a rubric. Don't worry—the scoring guide is a lot like a rubric. It lists everything you need to think about to write a good paper. Many scoring guides will include the six important traits of writing that are in all of the rubrics in this book:

Information/Organization Content/Ideas Sentence Fluency

Voice/Audience Word Choice/Clarity Grammar/Mechanics

Imagine that you witnessed an amazing event or saw an incredible sight.

Write a descriptive essay about what you saw.

Be sure your essay

- describes an event and is well organized around a main idea.
- begins with a description that gets the audience's attention.
- includes sensory details (what the writer sees, hears, smells, touches, and tastes) to describe people, things, and events.
- includes only sentences that describe the subject of your essay.
- has no sentences that are too long.
- has correct grammar, spelling, and punctuation.

Writing Traits
in the Scoring Guide

The scoring guide in the writing prompt on page 169 has been made into this chart. How does the information relate to the writing traits in the rubrics you've been using? Test prompts won't always include all of the six writing traits, but this one does!

Information/Organization
• Be sure your descriptive essay describes an event and is well organized around a main idea.

Voice/Audience
• Be sure your essay begins with a description that gets the audience's attention.

Content/Ideas
• Be sure your essay includes sensory details (what the writer sees, hears, smells, touches, and tastes) to describe people, things, and events.

Word Choice/Clarity
• Be sure your essay includes only sentences that describe the subject of your essay.

Sentence Fluency
• Be sure your essay has no sentences that are too long.

Grammar/Mechanics
• Be sure your essay has correct grammar, spelling, and punctuation.

Let's look at Katy O'Connor's essay on the next page. Did she follow the scoring guide?

Dolphins at Play

by Katy O'Connor

The sky was blue, and the summer sun was hot and bright out on the ocean when we went looking for dolphins. The captain of our boat said the water was smooth, but waves rocked us from side to side. I was standing by the railing, the wind pulling at my jacket. Suddenly, a splash from a big wave cooled my face and I tasted salt.

Then—swoosh!

A dolphin leapt from the water just a few feet away. He flew through the air then dove back into the water. His back was dark gray, but his sides were tan-colored. His belly was smooth and white. He was so near that I could see the black stripe that circled his eye. Suddenly I saw another dolphin, and then another! I began to count. There were at least ten of them.

The captain stood next to me. "Those are called Common Dolphins," he said. "It looks like a group of young males."

The dolphins looked like they were surfing the waves that came off the front of the boat. Then they seemed to play a game of tag. Sometimes one dolphin would chase another. If he got close enough, he'd nip at the other's tail! Then the group of dolphins swam as fast as they could toward each other. I was sure they were going to crash, but at the very last second they'd bend sharply away and disappear in the waves.

Every now and then we'd see a piece of seaweed floating by. Suddenly one of the dolphins caught a piece of seaweed on his nose. He tossed it into the air, and another dolphin jumped out of the water and batted it back! More dolphins joined them in this funny game of catch.

We could just see the shore in the distance. Before the dolphins left, however, they put on one last performance. The biggest dolphin rose straight up out of the deep blue water then crashed back down, making a huge splash. The sea spray dampened my face. A smaller one followed him. A third dolphin rose up on his tail and traveled backwards across the waves while another did a spin in the air. They looked like clowns at a circus, each one trying to do the most amazing trick. Their chatter sounded like squeaky laughter, as they disappeared.

Using the Scoring Guide to Study the Model

Now, let's use the scoring guide to check Katy's writing test, "Dolphins at Play." See if you can find examples from her writing to show how well she did on each part of the scoring guide.

Information/Organization

- **The essay describes an event. The essay is well organized around a main idea.**

Katy writes about an exciting event. Her essay describes the day she went out on the ocean in a boat, looking for—and finding—dolphins. She organizes her essay around this main idea. Here's how she describes her first dolphin sighting. Notice that this is the perfect time to tell the reader what the dolphins looked like.

Then—swoosh!
A dolphin leapt from the water just a few feet away. He flew through the air then dove back into the water. His back was dark gray, but his sides were tan-colored. His belly was smooth and white. He was so near that I could see the black stripe that circled his eye.

Voice/Audience

- **The essay begins with a description that gets the audience's attention.**

The scoring guide reminds you that it's important to grab your audience's attention with your beginning description. See how her description puts the reader on a boat, out in the ocean, on a hot summer's day.

The sky was blue, and the summer sun was hot and bright out on the ocean when we went looking for dolphins. The captain of our boat said the water was smooth, but waves rocked us from side to side. I was standing by the railing, the wind pulling at my jacket. Suddenly, a splash from a big wave cooled my face and I tasted salt.

Content/Ideas

- The essay includes sensory details (what the writer sees, hears, smells, touches, and tastes) to describe people, things, and events.

Katy brings her paragraph to life with details related to the five senses. She tells how something looks, sounds, smells, feels, or tastes. She creates word pictures. Here is an example.

The biggest dolphin rose straight up out of the deep blue water then crashed back down, making a huge splash. The sea spray dampened my face. A smaller one followed him. A third dolphin rose up on his tail and traveled backwards across the waves while another did a spin in the air. They looked like clowns at a circus, each one trying to do the most amazing trick. Their chatter sounded like squeaky laughter, as they disappeared.

Word Choice/Clarity

- The essay includes only sentences that describe the subject of the essay.

In her essay, Katy used only sentences that were related to her main idea: looking for and finding dolphins. This is important because unrelated sentences can be confusing to the reader. In this example, she describes how a piece of seaweed becomes the focus for a game of catch.

Every now and then we'd see a piece of seaweed floating by. Suddenly one of the dolphins caught a piece of seaweed on his nose. He tossed it into the air, and another dolphin jumped out of the water and batted it back! More dolphins joined them in this funny game of catch.

Using the Scoring Guide to Study the Model

• **The essay has no sentences that are too long.**

The scoring guide reminds you that sentences in your essay should not be too long. Sentences that are too long should be broken into shorter ones. Katy made sure that her sentences were not too long and that each expressed one clear thought, feeling, or idea.

The dolphins looked like they were surfing the waves that came off the front of the boat. Then they seemed to play a game of tag. Sometimes one dolphin would chase another. If he got close enough, he'd nip at the other's tail!

• **The essay has correct grammar, spelling, and punctuation.**

The scoring guide reminds you to check grammar, spelling, and punctuation. Look for any mistakes you often make, such as forming plural nouns incorrectly or using incorrect punctuation at the end of a sentence. Katy seems to have caught any mistakes she made in her first draft. Her final draft doesn't have any errors.

Planning My Time

Before giving us a writing test prompt, my teacher tells us how much time we'll have to complete the test. First, I'll think about how much time I'll have. Then I'll divide the time into the different parts of the writing process. I'll also make sure I give myself some time to study the writing prompt. Here's how I've divided my time into four steps.

Step 4:
Editing
10 minutes

Step 1:
Prewriting
25 minutes

Step 3:
Revising
10 minutes

Step 2:
Drafting
15 minutes

Prewriting Study the Writing Prompt

Information/ Organization

Writing Strategy Study the writing prompt to be sure I know what to do.

Once I have my writing prompt, I study it and make sure I know exactly what I'm supposed to do. Most writing prompts have a setup, a task, and a scoring guide. You should find these and label them on the writing prompt, just like I did. Then you can circle key words that tell what kind of writing you need to do. I circled **an essay that describes** because these words tell me what kind of writing I'll be doing. I circled the word **celebration** because that tells me what I'll be describing.

My Descriptive Test Prompt

Setup — Think about how we celebrate an important national holiday.

Task — Write (an essay that describes) a memorable (celebration) you witnessed and enjoyed.

Scoring Guide — Be sure your essay

- describes an event and is well organized around a main idea.
- begins with a description that gets the audience's attention.
- includes sensory details (what the writer sees, hears, smells, touches, and tastes) to describe people, things, and events.
- includes only sentences that describe the subject of your essay.
- has no sentences that are too long.
- has correct grammar, spelling, and punctuation.

Next I'll think about how the scoring guide relates to the six writing traits I've studied in the rubrics. All of the traits might not be included in every scoring guide, but I need to remember them all to write a good essay.

Information/Organization
- Be sure your descriptive essay describes an event and is well organized around a main idea.

When I describe an event, it's important to put down the details in an organized way around the main idea.

Voice/Audience
- Be sure your essay begins with a description that gets the audience's attention.

I know that it's important that I grab the reader's attention right away with my opening description.

Content/Ideas
- Be sure your essay includes sensory details (what the writer sees, hears, smells, touches, and tastes) to describe people, things, and events.

I need to think about details such as sights, sounds, smells, tastes, and the feel of things related to my essay's topic.

Word Choice/Clarity
- Be sure your essay includes only sentences that describe the subject of your essay.

I don't want to confuse my reader. I need to make sure all my sentences are related to the subject of my essay.

Sentence Fluency
- Be sure your essay has no sentences that are too long.

I know that if some of my sentences are too long, I need to break them into shorter ones.

Grammar/Mechanics
- Be sure your essay has correct grammar, spelling, and punctuation.

Whenever I write anything, I need to check my grammar, spelling, and punctuation!

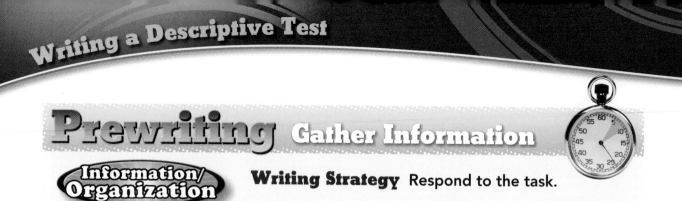

Prewriting Gather Information

Information/Organization

Writing Strategy Respond to the task.

I know that writers gather information before they begin writing. When you write for a test, you can gather information from the writing prompt. Look at the task in the writing prompt. This is the part that explains what you are supposed to write. Remember, you won't have much time when writing for a test. That's why it's important to think about how you'll respond before you begin to write.

I know that I have to write an essay. I need to describe a celebration. Jotting down notes will help. I have to do this step quickly because the clock is ticking!

Task — Write an essay that describes a memorable celebration you witnessed and enjoyed.

Fireworks on New Year's Eve

- midnight
- cold night air
- Mom and Dad counting down
- exploding rockets
- sparks in the air

- lots of colors
- fireworks like flowers and fountains
- loud booming sounds
- people saying "ooh"
- spinning fireworks
- a burning smell
- smoke
- silence

Remember! Think about how you'll respond to the task part of your writing prompt before you write. Then jot down some notes to gather information.

Prewriting Organize Ideas

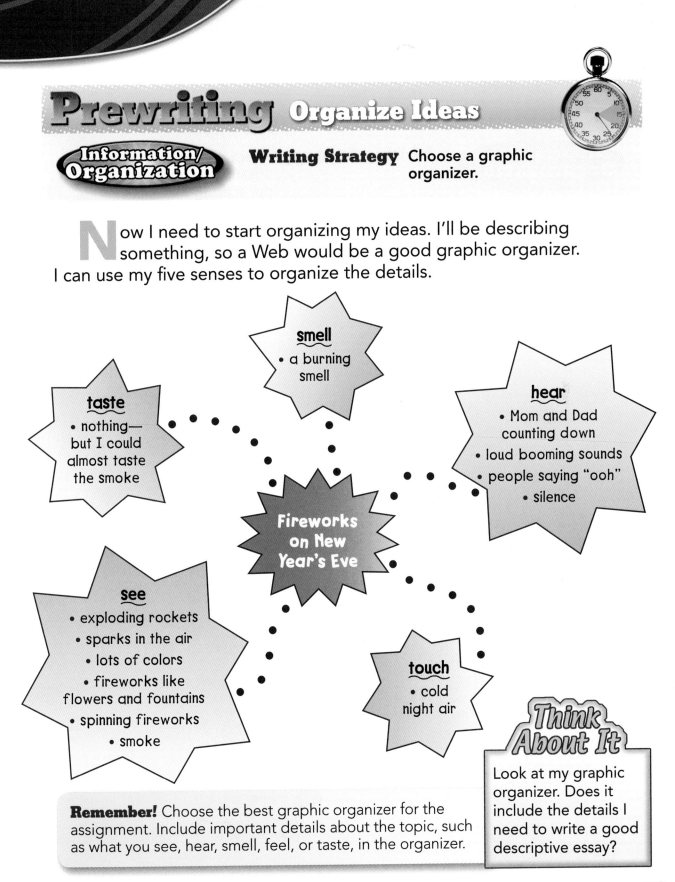

Information/Organization

Writing Strategy Choose a graphic organizer.

Now I need to start organizing my ideas. I'll be describing something, so a Web would be a good graphic organizer. I can use my five senses to organize the details.

smell
• a burning smell

taste
• nothing—but I could almost taste the smoke

hear
• Mom and Dad counting down
• loud booming sounds
• people saying "ooh"
• silence

Fireworks on New Year's Eve

see
• exploding rockets
• sparks in the air
• lots of colors
• fireworks like flowers and fountains
• spinning fireworks
• smoke

touch
• cold night air

Think About It
Look at my graphic organizer. Does it include the details I need to write a good descriptive essay?

Remember! Choose the best graphic organizer for the assignment. Include important details about the topic, such as what you see, hear, smell, feel, or taste, in the organizer.

Prewriting Check the Scoring Guide

Information/Organization

Writing Strategy Check my graphic organizer against the scoring guide.

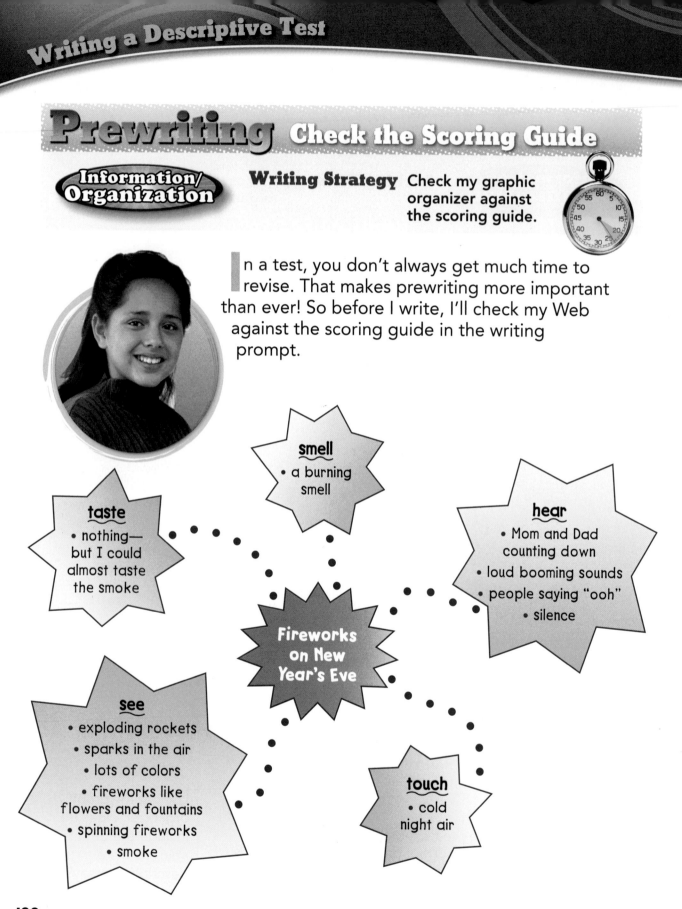

In a test, you don't always get much time to revise. That makes prewriting more important than ever! So before I write, I'll check my Web against the scoring guide in the writing prompt.

smell
• a burning smell

taste
• nothing—but I could almost taste the smoke

hear
• Mom and Dad counting down
• loud booming sounds
• people saying "ooh"
• silence

Fireworks on New Year's Eve

see
• exploding rockets
• sparks in the air
• lots of colors
• fireworks like flowers and fountains
• spinning fireworks
• smoke

touch
• cold night air

 **Information/Organization** • describes an event and is well organized around a main idea.

I'll use my Web as my guide when I write my draft.

 **Voice/Audience** • begins with a description that gets the audience's attention.

I'll use the beginning of my description to grab the reader's attention.

 **Content/Ideas** • includes sensory details (what the writer sees, hears, smells, touches, and tastes) to describe people, things, and events.

In my Web, I used my five senses to organize my notes. When I begin writing my draft, I'll use these details to create word pictures for my reader.

 **Word Choice/Clarity** • includes sentences that describe the subject of your essay.

As I'm writing my draft, I'll make sure all my sentences are about my subject.

 **Sentence Fluency** • has no sentences that are too long.

I'll have to check this after I write my draft. If some of my sentences are too long, I'll break them into shorter ones.

 **Grammar/Mechanics** • has correct grammar, spelling, and punctuation.

I need to check my grammar, spelling, and punctuation when I edit my draft.

Think About It

Does my graphic organizer cover all the points in the scoring guide? What else do I need to include?

Remember! Before you begin writing, look back at the scoring guide in the writing prompt to make sure you know everything you need to do.

Drafting Write a Draft

Voice/Audience

Writing Strategy Remember my purpose as I write.

The purpose of my essay is to describe the important details of an event. I'll begin with a description that gets my audience's attention. It will also tell what the essay is about and when and where the event takes place.

[DRAFT] Fireworks for the New Year
by Marta

On New Year's Eve, my town lit up the sky with the biggest display of fireworks anyone had ever seen. And why not. It was about to become a new year.

It was getting close to midnight. I shivered in the crisp, cold air. I pulled my hat over my ears and zipped my jacket up tight. my mom and dad started to count down: "ten, nine, eight, seven, six . . ." Then—WOW!

A rocket exploded in the sky. There were sparks in the air. A split-second later came a gigantic boom. It was so loud I had to cover my ears. I could see smoke in the light from the sparks. A smell like something burning was in the air.

Then three more fireworks exploded at the same time. they were blue and green and opened out like a flower. I heard more booms and the burning smell got stronger. All around me

Proofreading Marks

⊐ Indent   ℓ Take out something
≡ Make a capital   ⊙ Add a period
/ Make a small letter   ¶ New paragraph
∧ Add something   SP Spelling error

[DRAFT]

people were saying, "ooh!" and "ah!" My little brother got scared and Dad had to pick him up and hold him. We probably should have left him at home with a babysitter.

I couldn't believe all the colors. Purple and yellow and orange glowed in the sky. Each firework exploded a different way. Some went up like big water fountains and others spread out sideways and some even spun around in circles. The light was so bright I could see everyone around me, even though it was late at night.

It seemed like the explosions went on forever. I got used to the loud booms and the smell and didn't notice them after a while. Then the fireworks got bigger. Rocketes went up more and more fast. A giant silver explosion made it seem as bright as day.

Then the show stopped. The silence sounded strange after all the noise. The burning smell seemed to come back. I could almost taste the smoke that drifted across the field. The fireworks were over. A new year had arrived. It was time to go home and go to bed.

Remember! The purpose of the essay is to describe the important, memorable details of an event. Start with a description that gets the reader's attention. Follow with details that help the reader picture what happened.

Think About It

Read my draft. Did I remember my purpose as I wrote?

Revising Extend Writing

Writing Strategy Add sensory words.

I've written my draft. Now I'll look back at the scoring guide and make sure I've included all the points I'll be graded on. The rubric reminds me that adding sensory details always makes a description better. My description of how the fireworks show began doesn't really give the reader a clear picture of how beautiful and exciting it was. I'll add more details to improve my description.

[DRAFT]

added details

huge

black

A rocket exploded in the sky. ~~There were sparks in the air.~~

Red and gold sparks sprayed through the air.

A split-second later came a gigantic boom. It was so loud I

a puff of

had to cover my ears. I could see smoke in the light from the

sparks. A smell like something burning was in the air.

added details

Remember! Read your draft. Add sensory words to paint a vivid picture that your reader can "see, feel, hear, smell, and taste."

Revising   Clarify Writing

Word Choice/ Clarity    **Writing Strategy**   Get rid of sentences that don't describe my subject.

Now I'll read my paper again. This time I'll check to be sure all my sentences are related to my subject. If I find any sentences that don't describe something important or memorable about the fireworks show, I'll take them out.

[DRAFT]

Then three more fireworks exploded at the same time. They were blue and green and opened out like a flower. I heard more booms and the burning smell got stronger. All around me people were saying, "ooh!" and "ah!" My little brother got scared and Dad had to pick him up and hold him. ~~We probably should have left him at home with a babysitter.~~

unrelated detail

Remember! Make sure all of the sentences in your essay relate to the subject. Remove sentences that don't describe your subject.

Think About It

Look at my revisions. Do the sensory words that I added make my description better? Did I remove sentences that don't describe my subject?

Editing   Check Sentences

Sentence Fluency

Writing Strategy Separate sentences that are too long into shorter sentences.

The scoring guide reminds me to separate sentences that are too long into shorter sentences. I know that each sentence should express a complete thought, feeling, or idea. When I read my draft again, I noticed one sentence that described three different ways that the fireworks exploded. The sentence went on and on. Here's how I broke that long sentence into shorter ones.

[DRAFT]

I couldn't believe all the colors. Purple and yellow and orange glowed in the sky. Each firework exploded a different way. Some went up like big water fountains ~~and~~ others spread out sideways ~~and~~ some even spun around in circles. The light was so bright I could see everyone around me, even though it was late at night.

separate sentences that are too long

Remember! Each sentence should have one complete thought, feeling, or idea. If some of your sentences are too long, you need to break them into shorter ones.

Editing Proofread Writing

Grammar/ Mechanics

Writing Strategy Check the grammar, spelling, capitalization, and punctuation.

The scoring guide reminds me to use correct grammar and spelling. I also need to check my capitalization and punctuation. That's a lot to do, but I scheduled plenty of time to check for errors in these important areas. I'll read my draft carefully one more time.

[FINAL DRAFT]

Fireworks for the New Year
by Marta

On New Year's Eve, my town lit up the sky with the biggest display of fireworks anyone had ever seen. And why not? It was about to become a new year.

It was getting close to midnight. I shivered in the crisp, cold air. I pulled my hat over my ears and zipped my jacket up tight. my mom and dad started to count down: "ten, nine, eight, seven, six . . ." Then—WOW! A rocket exploded in the sky. There were sparks in the air. Red and gold sparks sprayed through the air. A split-second later came a gigantic boom. It was so loud I had to cover my ears. I could see a puff of smoke in the light from the sparks. A smell like something burning was in the air.

Remember! Every time you write for a test, you need to check your grammar, spelling, capitalization, and punctuation.

Descriptive Writing ■ Descriptive Test **187**

Then three more fireworks exploded at the same time. they were blue and green and opened out like a flower. I heard more booms, and the burning smell got stronger. All around me people were saying, "ooh!" and "ah!" My little brother got scared, and Dad had to pick him up and hold him. ~~We probably should have left him at home with a babysitter.~~

I couldn't believe all the colors. Purple and yellow and orange glowed in the sky. Each firework exploded a different way. Some went up like big water fountains, others spread out sideways, some even spun around in circles. The light was so bright I could see everyone around me, even though it was late at night.

It seemed like the explosions went on forever. I got used to the loud booms and the smell and didn't notice them after a while. Then the fireworks got bigger. Rockets went up faster and faster ~~more and more fast~~. A giant silver explosion made it seem as bright as day.

Then the show stopped. The silence sounded strange after all the noise. The burning smell seemed to come back. I could almost taste the smoke that drifted across the field. The fireworks were over. A new year had arrived. It was time to go home and go to bed.

[FINAL DRAFT]

Think About It

Check my essay against the scoring guide. Did I include everything I will be graded on?

We're finished! With the help of the prompt and scoring guide, we wrote an exciting descriptive essay. Remember these important tips when you write for a test.

TEST TIPS

1. **Study the writing prompt before you begin to write.** Most writing prompts will have three parts: the setup, the task, and the scoring guide. Look for these three parts and label them. Use the helpful information they give you.

2. **Make sure you understand the task before you start to write.**
   - Read all three parts of the writing prompt carefully.
   - Circle key words in the task part of the writing prompt that tell you what kind of writing you need to do. The task might also tell you who your audience is.
   - Make sure you know how you'll be graded.
   - Say the assignment in your own words to yourself.

3. **Keep an eye on the clock.** Decide how much time you'll spend on each part of the writing process, and try to stick to your plan. Don't spend so much time on prewriting that you don't have enough time left to write.

4. **Reread your writing. Compare it to the scoring guide at least twice.** Remember the rubrics you've used all year? A scoring guide on a writing test is like a rubric. It reminds you of what is important.

5. **Plan, plan, plan!** You don't get much time to revise during a test, so planning is more important than ever.

6. **Write neatly.** Remember, if the people who score your test can't read your writing, it won't matter how good your essay is!

EXPOSITORY
writing gives information.

Hi, my name is Alika. I'm learning all about expository writing, and I really like it! One of my favorite things to do is to observe nature along the Hawaiian coast. I also love the Hawaiian culture—especially the great food! My writing skills are getting better. Now, I can do a better job of reporting about the sea animals, landforms, and interesting culture around me.

IN THIS UNIT

1. **Compare-and-Contrast Essay**
2. **Factual Report**
3. **How-To Essay**
4. **Writing for a Test**

Name: Alika

Home: Hawaii

Favorite Activities: observing nature, snorkeling, fishing

Favorite Sports: baseball, beach volleyball

Hobbies: baking, photography

Favorite School Subjects: science and language arts

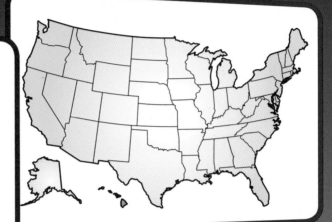

What's a Compare-and-Contrast Essay?

A compare-and contrast essay tells how two or more things are alike (compare) and different (contrast).

What's in a Compare-and-Contrast Essay?

Two (or more) Topics
A topic is what I'm writing about. A compare-and-contrast essay usually has at least two topics. I could compare and contrast my pet bird and my pet dog.

Comparisons
When I compare two things, I tell the ways that they are alike or similar.

Contrasts
When I contrast two things, I tell how they are different.

Why write a Compare-and-Contrast Essay?

There are lots of reasons for writing a compare-and-contrast essay. Here are two good reasons.

Information
I can explain something that's new to my reader by comparing and contrasting it with something that's familiar to the reader. I might teach my classmates about seasons in Alaska by comparing and contrasting them with seasons in Hawaii.

Evaluation
If I compare and contrast two things fairly and without bias, my reader can decide which one he or she thinks is better.

Compare-and-Contrast Essay
Writing Traits

What makes a good compare-and-contrast essay? A compare-and-contrast essay is well balanced. Both topics are mentioned to make each comparison and to show each contrast. Here are some traits of a good compare-and-contrast essay.

Information/Organization	The essay has two topics. Similarities and differences are well organized.
Voice/Audience	The essay begins with a compare-and-contrast lead that gets the reader's attention.
Content/Ideas	The essay has good examples of similarities and differences.
Word Choice/Clarity	The essay has signal words to make comparisons and contrasts clear.
Sentence Fluency	Variety in length and type of sentences helps the essay flow.
Grammar/Mechanics	Spelling, punctuation, and capitalization are correct. Homophones are used correctly.

Let's read Taisha Moore's compare-and-contrast essay on the next page. Did she follow all of the writing traits?

As Different as Day and Night

Compare-and-
MODEL
Contrast Essay

by Taisha Moore

Which two objects in the sky are as different as day and night? One answer to this question is "the sun and the moon." The sun is a bright daytime light. The moon is a beautiful and changing light in the night sky.

two topics

The sun and the moon both give light, but the sun is a star. Earth and the other planets in the solar system revolve around the sun. All life on Earth depends on the sun. Plants need the sun to grow, and animals and people need the sun's heat and light. Unlike the sun, the moon is a satellite. It revolves around Earth. Life on Earth does not depend on the moon, but the moon affects many things on Earth, including the tides.

comparison

Both the sun and the moon seem to change or to move in the sky. The sun seems to rise and set. The moon appears in different places at different times of year and even at different times of night.

The moon has a 29-day cycle. Phases of the moon make its circular shape look different at different times of the month. It sometimes looks like a thin crescent, half of a moon, or a full moon. We see only the part of the moon that is lit by sunlight. The sun doesn't have a cycle.

contrast

The moon and the sun also differ in how far away they are from Earth. About one quarter of a million miles away, the moon is Earth's closest neighbor in space. That is one reason we see it so easily. On the other hand, the sun is 93 million miles away. Only its brightness makes it easy to see.

There is no life on either the sun or the moon. The sun has a boiling, busy, bubbling surface. The center of the sun can get as hot as 27 million degrees. The moon, on the other hand, has no activity. It has no air, no clouds, and no water.

The sun provides our daytime light, and the moon sometimes lights up the darkness. We sometimes use the sun as our symbol for "day" and the moon as our symbol for "night."

Compare-and-Contrast Essay Rubric

The rubric below was made using the traits of a good compare-and-contrast essay on page 194. To score a compare-and-contrast essay, assign one to four stars for each trait. Four stars mean that trait is excellent! Three stars mean it is very good. One or two stars mean that trait needs more work.

	Excelling	Achieving	Developing	Beginning
Information/Organization	The essay has two topics. Similarities and differences are well organized.	The essay has two topics. Most similarities and differences are well organized.	The essay has two topics. Some similarities and differences are organized.	The essay needs two topics. It needs to be organized.
Voice/Audience	A very interesting compare-and-contrast lead gets the reader's attention.	A good compare-and-contrast lead gets the reader's attention.	A compare-and-contrast lead begins the essay.	The essay needs a good compare-and-contrast lead.
Content/Ideas	The essay has many excellent examples of similarities and differences.	The essay has some examples of similarities and differences.	The essay has a few examples of similarities and differences, but more are needed.	The essay needs examples of similarities and differences.
Word Choice/Clarity	Signal words make comparisons and contrasts clear throughout.	Signal words make comparisons and contrasts clear most of the time.	A few signal words make comparisons and contrasts clear.	The essay needs signal words to make comparisons and contrasts clear.
Sentence Fluency	Great variety in length and type of sentences helps the essay flow.	Variety in length and type of sentences helps the essay flow most of the time.	Some variety in length and type of sentences helps the essay flow sometimes.	Variety in length and type of sentences is needed to help the essay flow.
Grammar/Mechanics	Spelling, punctuation, and capitalization are correct. Homophones are used correctly.	There are a few errors in spelling, punctuation, capitalization, or homophones.	There are some errors in spelling, punctuation, capitalization, or homophones.	There are many errors in spelling, punctuation, capitalization, or homophones.

Compare-and-Contrast Essay

Using the Rubric to Study the Model

Now, let's use the rubric to check Taisha Moore's compare-and-contrast essay, "As Different as Day and Night." What score would you give Taisha for each category in the rubric?

Information/Organization

• **The essay has two topics.**
• **Similarities and differences are well organized.**

Taisha makes the topics clear in the first two sentences of her essay. Her similarities and differences are well organized and easy to follow. Each paragraph compares and contrasts different features of the sun and the moon. In the following paragraph, Taisha talks about differences in distance.

The moon and the sun also differ in how far away they are from Earth. About one quarter of a million miles away, the moon is Earth's closest neighbor in space. That is one reason we see it so easily. On the other hand, the sun is 93 million miles away. Only its brightness makes it easy to see.

Voice/Audience

• **The essay begins with a compare-and-contrast lead that gets the reader's attention.**

Taisha's lead—the first sentence—asks an interesting question. It got my attention right away. I wanted to find out the answer. I knew if I kept reading I would learn the answer.

Which two objects in the sky are as different as day and night?

Content/Ideas

- The essay has good examples of similarities and differences.

Taisha gives plenty of examples to explain the comparisons and contrasts. In this paragraph, Taisha compares and contrasts the light of the sun and the moon. She gives examples to explain why and how the light is different.

The sun and the moon both give light, but the sun is a star. Earth and the other planets in the solar system revolve around the sun. All life on Earth depends on the sun. Plants need the sun to grow, and animals and people need the sun's heat and light. Unlike the sun, the moon is a satellite. It revolves around Earth. Life on Earth does not depend on the moon, but the moon affects many things on Earth, including the tides.

Word Choice/Clarity

- The essay has signal words to make comparisons and contrasts clear.

Taisha uses signal words all through the essay. In this paragraph, she contrasts the surface and heat of the sun and the moon. The words **on the other hand** signal the reader that a contrast is coming up.

There is no life on either the sun or the moon. The sun has a boiling, busy, bubbling surface. The center of the sun can get as hot as 27 million degrees. The moon, on the other hand, has no activity. It has no air, no clouds, and no water.

Compare-and-Contrast Essay

Using the Rubric to Study the Model

• **Variety in length and type of sentences helps the essay flow.**

The writer uses lots of different kinds of sentences in her essay. Some are short, simple sentences. Some are longer and complex. This makes reading her essay interesting and easy. This next paragraph is a good example.

> The moon has a 29-day cycle. Phases of the moon make its circular shape look different at different times of the month. It sometimes looks like a thin crescent, half of a moon, or a full moon. We see only the part of the moon that is lit by sunlight. The sun doesn't have a cycle.

• **Spelling, punctuation, and capitalization are correct. Homophones are used correctly.**

I looked through the whole essay and every word is spelled correctly. All the sentences are capitalized and punctuated correctly. Taisha uses homophones correctly. In this example, she does not confuse **its** (belonging to **it**) with **it's** (the contraction for **it is**).

> On the other hand, the sun is 93 million miles away. Only its brightness makes it easy to see.

My Turn!

Now I'm going to write my own compare-and-contrast essay! Follow along to see how I use good writing strategies. I will use the model and the rubric to help me, too.

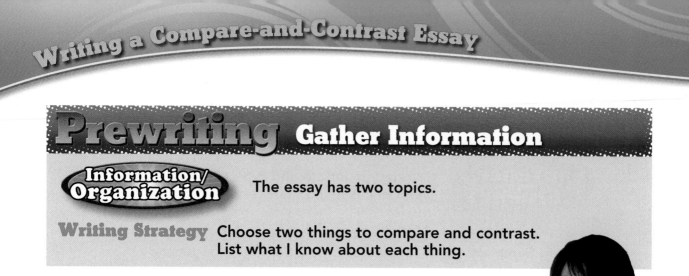

Prewriting Gather Information

Information/Organization The essay has two topics.

Writing Strategy Choose two things to compare and contrast. List what I know about each thing.

When my teacher asked us to write a compare-and-contrast essay, I decided to compare sharks and whales. Sharks are really interesting fish, and whales are the biggest creatures in the ocean. I've already read a lot about both of them. I decided to list everything I know about sharks and whales.

What I Know About Sharks and Whales

Sharks	Whales
• are fish	• make sounds—humpbacks "sing"
• breathe through gills	• are mammals
• 6 inches to about 40 feet long	• have great eyesight, great hearing
• do not make sounds	• have lungs and blowholes
• very good hearing and vision	• can be 10 feet to 100 feet long
• excellent sense of smell	• hardly any sense of smell
	• huge!

Practice!

Brainstorm a list of topics that you would like to compare and contrast. Select the pair that you think will be the most interesting. Jot down some notes.

Prewriting Organize Ideas

Information/Organization   Similarities and differences are well organized.

Writing Strategy   Make an Attribute Chart to show similarities and differences.

The rubric reminds me that I need to organize my ideas. For example, sharks breathe underwater, but whales have to come up for air. How sharks and whales breathe is an attribute. I took the ideas on my list and made an Attribute Chart.

Writer's Term ———

Attribute Chart
An **attribute** (at•ruh•byoot) is a quality of something. An **Attribute Chart** organizes information about how two things are alike or different.

Attribute Chart

Shark	Attribute	Whale
fish	kind of animal	mammal
underwater with gills	how it breathes	above water with lungs and blowhole
6 inches to 40 feet	its length	10 to 100 feet
none	sounds it makes	many sounds
great vision and hearing	hearing and vision	great vision and hearing
excellent	sense of smell	poor

Look at your notes on the topics that you chose to compare and contrast. What attributes do the two topics have in common? How are they different? Use your notes to make an Attribute Chart.

Look at my notes and my Attribute Chart. Will the attributes in my chart help me to write a good compare-and-contrast essay?

Drafting — Write a Draft

Voice/ Audience

The essay begins with a compare-and-contrast lead that gets the reader's attention.

Writing Strategy   Begin with a compare-and-contrast lead that gets the reader's attention.

Now I'm ready to write. I'll use my Attribute Chart to write a draft. I need to remember that a compare-and-contrast essay shows both differences and similarities. I need to organize my ideas so that they won't be confusing.

The rubric reminds me that I need to think about my audience. My reader should want to keep reading my paper. That means I have to start with a great compare-and-contrast sentence, or lead!

As I'm writing, I'll do the best I can with grammar and spelling, but I won't worry about mistakes. I'll fix them later. Here is part of my draft.

Writer's Term

Lead

A **lead** is the first sentence of a piece of writing. A good lead grabs the reader's attention and makes him or her want to read more. A lead can be a question or a surprising statement.

Question Lead: Do you know which of the five senses is the shark's best and the whale's worst?

Surprise Lead: Not everyone knows that a shark can be six inches long or that a whale can sing!

[DRAFT] Whales and Sharks

Have you ever heard of a six-inch shark or a ten-foot whale?

A tiny shark is only six inches long! Its called a dwarf shark.
The smallest whale is about ten feet long.

compare-and-contrast lead

Whales and sharks are alike in many ways. They are usually
both very large. Whales are larger than sharks. Sharks can
grow to 40 feet long. Whales can grow to 100 feet long. Whales
and sharks both have excellent hearing and vision. Sharks have
a terrific sense of smell while whales have almost no sense of
smell at all.

Whales and sharks have other differences, to. A big
difference is that sharks are fish. They breathe underwater
through gills. Whales are mammals, so they have lungs. They
have to rise to the surface of the water to breathe.

Practice!

Write a draft of a compare-and-contrast essay.
Remember to begin with a lead that catches your
reader's attention. Use your Attribute Chart to help
you organize your ideas.

Think About It

Read my draft. Does
my first sentence get
the reader's attention?
How well did I
organize my ideas?

Revising Extend Writing

Content/Ideas

The essay has good examples of similarities and differences.

Writing Strategy Add examples.

After I wrote my first draft, I read it to my friend Lauren. I know from the rubric that I need examples to explain my points. Lauren thought I had really good examples of how whales and sharks are alike and different, except for the sounds they make while they swim. I saw that Lauren was right. I can give examples.

Writer's Term

Example

An **example** is something that helps explain a larger idea or thought. A whale and a shark are examples of fascinating sea animals.

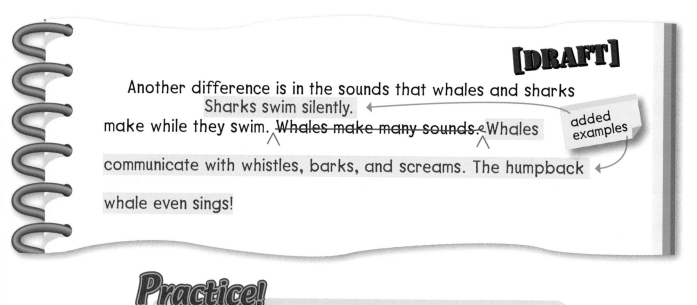

[DRAFT]

Another difference is in the sounds that whales and sharks
            Sharks swim silently.
make while they swim. ~~Whales make many sounds.~~ Whales

communicate with whistles, barks, and screams. The humpback

whale even sings!

added examples

Practice!

Read your draft. Look for places to add interesting examples to your compare-and-contrast essay. Add these examples to your draft.

Revising Clarify Writing

Word Choice/ Clarity The essay has signal words to make comparisons and contrasts clear.

Writing Strategy Use signal words to make the comparisons and contrasts clear.

The rubric reminds me to use signal words. I found places in my draft to add signal words. They will help make some of my comparisons and contrasts clearer.

Writer's Term

Signal Words

A **signal word** helps tie ideas together. It signals the reader that the writing is going from one idea to another.

[DRAFT]

Whales and sharks are alike in many ways. They are usually

both very large. ^ However, Whales are larger than sharks.

added contrast signal word

Practice!

Read your draft again. Look for places where adding compare-and-contrast signal words would make your writing clearer.

Think About It

Look at my revisions. Have I included good examples of similarities and differences? Did I choose signal words that made my comparisons and contrasts clearer?

Editing Check Sentences

Sentence Fluency Variety in length and type of sentences helps the essay flow.

Writing Strategy Vary the length and type of sentences.

The next step is to edit my writing. The rubric tells me that it's important to vary the length of my sentences. This will make my essay sound more natural and easier for my readers to read.

I read through my essay and found a few places where a longer, compound sentence would add variety. Here's an example.

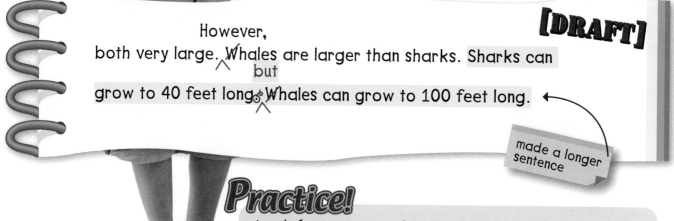

[DRAFT]

However,
both very large. ^ Whales are larger than sharks. Sharks can
                      but

grow to 40 feet long ^ Whales can grow to 100 feet long. ←

made a longer sentence

Practice!

Look for a variety of sentence lengths in your draft. Carefully choose places to lengthen or shorten sentences to add variety to your writing.

Editing Proofread Writing

Grammar/Mechanics

Spelling, punctuation, and capitalization are correct. Homophones are used correctly.

Writing Strategy Make sure that homophones are used correctly.

Now I need to check for errors. I always check spelling, punctuation, and capitalization. I'll also make sure that I've used every homophone correctly. Here's the end of my draft.

Writer's Term

Homophones

Homophones are words that sound the same but have different spellings and meanings.

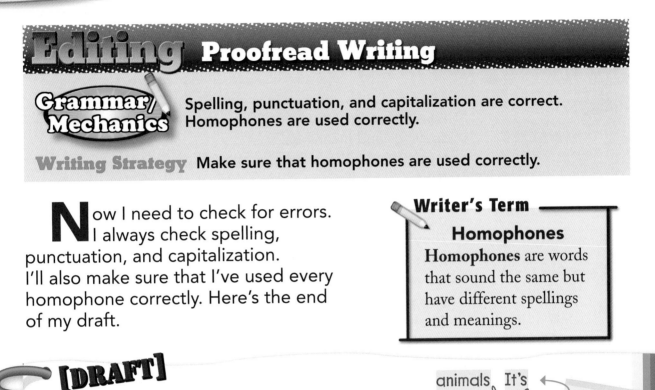

[DRAFT]

Both whales and sharks are fascinating ~~aminals~~ animals. ~~Its~~ It's not surprising that ~~their~~ they're the subjects of poems, stories, and

compare-and-contrast essays!

corrected homophones

Practice!

Edit your draft for spelling, punctuation, and capitalization. Make sure that you have used every homophone correctly.

Grammar/Mechanics

For more practice identifying and using homophones correctly, use the exercises on the next two pages.

Think About It

Look at my editing. Does the sentence that I lengthened add variety to my writing? Did I fix the spelling, punctuation, and capitalization problems? Are homophones used correctly?

Homophones

Homophones are words that sound alike but have different spellings and meanings.

Your is a possessive pronoun that means "belonging to you." **You're** is a contraction made from the words "you are."

Their is a possessive pronoun that means "belonging to them." **There** is an adverb that means "in that place." **They're** is a contraction made from the words "they are."

Its is a possessive pronoun that means "belonging to it." **It's** is a contraction made from the words "it is" or "it has."

Two is a number. **Too** means "also" or "more than enough." **To** often means "towards."

Practice the Rule

Number a piece of paper 1.–10. Write the word in parentheses that completes each sentence correctly.

1. My class went (two/too/to) a natural history museum.
2. We went to a whale exhibit (their/there/they're).
3. We learned that a whale isn't a fish; (its/it's) a mammal.
4. A whale has a blowhole on the top of (its/it's) head.
5. Whales use (their/there/they're) blowholes to breathe air.
6. A whale's flipper is a little like (your/you're) hand.
7. We found that there are (two/too/to) kinds of whales.
8. The whale that (your/you're) looking at is a baleen whale.
9. Large amounts of seawater go into (their/there/they're) mouths.
10. The baleen hangs (their/there/they're) like a loose fringe curtain.

Apply the Rule

Read the following paragraphs. Rewrite the paragraphs on a separate sheet of paper, correcting any homophones that are used incorrectly.

Whales do not swim the same way that fish do. Fish move there tails from side to side. However, whales move their tails up and down. This moves the whale forward through the water. A whale's tail must be very strong to move such a huge creature. In fact, it's largest muscles are their. Notice the too flukes at the end of a whale's tail. These flukes are very strong. They are stronger than any part of you're body.

Because whales are powerful swimmers, they're able too travel great distances. In fact, whales are known for there long distance migrations. They often travel thousands of miles each year from cool waters two warm waters and back. For example, the Gray Whale makes a seasonal migration of 10,000 to 14,000 miles round trip. Its one of the longest migrations of any mammal.

Publishing Share Writing

Display my essay on the classroom bulletin board.

I finished my essay! Some of my classmates asked to read my paper. There are many ways to publish a compare-and-contrast essay. I could post it on our school's Web site or put it with other classmates' essays in a book. I decided that I am going to put it on the class bulletin board. Before I publish it, though, I'm going to read it over one more time. Here's my final checklist.

My Checklist

✔ The title of the essay and my name are at the top of the page.

✔ The similarities and differences that I discuss are well organized.

✔ I've included good examples of similarities and differences between the topics.

✔ Signal words make the comparisons and contrasts clear.

✔ Spelling, punctuation, and capitalization are all correct. I've used homophones correctly.

✔ My handwriting is neat.

Practice!

Make a checklist to review your own compare-and-contrast essay. Be sure to check your essay carefully one last time before publishing it. Then make a final draft to post on your classroom bulletin board.

Whales and Sharks
by Alika

Have you ever heard of a six-inch shark or a ten-foot whale? The smallest shark is only six inches long! It's called a dwarf shark. The smallest whale is about ten feet long.

Whales and sharks are alike in many ways. They are usually both very large. However, whales are larger than sharks. Sharks can grow to 40 feet long, but whales can grow to 100 feet long. Whales and sharks both have excellent hearing and vision. However, sharks have a terrific sense of smell, while whales have almost no sense of smell at all.

Whales and sharks have other differences, too. A big difference is that sharks are fish. They breathe underwater through gills. Whales are mammals, so they have lungs. They have to rise to the surface of the water to breathe. They breathe through one or two nostrils at the top of their head called blowholes.

Another difference is in the sounds that whales and sharks make while they swim. Sharks swim silently, while whales communicate with whistles, barks, and screams. The humpback whale even sings!

Both whales and sharks are fascinating animals. It's not surprising that they're the subjects of poems, stories, and compare-and-contrast essays!

Think About It

Use the rubric to check my paper. Are all the traits of a good compare-and-contrast essay there? How does your essay compare against the rubric?

Ways to Publish a Compare-and-Contrast Essay

There are all kinds of ways to publish your compare-and-contrast essay. Think about the people who will enjoy the information in your essay. Then pick the best way to share it. Let's look at some ways for you to publish your work.

✓ **Post your compare-and-contrast essay in the school library.**

✓ **Submit your essay to your school newspaper or Web site for publication.**

✓ **Read your essay to a younger student. Then ask the student to share something interesting that he or she learned from the essay.**

✓ **Create a PowerPoint presentation with bullet-pointed text, pictures, or charts that highlight the details of your essay. Use this during a classroom reading of your essay.**

✓ **Submit your essay to a magazine that publishes student work.**

Writing Across the Content Areas
Compare-and-Contrast Essay

Pick any school subject and brainstorm some topics. You'll think of a good compare-and-contrast topic before you know it! Here are some examples.

Art and/or Music

- Write an essay that compares and contrasts dance with sports.
- Write about the similarities and differences between two styles of art or two works of art.

Social Studies

- Compare and contrast family life today and during colonial days in America.
- Write an essay that compares and contrasts two important historical figures or events.

Science

- Compare and contrast the life cycles of plants and animals.
- Write about the similarities and differences between Earth and another planet.

What's a Factual Report?

A factual report is a piece of writing that gives facts and details about a topic.

What's in a Factual Report?

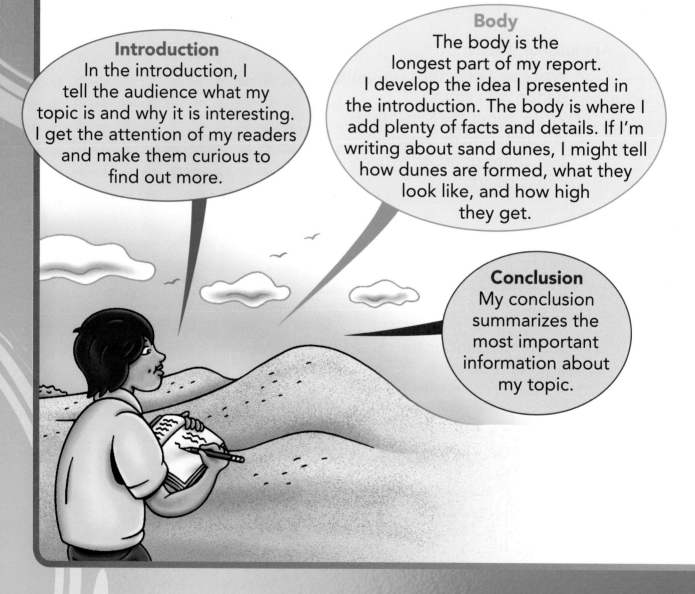

Introduction
In the introduction, I tell the audience what my topic is and why it is interesting. I get the attention of my readers and make them curious to find out more.

Body
The body is the longest part of my report. I develop the idea I presented in the introduction. The body is where I add plenty of facts and details. If I'm writing about sand dunes, I might tell how dunes are formed, what they look like, and how high they get.

Conclusion
My conclusion summarizes the most important information about my topic.

Why write a Factual Report?

There are many reasons to write a factual report. Here are three reasons.

Information

People in many different careers make factual reports. Police make factual reports to tell how an investigation is going. People in business make factual reports about training programs for new workers.

Entertainment

Many people enjoy learning about topics that interest them. Nonfiction writers may publish factual reports in magazines, newspapers, and books.

Change

Factual reports are often used to support arguments when people want to convince others to make changes. Factual reports that show how certain animals are becoming extinct have led to the Endangered Species Act.

Factual Report
Writing Traits

What makes a good factual report? A factual report should be well organized with clear ideas and plenty of interesting facts. Here are some traits of a factual report.

Information/ Organization	The report has information on one topic. It is well organized and has an introduction, body, and conclusion.
Voice/ Audience	The report contains plenty of details to interest the audience.
Content/ Ideas	The report contains many important facts.
Word Choice/ Clarity	The report has appositives to enrich the writing.
Sentence Fluency	All detail sentences relate to the topic sentences.
Grammar/ Mechanics	Spelling and punctuation are correct. Capital letters are used correctly.

Let's read author Bob Yang's factual report about a famous tower in Pisa, Italy. Then, we can check to see if he followed all of the writing traits.

Fixing the Leaning Tower of Pisa

by Bob Yang

Pisa is a city in Italy. This city has become famous for its leaning bell tower, an architectural mistake. In fact, the bell tower is known as the Leaning Tower of Pisa. It began to lean soon after it was built 800 years ago.

The Leaning Tower of Pisa is a very special place. Made of white marble with 207 columns, the tower is very beautiful. It is also very heavy. Most of the walls are nine to ten feet thick. With its thick walls and marble, the tower weighs about 16,000 tons.

Many attempts have been made to straighten the tower. The south side of the tower leans, so the most common solution has been to put weights on the north side. This has never worked. People also tried putting concrete around the base of the tower. Then they attached cables to support the tower. At one time, 80 tons of concrete were poured into the foundation, but that solution didn't work either. People have also suggested putting huge weights against the tower to hold it upright.

Recently, the tower was leaning so much that it had to be closed. A committee was formed to solve the problem.

Finally, an attempt to save the Leaning Tower of Pisa worked. It seemed to be an unlikely plan at first. It involved moving sand. Led by a chief engineer named Dr. Paolo Heiniger, work crews removed almost 80 tons of soil from under the tower. They took away the soft sand that had caused the tower to lean in the first place. As they did, they slowly moved the south side of the tower toward the north.

Today, the tower still leans. The top is still more than 15 feet out over the base. Nevertheless, this is less than the 17 feet of "lean" in 1990. It is also a big enough improvement to reopen the tower. Besides, people didn't really want the tower to stop leaning. They just didn't want it to fall.

Factual Report Rubric

The rubric below was made using the traits of a factual report on page 216. To score a factual report, assign one to four stars for each trait. Four stars mean that trait is excellent! Three stars mean it is very good. Two stars mean that trait needs some more work. One star means it still needs a lot of work.

	Excelling	Achieving	Developing	Beginning
Information/ Organization	The report has information on one topic. It is very well organized with an excellent introduction, body, and conclusion.	The report has information on one topic. It is mostly organized with a clear introduction, body, and conclusion.	The report has some information on one topic. Some of the report is organized with a body and an introduction or a conclusion.	The report has a little information on one topic. It needs organization and a clear introduction, body, and conclusion.
Voice/ Audience	The report contains many excellent supporting details to interest the audience.	The report contains supporting details to interest the audience.	The report contains some supporting details to interest the audience.	The report needs supporting details to interest the audience.
Content/ Ideas	The report contains many important facts.	The report contains some important facts.	The report contains a few important facts.	The report needs important facts.
Word Choice/ Clarity	Appositives are used correctly to enrich the writing.	Some appositives are used correctly to enrich the writing.	A few appositives are used correctly to enrich the writing.	Appositives are needed to enrich the writing.
Sentence Fluency	All detail sentences relate to the topic sentences.	Most detail sentences relate to the topic sentences.	Some detail sentences relate to the topic sentences.	Detail sentences need to relate to the topic sentences.
Grammar/ Mechanics	Spelling and punctuation are correct. Capital letters are used correctly.	There are a few errors in spelling or punctuation. Capital letters are used correctly.	There are some errors in spelling and punctuation. Some capital letters are used incorrectly.	There are many errors in spelling and punctuation. Many capital letters are used incorrectly.

Using the Rubric to Study the Model

Factual Report

Now, let's use the rubric to check Bob Yang's factual report, "Fixing the Leaning Tower of Pisa." What score would you give Bob for each category in the rubric?

 **Information/Organization**

- The report has information on one topic.
- It is well organized and has an introduction, body, and conclusion.

I really enjoyed reading this report. The information is interesting, and the report is well organized. The writer introduces the topic in the first paragraph then follows with interesting details in the body of the report. He finishes with a concluding paragraph. Look at how the writer introduces the topic.

> Pisa is a city in Italy. This city has become famous for its leaning bell tower, an architectural mistake. In fact, the bell tower is known as the Leaning Tower of Pisa. It began to lean soon after it was built 800 years ago.

 **Voice/Audience**

- The report contains plenty of details to interest the audience.

I learned a lot about the Leaning Tower of Pisa from this report. The writer explains why the tower leans and tells how people have tried to fix it. The body has some interesting details about attempts to straighten the tower that didn't work.

> Many attempts have been made to straighten the tower. The south side of the tower leans, so the most common solution has been to put weights on the north side. This has never worked. People also tried putting concrete around the base of the tower. Then they attached cables to support the tower.

Content/Ideas

- **The report contains many important facts.**

There are many important facts in the report. The writer tells where the tower is located and when it was built. He describes the tower and the problem. He tells about some failed attempts to fix it, and then he describes a successful solution. This is a good example of a paragraph with some of those important facts.

The Leaning Tower of Pisa is a very special place. Made of white marble with 207 columns, the tower is very beautiful. It is also very heavy. Most of the walls are nine to ten feet thick. With its thick walls and marble, the tower weighs about 16,000 tons.

Word Choice/Clarity

- **The report has appositives to enrich the writing.**

In this report, the writer uses appositives to add more information about the nouns in his sentences. In the sentence below, *an architectural mistake* is an appositive that provides more information about the tower.

This city has become famous for its leaning bell tower, an architectural mistake.

Using the Factual Report Rubric to Study the Model

Sentence Fluency

• All detail sentences relate to the topic sentences.

I checked, and every paragraph has a topic sentence. The detail sentences in each paragraph explain the topic sentence. In this paragraph, the topic sentence is the first sentence. See how the detail sentences that follow explain the topic sentence.

> Finally, an attempt to save the Leaning Tower of Pisa worked. It seemed to be an unlikely plan at first. It involved moving sand. Led by a chief engineer named Dr. Paolo Heiniger, work crews removed almost 80 tons of soil from under the tower. They took away the soft sand that had caused the tower to lean in the first place. As they did, they slowly moved the south side of the tower toward the north.

Grammar/ Mechanics

• Spelling and punctuation are correct. Capital letters are used correctly.

I checked the spelling and every word is spelled correctly. Also, the punctuation is correct. The writer capitalizes the first word of every sentence, all the proper nouns, and the one abbreviation of a person's title.

> Led by a chief engineer named Dr. Paolo Heiniger, work crews removed almost 80 tons of soil from under the tower. They took away the soft sand that had caused the tower to lean in the first place.

Now it's my turn to write a factual report! I'll use the rubric and good writing strategies to help me. Follow along to see how I do it.

Prewriting Gather Information

Information/Organization The report has information on one topic.

Writing Strategy Take notes from a book about my topic.

My teacher asked us to write a factual report on something about volcanoes. We had to narrow the topic from volcanoes in general to something specific.

First, I skimmed an encyclopedia article about volcanoes to narrow my topic. One thing about volcanoes that interests me most is living near one.

Then I found a book that told more about my topic. I took notes on what people keep in mind if they live near a volcano.

My Book Notes on Living Near Volcanoes

escape plans	emergency supplies	dangers
routes to take	flashlight	blasts
higher land	radio	ash
away from wind	batteries	lava
place to meet	food and water	
	can opener	
	first-aid kit	

Practice!

Do some research and narrow your topic. Then make a list of important things to remember about your topic.

Prewriting Organize Ideas

Information/Organization The report is well organized and has an introduction, body, and conclusion.

Writing Strategy Use a Web to organize my notes.

I know from the rubric that every main idea needs information to back it up. I'll use a Web to organize my report. I can put the main idea in the center. The categories from my notes will go in the next set of circles. Then the details for each category will go in smaller circles connected to the categories.

Writer's Term

Web

A **Web** organizes information about one main topic. The main topic goes in the center. Related details go in outside circles connected to the center.

Web

- place to meet
- routes to take
- higher land
- escape plans
- away from wind
- blasts
- lava
- dangers
- ash
- living near a volcano
- radio
- first-aid kit
- food and water
- emergency supplies
- can opener
- batteries
- flashlight

Practice!

Look at your list of important things to remember about your topic. Use these to make a Web.

Think About It

Look at my notes and my Web. Will they help me write a good report?

Drafting Write a Draft

Voice/Audience The report contains plenty of details to interest the audience.

Writing Strategy Provide supporting details to interest my audience.

It's time to write my first draft. I know from the rubric that my report should have plenty of details. By using my Web, I'll be sure that the topic of my report is clear and that my draft includes all the categories and details that I found. Each category and related details should have its own paragraph.

I'll do my best with spelling and grammar, but I won't worry about mistakes. I'll get a chance to fix them later. Look at the start of my draft on the next page.

> **Writer's Term**
>
> **Paragraph**
>
> A **paragraph** is a group of sentences that share a common topic or purpose and focus on a single main idea or thought.

[DRAFT]

In the Shadow of a Volcano

introduction

Living near a volcano can be risky. People who live near a volcano learn to live near danger by being ready to act quickly they must also be prepared in other ways.

The danger from an erupting volcano is real. When authorities tell people to leave there homes, residents move fast.

category

Those who live near a volcano have their emergency items ready. people keep a Flashlight and extra batteries handy. they have a radio that runs on batteries, too. They keep Canned Food and Bottled Water on hand. a first-aid kit and a can opener that is not electric can save lifes.

supporting detail

supporting detail

Practice!

Use your Web to write a draft of your factual report. Be sure the main topic is clear. Give each category its own paragraph and include all the details.

Think About It

Read my draft. Is the main topic clear? Did I include details?

Revising Extend Writing

Content/Ideas

The report contains many important facts.

Writing Strategy Add facts.

This is a factual report. I have to be sure I've included all the important facts. If I add facts, I have to put them in the right place, too. I added facts to explain more about the danger of volcanoes. I also noticed that I made a mistake with a homophone, so I corrected it. I'll have to watch out for those when I write.

Writer's Term

Facts

A **fact** is a statement that can be proven to be true.

Fact: Lava and mud flow downhill from a volcano. (can be proven)

Not a fact: Volcanoes are beautiful at night. (cannot be proven)

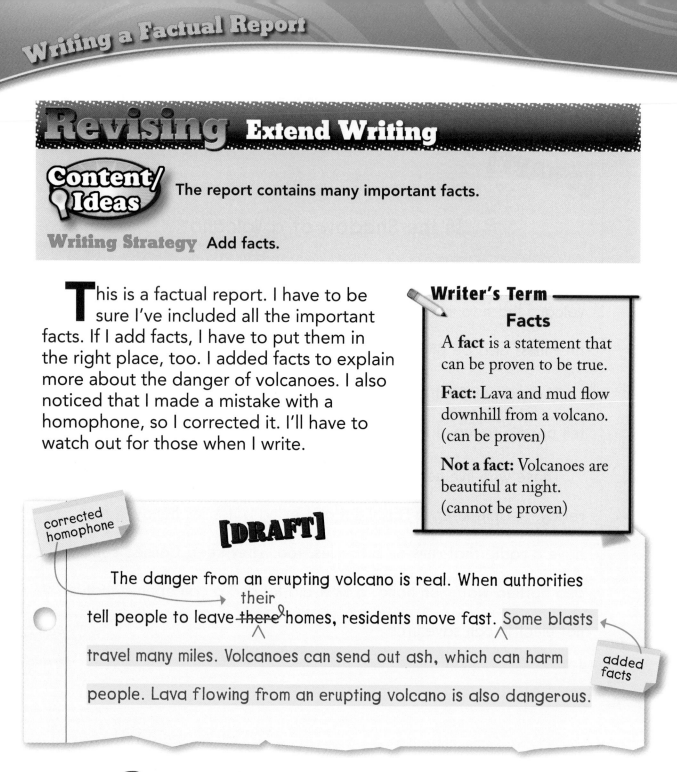

corrected homophone

[DRAFT]

The danger from an erupting volcano is real. When authorities

their

tell people to leave ~~there~~ homes, residents move fast. Some blasts

added facts

travel many miles. Volcanoes can send out ash, which can harm

people. Lava flowing from an erupting volcano is also dangerous.

Practice!

Read your draft. Then go back to your research notes and your Web. Find other interesting facts you can add to your report.

Revising Clarify Writing

Word Choice/Clarity The report has appositives to enrich the writing.

Writing Strategy Be sure my report has appositives.

I know from the rubric that my report should have appositives. I checked my report. My second paragraph has a word that I should identify. Take a look at how I edited that sentence.

Writer's Term

Appositives

An **appositive** is a word or phrase that follows a noun and helps identify or describe it.

added appositive

, the officials in control,

The danger from an erupting volcano is real. When authorities ∧

their

tell people to leave ~~there~~ homes, residents move fast.

[DRAFT]

Practice!

Read your draft again. Be sure that your report has appositives where needed.

Think About It

Look at my revisions. Are important facts included in the report? Does the appositive identify the word?

Editing Check Sentences

 **Sentence Fluency**

All detail sentences relate to the topic sentences.

Writing Strategy Make sure that detail sentences relate to the topic sentences.

I know from the rubric that detail sentences tell about a topic sentence.

When I read my report to myself, I noticed that my fourth paragraph did not have a topic sentence! I never said that the paragraph was about having an escape plan.

> **Writer's Term**
>
> **Topic Sentence/ Detail Sentences**
>
> A **topic sentence** states the main idea of the whole paragraph.
>
> **Detail sentences** go with, tell about, or give examples that support the topic sentence.

Having an escape plan is important for people who live near a volcano. ← topic sentence

∧They decide on a route to take if they have to leave their home.

They always head toward higher grownd because lava and mud flow downhill. Also, they try to stay away from the wind. The wind can carry objects and harmful gas. The plan includes a place for everyone to meet later.

[DRAFT]

 **Practice!**

Check your draft. Do the detail sentences explain the topic sentence?

Grammar/ Mechanics

Spelling and punctuation are correct. Capital letters are used correctly.

Writing Strategy Make sure capital letters are used correctly.

When I proofread, I always check spelling and punctuation. This time I'm going to pay special attention to capitalization. I want to be sure I've started every sentence with a capital letter. I'm also going to check that I've capitalized all proper nouns, all important words in titles, and all abbreviations of personal titles.

have a radio that runs on batteries, too. They keep ¢anned ƒood

and ƀottled Ⱳater on hand. a first-aid kit and a can opener that is
                                                              lives
not electric can save lifes.   **[DRAFT]**

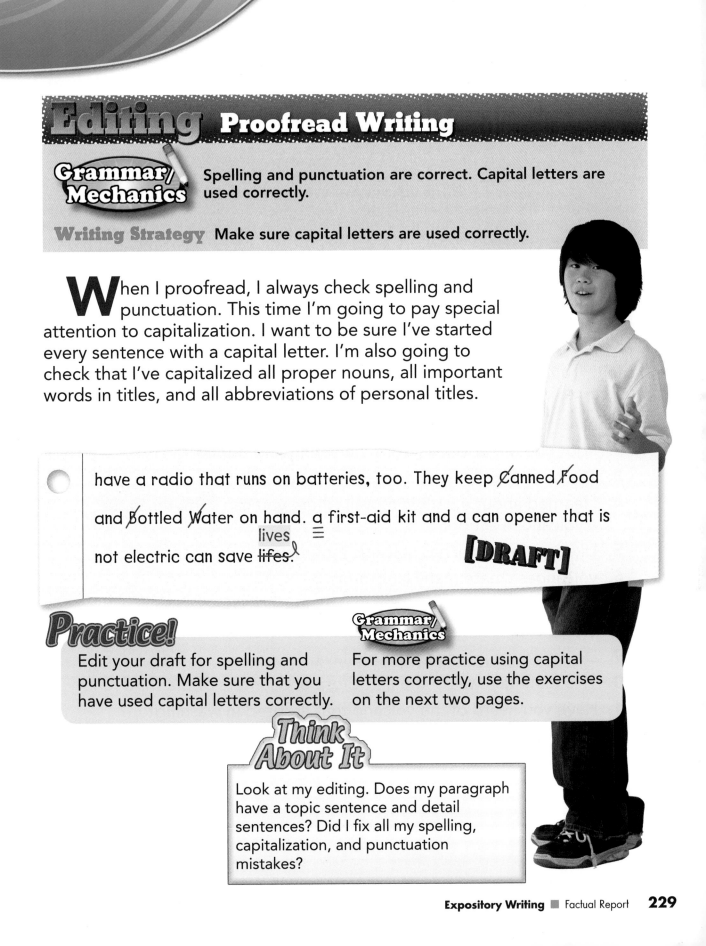

Practice!

Edit your draft for spelling and punctuation. Make sure that you have used capital letters correctly.

Grammar/ Mechanics

For more practice using capital letters correctly, use the exercises on the next two pages.

Think About It

Look at my editing. Does my paragraph have a topic sentence and detail sentences? Did I fix all my spelling, capitalization, and punctuation mistakes?

Capitalization

1. The first word of every sentence begins with a capital letter.
2. All proper nouns and the first word, the last word, and all important words in titles begin with capital letters.
3. Capitalize abbreviations of personal titles.

Practice the Rule

Number a piece of paper 1.–12. Correct any errors in capitalization. Write the corrected words and the number of the rule for capitalizing them. If a sentence is correct, write **Correct**.

1. have you read any books by ms. Margaret Poynter?
2. I got one of her books from the springfield public library.
3. The book is called *volcanoes: The fiery mountains.*
4. I learned about a park in hawaii where you can sometimes see a volcano in action.
5. Like japan, Hawaii has volcanic mountains.
6. volcanoes create many landforms.
7. There is an odd mountain in wyoming called devil's tower.
8. This is a famous landmark in north America.
9. Devil's Tower is made from old lava.
10. This mountain was in the film *Close encounters of the third Kind.*
11. Have you heard of the volcano that erupted in washington?
12. This mountain erupted on may 18, 1980.

Apply the Rule

Read the following paragraphs. Check for capitalization errors. Write the paragraphs with correct capitalization on a separate piece of paper.

Last year I read a book about the great Krakatoa volcano. Krakatoa was an island in indonesia. In 1883, its volcano erupted. This was one of the largest eruptions in History.

Krakatoa's eruption was Extremely explosive and Very destructive. It began on august 26, 1883, and ended on august 27 with one last spectacular eruption that blew Krakatoa apart. two thirds of the island collapsed beneath the sea. The sound of it was heard as far away as australia.

Krakatoa was an uninhabited Island. Even so, its eruption killed thousands of people on nearby islands. The final eruption and collapse of krakatoa caused huge sea waves. these gigantic sea waves destroyed hundreds of villages and towns on the neighboring islands.

Publishing Share Writing

Publish my report on the school's Web site.

My factual report is finished! If I publish my report on my school's Web site, other people could read it. I want people to know how to stay safe if they live near a volcano. Before I publish, I'll read my report one more time. Here is my final checklist.

My Checklist

✔ The title of my factual report and my name are at the top of the page.

✔ The report gives information on one topic and is well organized.

✔ I've supplied lots of details to interest my audience.

✔ The detail sentences explain the topic sentence.

✔ Spelling, grammar, and punctuation are all correct. Capital letters are used correctly.

Practice!

Make a checklist to check your own factual report one last time before you publish it. Then, publish your factual report.

In the Shadow of a Volcano
by Alika

Living near a volcano can be risky. People who live near a volcano learn to live near danger by being ready to act quickly. They must also be prepared in other ways.

The danger from an erupting volcano is real. When authorities, the officials in control, tell people to leave their homes, residents move fast. Some blasts travel many miles. Volcanoes can send out ash, which can harm people. Lava flowing from an erupting volcano is also dangerous.

Those who live near a volcano have their emergency items ready. People keep a flashlight and extra batteries handy. They have a radio that runs on batteries, too. They keep canned food and bottled water on hand. A first-aid kit and a can opener that is not electric can save lives.

Having an escape plan is important for people who live near a volcano. They decide on a route to take if they have to leave their home. They always head toward higher ground because lava and mud flow downhill. Also, they try to stay away from the wind. The wind can carry objects and harmful gas. The plan includes a place for everyone to meet later.

People who live on or near active volcanoes usually adjust to their dangerous neighbors. In the book *Volcanoes and Earthquakes*, Jon Erickson says that people learn to treat volcanoes "as though they were just a normal part of their lives."

Think About It

Use the rubric to check my report. Are the traits of a good factual report there? How does your report compare against the rubric?

Ways to Publish a Factual Report

There's more than one way to publish your factual report. As you decide how to publish your report, keep in mind who will be reading it. That will help you pick the best way to share your work. Here are a few ideas for publishing your factual report.

✓ **Read your factual report to your class. Have related pictures, artwork, maps, or charts available for the class to see.**

✓ **Add your report to the class or school Web site. Provide the Web master with an image to include with your report.**

✓ **Use a computer to type up and print your report. Make a folder for it, and include pictures, artwork, maps, or charts.**

✓ **Submit your report to a magazine that publishes student work.**

✓ **Post your report in the school library, and print extra copies as handouts for students to take.**

Writing Across the Content Areas
Factual Report

The subjects that you study in school are an excellent source of ideas for factual reports. Any subject will have a variety of topics to choose from. Let's look at some examples.

Social Studies

- Write a factual report about an influential person in the history of your state.
- Write a report about a historical event in your country or state.

Language Arts

- Write a factual report about an author whose books, stories, or poetry you like.
- Write a report about a book or story that has been made into a cartoon, film, or television program.

Math

- Write a factual report about ways that decimals, fractions, or math processes like multiplication and division are used in everyday life.
- Research and write a report about the history of numbers.

What's a How-To Essay?

It's an essay that explains how to do something or make something.

What's in a How-To Essay?

Materials
These are the things I will need to do my project. I might explain how to make a birdhouse. My materials for that project would be pieces of wood, a saw, a ruler, a pencil, and a hammer and nails.

Steps
Steps tell what you have to do to complete the task. To explain my project I have to tell you the steps in order.

Why write a How-To Essay?

People write how-to essays for a lot of different reasons. Here are two—information and entertainment.

Information

Sometimes I want to share what I know how to do with others. I can write up the instructions in a how-to essay.

People have written how-to essays on many topics, from studying for a test to coaching a basketball team. If you want to know how to do something, you can probably find a how-to essay in a book or on the Internet.

Entertainment

My readers may want the instructions in a how-to essay for entertainment. I may write a how-to essay about origami so readers can enjoy making paper animals and flowers. I may write a how-to essay about building a birdhouse. The reader may build one in order to enjoy watching birds from the window.

How-To Essay
Writing Traits

What makes a good how-to essay? A how-to essay should tell everything the reader needs to know simply and clearly. Here are some traits of a how-to essay.

Information/ Organization	The essay tells how to do or make something. All of the steps are in the right order.
Voice/ Audience	The essay's tone helps the reader picture the process.
Content/ Ideas	All necessary information is included.
Word Choice/ Clarity	All details are related to the process.
Sentence Fluency	Each sentence leads clearly to the next sentence.
Grammar/ Mechanics	Spelling, punctuation, and capitalization are correct. Pronouns are used correctly.

Let's read Carlos Ortiz's how-to essay about writing a research report. Then, we can check to see if he followed all of the writing traits.

Doing Research for a Town History Report

by Carlos Ortiz

What was your town like when it was brand-new? Many towns have an interesting history. Research your town's history, and write a report that tells about the "early days."

A good place to begin your report is with the founding of the town. Before you start your research, you should make a list of questions you want to answer. Here are some important questions: Where is the town located? When was the town built? Who were the first people who lived there? Why did they think this was a good place to start a community? What were their plans for the future?

step

There are many places to look for this information. Start by visiting the town hall or the library. Some towns also have a local history museum. Town records and old newspapers are great sources of information.

materials

step

After you have collected a lot of facts about the early days of your town, you can look for pictures to put in your report. Maps and photographs can show how the town has grown and how buildings have changed.

materials

While you do your research, make sure to write down the sources for all your facts and stories. A good research report ends with a list of all the sources the writer used.

Don't start writing your report just yet, though! The next step is likely to be the most fun. Seek out the "living memory" of your town. A town's "living memory" is the oldest members of the community. They have seen a lot during their own lifetimes. They might even remember stories told by their parents or grandparents. Maybe some of their ancestors helped settle the town.

final step

Finally it's time to write your report. By this time you should be quite an expert on your town's early days.

How-To Essay Rubric

The rubric below was made using the traits of a how-to essay on page 238. To score a how-to essay, assign one to four stars for each trait. Four stars mean that trait is excellent! Three stars mean it is very good. One or two stars mean that trait needs more work.

	Excelling	Achieving	Developing	Beginning
Information/Organization	The essay tells how to do or make something. All of the steps are in the right order.	The essay tells how to do or make something. Most steps are in order.	The essay tells how to do or make something. Some steps are in order.	The essay needs to tell how to do or make something. Very few steps are in order.
Voice/Audience	The essay's tone helps the reader picture the whole process.	The essay's tone helps the reader picture most of the process.	The essay's tone helps the reader picture some of the process.	The essay's tone needs to help the reader picture the process.
Content/Ideas	All necessary information is included.	Most necessary information is included.	Some necessary information is included.	A little of the necessary information is included.
Word Choice/Clarity	All details are related to the process.	Most details are related to the process.	Some details are related to the process.	A few details are related to the process.
Sentence Fluency	Each sentence leads clearly to the next sentence.	Most sentences lead clearly to the next.	Some sentences lead clearly to the next.	Few sentences lead clearly to the next.
Grammar/Mechanics	Spelling, punctuation, and capitalization are correct. Pronouns are correct.	There are a few errors in spelling, punctuation, or capitalization. Pronouns are correct.	There are some errors in spelling, punctuation, or capitalization. Some pronouns are incorrect.	There are many errors in spelling, punctuation, or capitalization. Many pronouns are incorrect.

How-To Essay
Using the Rubric to Study the Model

Now, let's use the rubric to check Carlos Ortiz's how-to essay: "Doing Research for a Town History Report." What score would you give Carlos for each category in the rubric?

Information/ Organization

- **The essay tells how to do or make something.**
- **All of the steps are in the right order.**

This essay gave me lots of good information on how to do a research report for a town history report. The writer explains all the important steps for gathering materials. He organizes the steps from first to last, so they are easy to follow. Each step has a separate paragraph. In this paragraph, he talks about how to get started.

A good place to begin your report is with the founding of the town. Before you start your research, you should make a list of questions you want to answer. Here are some important questions: Where is the town located? When was the town built? Who were the first people who lived there?

Voice/ Audience

- **The essay's tone helps the reader picture the process.**

Reading the essay, I could picture the different steps in researching a town history report. For each step, the writer explains what to do and what materials would be useful. He uses a friendly, natural tone to make it easy for the reader to follow the process. Here's an example.

After you have collected a lot of facts about the early days of your town, you can look for pictures to put in your report. Maps and photographs can show how the town has grown and how buildings have changed.

Content/Ideas

- **All necessary information is included.**

I like the way Carlos gives me specific sources of information. He also tells me why the step or materials are important. Here's a good example. In this paragraph, he explains what to do, when to do it, and why it's important.

> While you do your research, make sure to write down the sources for all your facts and stories. A good research report ends with a list of all the sources the writer used.

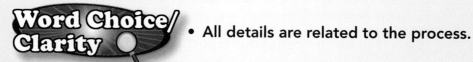

Word Choice/Clarity

- **All details are related to the process.**

There are lots of details in this essay, and all of them are related to doing research for a town history report. Unrelated details can be confusing to the reader. This paragraph has loads of details, but each one is related to seeking out a "living memory."

> The next step is likely to be the most fun. Seek out the "living memory" of your town. A town's "living memory" is the oldest members of the community. They have seen a lot during their own lifetimes. They might even remember stories told by their parents or grandparents. Maybe some of their ancestors helped settle the town.

Using the Rubric to Study the Model
How-To Essay

Sentence Fluency

- Each sentence leads clearly to the next sentence.

In this essay, each sentence leads clearly into the next. Also, even though each paragraph talks about a different step, the writer moves in a logical way from one paragraph to the next. Look at this example.

> There are many places to look for this information. Start by visiting the town hall or the library. Some towns also have a local history museum. Town records and old newspapers are great sources of information.
>
> After you have collected a lot of facts about the early days of your town, you can look for pictures to put in your report.

Grammar/Mechanics

- Spelling, punctuation, and capitalization are correct. Pronouns are used correctly.

Every word in the essay is spelled correctly. All the sentences begin with a capital letter and end with the correct punctuation. When Carlos uses a pronoun in place of a noun, he uses it correctly.

> A town's "living memory" is the oldest members of the community. They have seen a lot during their own lifetimes. They might even remember stories told by their parents or grandparents.

My Turn!

Now it's my turn to write a how-to essay! I'll use the rubric and good writing strategies to help me. Read along to see how I do this.

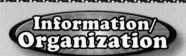

Prewriting Gather Information

Information/Organization The essay tells how to do or make something.

Writing Strategy Choose something to do or make. Make a list of all the important steps.

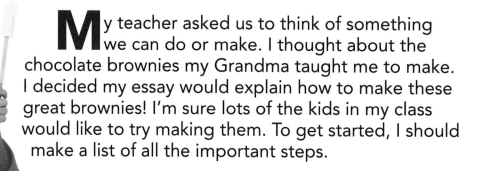

My teacher asked us to think of something we can do or make. I thought about the chocolate brownies my Grandma taught me to make. I decided my essay would explain how to make these great brownies! I'm sure lots of the kids in my class would like to try making them. To get started, I should make a list of all the important steps.

Important Steps for Making Brownies

- Melt butter, semisweet chocolate, and milk chocolate chips.
- Use a saucepan.
- Put in eggs and vanilla (beat the eggs).
- Add brown sugar and honey.
- Add flour and salt.
- Put in the macadamia nuts.

- Spread the batter in a baking pan, and bake for 30 minutes.
- You need a square baking pan.
- Put a little butter and parchment paper in the bottom of the pan.
- Cool brownies before you cut them into squares.

Practice!

Brainstorm a list of things that you like to do or make. Pick one that you think would be interesting to write about in a how-to essay. Then, make a list of all the important steps.

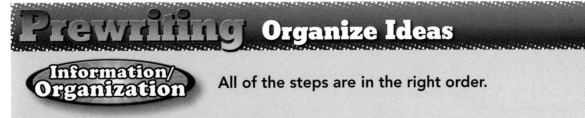

Prewriting Organize Ideas

Information/Organization All of the steps are in the right order.

Writing Strategy Make an Outline to organize the steps from first to last.

The rubric says that my steps need to be in order. I can use an Outline to put my list of steps for making brownies in order, from first to last.

Outline

I. **Introduction**
   A. I make chocolate brownies that taste like Hawaii to me.

II. **Body**
   A. Put butter and parchment paper in the bottom of a square baking pan.
   B. Melt butter, semisweet chocolate, and milk chocolate chips together in a saucepan.
   C. Add brown sugar and honey.
   D. Put in beaten eggs and vanilla.
   E. Add flour, salt, and nuts.
   F. Spread the batter in a baking pan, and bake for 30 minutes.

III. **Conclusion**
   A. Let the brownies cool, and then cut them into squares and eat them.

Writer's Term

Outline

An **Outline** is a writing plan that lists the main ideas. It has three sections: an introduction, a body, and a conclusion.

Practice!

Look at the list of important steps that you made. Use an Outline to organize your steps. Put them in order, from first step to last step.

Think About It

Look at my notes and my Outline. Did they help me organize my information? Will they help me write a good essay?

Drafting   Write a Draft

Voice/ Audience

The essay's tone helps the reader picture the process.

Writing Strategy   Use a friendly, natural tone so that the reader can picture the process.

Now it's time to write the first draft of my how-to essay. I'll use my Outline to keep the steps in my essay organized. I know from the rubric that I need to use a tone that helps my reader picture the process. I'll keep my writing sounding friendly and natural by "talking" to my reader directly. I always do my best with spelling and grammar, but I won't worry about mistakes right now. I'll get a chance to fix them later. The beginning of my draft is on the next page.

used a friendly, natural tone

[DRAFT]

Fantastic Chocolate Macadamia Nut Brownies

These great fantastic Chocolate Macadamia Nut Brownies that I make taste like Hawaii to me. Try making some and see if you agree!

used a friendly, natural tone

Start by wiping a little butter inside of a square baking pan. After you do that, it's important to cover the bottom of the pan with a piece of parchment paper.

correct homophone

Now it's time to make the batter. first we you melt half a stick of butter, 3 ounces of semisweet chocolate and three-fourths cup of milk chocolate chips in a large saucepan. Set the heat low. and keep stirring so that nothing burns.

After the butter and chocolate melt together, remove the pan from the stove. Then add half a cup of brown sugar and two tablespoons of honey to the pan.

Practice!

Use your Outline to write a draft of your how-to essay. Remember to explain each step clearly. Try using some time-order signal words to help clarify when each step happens.

Think About It

Read my draft. Did I explain things in a friendly tone? Can the reader picture what to do?

Revising Extend Writing

Content/Ideas All necessary information is included.

Writing Strategy Add any missing information.

I know from the rubric that I should make sure my essay has all the necessary information. If any important information is missing, I should add it.

I read my draft to my friend Maya. As I was reading, I realized I had forgotten to put in the size of the baking pan for the brownies. Maya noticed that I didn't give some important details about cooking the brownies—how hot the oven should be and when to heat up the oven! Here's how I added in that information.

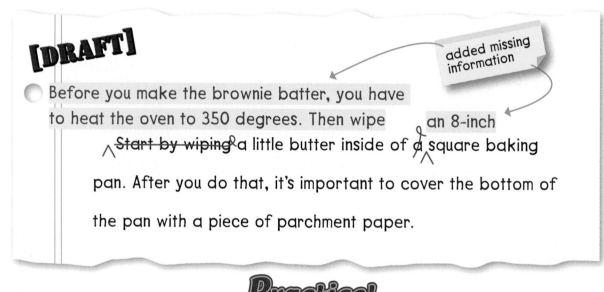

[DRAFT]

added missing information

Before you make the brownie batter, you have to heat the oven to 350 degrees. Then wipe ~~Start by wiping~~ a little butter inside of a an 8-inch square baking pan. After you do that, it's important to cover the bottom of the pan with a piece of parchment paper.

Practice!

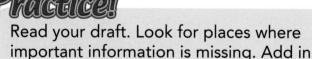

Read your draft. Look for places where important information is missing. Add in the necessary information.

Revising Clarify Writing

All details are related to the process.

Writing Strategy Take out details that are not related to the process.

The rubric says that all of the details in my essay should relate to the process. After reading my first draft again, I saw that in the middle of my draft, I had included information about macadamia nuts that doesn't relate to making brownies. I'll have to take it out of my essay. I also saw a mistake in capitalization. I'll correct that, too.

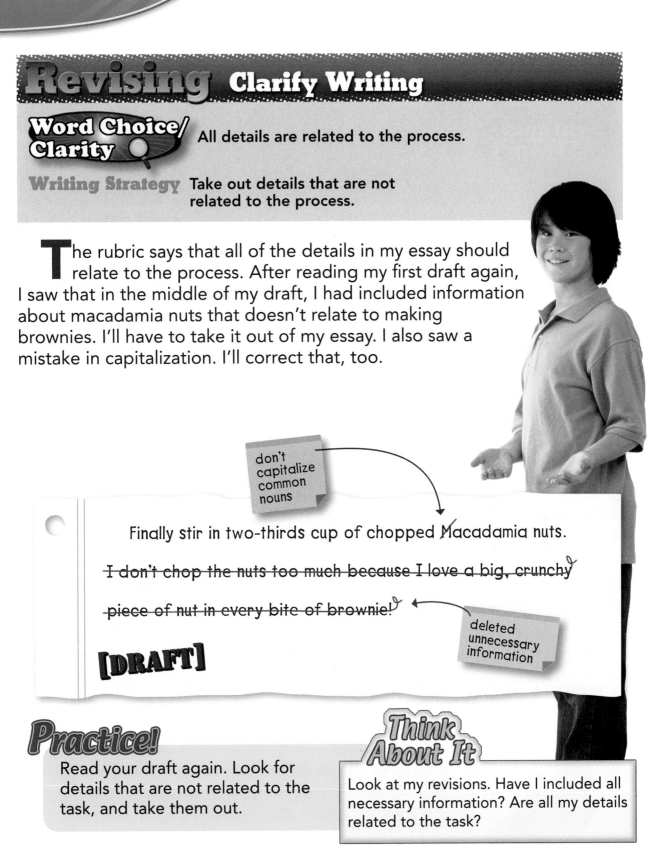

don't capitalize common nouns

Finally stir in two-thirds cup of chopped Macadamia nuts.

~~I don't chop the nuts too much because I love a big, crunchy~~

~~piece of nut in every bite of brownie!~~

deleted unnecessary information

[DRAFT]

Practice!

Read your draft again. Look for details that are not related to the task, and take them out.

Think About It

Look at my revisions. Have I included all necessary information? Are all my details related to the task?

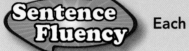

Editing Check Sentences

Sentence Fluency — Each sentence leads clearly to the next sentence.

Writing Strategy Be sure each sentence leads clearly to the next sentence.

It's important that ideas in my essay flow together—that each sentence leads clearly to the next. This means putting sentences in a logical order. I found one place in the middle of my essay where the sentences were not in logical order. One sentence didn't lead clearly to the next. This is how I fixed the problem.

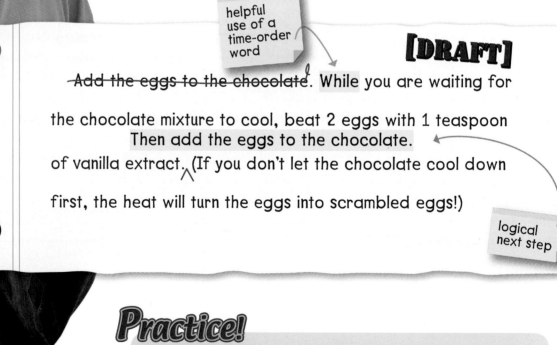

[DRAFT]

helpful use of a time-order word

~~Add the eggs to the chocolate.~~ While you are waiting for

the chocolate mixture to cool, beat 2 eggs with 1 teaspoon
Then add the eggs to the chocolate.
of vanilla extract. (If you don't let the chocolate cool down

first, the heat will turn the eggs into scrambled eggs!)

logical next step

Practice!

Read your draft. Check that each sentence leads clearly to the next sentence. Make sure that there is a logical flow to your ideas.

 **Proofread Writing**

Grammar/ Mechanics Spelling, punctuation, and capitalization are correct. Pronouns are used correctly.

Writing Strategy Check that all pronouns are used correctly.

The rubric tells me that I need to check my essay for errors. I'm going to check spelling, punctuation, and capitalization first. Then I'm going to make sure that I've used all the pronouns correctly.

Writer's Term

Pronouns

A **pronoun** can replace a noun naming a person, place, or thing. Pronouns include **I, me, you, we, us, he, she, it, they,** and **them**.

correct pronoun

set the pan of brownies on the kitchen counter to cool.

→ them

When they are cold, cut it into squares. (Don't forget to peel peel the parchment paper off the bottoms!)

[DRAFT]

 **Practice!**

Edit your draft for spelling, punctuation, and capitalization. Check that you have used all pronouns correctly.

 **Grammar/ Mechanics**

For more practice using pronouns correctly, use the exercises on the next two pages.

Think About It

Look at my editing. Does each sentence lead clearly to the next sentence? Did I proofread my writing? Are all pronouns used correctly?

Grammar/Mechanics Practice!

Subject and Object Pronouns

Know the Rule

A **pronoun** is a word that can take the place of one or more nouns in a sentence. A **subject pronoun** takes the place of one or more nouns in the subject of a sentence.

Use the pronouns **I, we, he, she,** and **they** as subjects in sentences.

An **object pronoun** follows action verbs or prepositions, such as **to, at, for, of,** and **with**.

Use the pronouns **me, us, him, her,** and **them** as objects in sentences. The pronoun **you** is used as a subject or an object. The pronoun **it** can be a subject or an object.

Practice the Rule

Number a piece of paper 1.–12. Write a pronoun that can take the place of the underlined word or words in each sentence.

1. <u>My friend Paulo and I</u> live in a small town on the island of Maui.
2. Every Saturday morning, <u>Paulo and I</u> run over to the bakery owned by Mr. and Mrs. Lee.
3. <u>The Lees</u> make the best fresh bread and pastries on Maui!
4. Mrs. Lee uses family recipes, and <u>Mrs. Lee</u> bakes a mango bread that is delicious.
5. <u>Mango bread</u> is made using fresh mangoes and macadamia nuts.
6. Mr. Lee runs the bakery shop, and <u>Mr. Lee</u> always has a loaf of mango bread waiting for me on Saturdays.
7. Paulo always buys papaya muffins and takes <u>the papaya muffins</u> home to his mother.
8. Sometimes Paulo eats one of <u>the papaya muffins</u> before he gets home. They're so good!

9. <u>Papaya muffins</u> are made from papaya, carrots, applesauce, and chopped walnuts.

10. If Mr. Lee has extra poi muffins on Saturday, he will give a few to <u>Paulo and me</u> for free.

11. <u>Poi muffins</u> are made from taro, the edible root of the taro plant.

12. When Mr. Lee gives <u>Paulo and me</u> those wonderful poi muffins, we usually eat them all on the walk back home.

Apply the Rule _____

Read this part of a story. Correct any pronoun errors that you find. Write the paragraphs correctly on a separate sheet of paper.

My sister loves to cook. A month ago, her decided to learn more about baking. She enrolled in a cooking class. She signed up for them at the local community center. The class was taught by a professional pastry chef. Him was the pastry chef for a fancy restaurant downtown.

Last night, my sister brought home an apple tart that her had made in class. They tasted delicious! My brother wanted all of it. I told him that the apple tart was for I. Our sister said that us should share it. We asked my sister if us could each have half of it. My sister said that we could. Her said she ate her share in class. They ate it together.

My brother and I think that she should take all the cooking classes she wants—as long as me get all the tasty results!

Publishing **Share Writing**

Publish my essay in a class how-to book.

I've completed my how-to essay! Now I have to decide how to publish it. I chose the topic of making brownies because I thought kids in my class would like to try making their own. Other kids want to share their how-to essays, too. We decided to put all our essays together in a class how-to book. The book will go in the class library. Before I publish my how-to essay, I'm going to check it over one last time. Here's the final checklist I'll use.

My Checklist

✔ The title of my how-to essay and my name are at the top of the page.

✔ The essay describes how to do or make something. It includes all the important steps in order.

✔ I've used a friendly tone so the reader can picture the process.

✔ I've included all necessary information and taken out details that are not related to the process.

✔ Each of my sentences leads clearly to the next sentence.

✔ Spelling, grammar, and punctuation are all correct. Pronouns are used correctly.

Practice!

Make a checklist to publish your own how-to essay. Be sure to check your essay one last time before publishing it.

Fantastic Chocolate Macadamia Nut Brownies
by Alika

These Fantastic Chocolate Macadamia Nut Brownies that I make taste like Hawaii to me. Try making some, and see if you agree!

Before you make the brownie batter, you have to heat the oven to 350 degrees. Then wipe a little butter inside of an 8-inch square baking pan. After you do that, cover the bottom of the pan with a piece of parchment paper.

Now it's time to make the batter. First you melt half a stick of butter, 3 ounces of semisweet chocolate and three-fourths cup of milk chocolate chips in a large saucepan. Set the heat low and keep stirring so that nothing burns.

After the butter and chocolate melt together, remove the pan from the stove. Then add half a cup of brown sugar and two tablespoons of honey to the pan. Mix everything well so that there aren't any lumps! Once that is done, let the mixture cool for a few minutes.

While you are waiting for the chocolate mixture to cool, beat 2 eggs with 1 teaspoon of vanilla extract. Then add the eggs to the chocolate. (If you don't let the chocolate cool down first, the heat will turn the eggs into scrambled eggs!)

Now sift one cup flour along with half a teaspoon of salt into the chocolate. Mix it all together gently. Finally stir in two-thirds cup of chopped macadamia nuts.

When the batter is completely mixed, spread it in the pan. Bake the brownies for about 30 minutes.

Set the pan of brownies on the kitchen counter to cool. When they are cold, cut them into squares. (Don't forget to peel the parchment paper off the bottoms!) Enjoy your Fantastic Chocolate Macadamia Nut Brownies with a glass of milk or a scoop of ice cream.

Think About It

Use the rubric to check my essay. Are the traits of a good how-to essay there? Check your own how-to essay with the rubric, too.

Ways to Publish a How-To Essay

You can publish your work in a variety of ways. It's important to think about who will enjoy reading about your topic. That will help you pick the best way to share it. Here are some ideas for publishing your how-to essay.

✓ **Present your essay as part of a classroom demonstration. Demonstrate each step as you read it.**

✓ **Create an electronic slide show of your essay for the class. Pictures and text should highlight details of each step.**

✓ **Submit your essay for publication on the school Web site or school newspaper.**

✓ **Send your essay to a magazine that publishes student work.**

✓ **As a class, create a how-to booklet of student essays. Make copies, and distribute them to other classrooms.**

Writing Across the Content Areas
How-To Essay

The subjects that you study in school can be a great source of topics for a how-to essay. Let's look at a few examples.

Science

- Explain each step in a science experiment that you observed or performed.
- Write a how-to essay that explains how to plan a science fair project.

Math

- Explain the step-by-step process for solving a word problem.
- Write a how-to essay that explains how you learned a new math skill.

Language Arts

- Describe the steps for writing a book report.
- Write a how-to essay that explains how to create a bibliography for a research report.

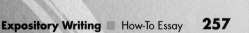

EXPOSITORY test writing

Read the Writing Prompt

As you begin a writing test, the first thing you'll read is the writing prompt. Look for three helpful parts in the writing prompt.

Setup This part of the writing prompt gives you the background information you need to get ready for writing.

Task This part of the writing prompt tells you exactly what you're supposed to write: a report about the history of a topic that you know about.

Scoring Guide This section tells how your writing will be scored. To do well on the test, you should include everything on the list.

You've used rubrics for each expository piece you've written using this book. When you take a writing test, you don't always have all the information that a rubric gives you. That's okay. The scoring guide is a lot like a rubric. It lists everything you need to think about to write a good paper. Many scoring guides will include the six important traits of writing that are in the rubrics we've looked at:

Information/Organization   Content/Ideas   Sentence Fluency

Voice/Audience   Word Choice/Clarity   Grammar/Mechanics

Everyone enjoys learning more about a topic that interests them. This topic might be something from sports, nature, or anything!

Write a report about the history of a topic that you know about.

Be sure your report

- provides interesting information on a topic and is well organized with a clear introduction, body, and conclusion.

- begins with a topic sentence and sticks to the topic so the reader can easily follow the ideas.

- includes examples or explanations that relate to the topic.

- is written using to-the-point language.

- includes a variety of lively, energetic sentences.

- has correct grammar, spelling, capitalization, and punctuation.

Writing Traits in the Scoring Guide

The scoring guide in the writing prompt on page 259 has been made into this chart. Notice how the information on this chart is similar to the writing traits in the rubrics you've been using. Test writing prompts won't always include all of the six writing traits, but this one does! They can help you write your best report.

Information/Organization
- Be sure your report provides interesting information on a topic and is well organized with a clear introduction, body, and conclusion.

Voice/Audience
- Be sure your report begins with a topic sentence and sticks to the topic so the reader can easily follow the ideas.

Content/Ideas
- Be sure your report includes examples or explanations that relate to the topic.

Word Choice/Clarity
- Be sure your report is written using to-the-point language.

Sentence Fluency
- Be sure your report includes a variety of lively, energetic sentences.

Grammar/Mechanics
- Be sure your report has correct grammar, spelling, capitalization, and punctuation.

Let's look at the report by Leilani Bishop on the next page. Did she follow the scoring guide?

Mighty Ships of the U.S. Navy

Writing Prompt MODEL Response

by Leilani Bishop

The United States Navy has had many "mighty ships." These ships have protected the United States for hundreds of years. As times changed, the ships did, too. When each vessel was built, it was the best and most modern battleship that could be made.

Work began on the first ships in 1794. These ships were called "frigates." Frigates protected American ships from pirates and attack by other countries. These ships had big cannons on board and could fight other warships. They were also fast and could get away if they were attacked by bigger ships. One of the frigates was built in Boston, Massachusetts. Its name is the *U.S.S. Constitution,* but most people know it as "Old Ironsides." The *Constitution* was used as a warship for more than 60 years. Then for about 40 years it was used to train sailors. Finally, around 1900, it went back to Boston. The *Constitution* is now a museum where people can learn about early warships.

America's warships kept getting bigger and better. Steam engines replaced sails in the late 1800s. Submarines became an important part of the Navy after 1914 and the start of World War I. When planes needed a safe place to land, the Navy built aircraft carriers. Aircraft carriers helped America win World War II in the 1940s.

Aircraft carriers are truly "mighty ships." These vessels are like a floating city with a runway area for launching and landing planes. They use nuclear energy for power. About 3,200 crew members can live on one aircraft carrier. Their jobs might be in the post office, a television or radio station, stores, a hospital, or a library. The *U.S.S. Ronald Reagan* is the most modern aircraft carrier in the Navy today. It is 1,092 feet long, which is more than three football fields put end-to-end! America's newest aircraft carrier is being built right now. It will go to sea in about the year 2008.

From frigate to huge aircraft carrier, time has seen many changes in America's warships. Yet one thing has not changed. The mighty ships of the United States Navy will keep on keeping America safe.

Using the Scoring Guide to Study the Model

Let's use the scoring guide to check Leilani's writing test. We'll look for examples from her writing to show how well she did on each part of the scoring guide.

Information/Organization

- **The report provides interesting information on a topic and is well organized with a clear introduction, body, and conclusion.**

Leilani's report provides a lot of interesting information about the history of her subject. The report is well organized. The writer introduces the topic in the first paragraph, follows with interesting details in the body of the report, and wraps up with some concluding thoughts. Here's how she introduced her topic.

> The United States Navy has had many "mighty ships." These ships have protected the United States for hundreds of years. As times changed, the ships did, too. When each vessel was built, it was the best and most modern battleship that could be made.

Voice/Audience

- **The report begins with a topic sentence and sticks to the topic so the reader can easily follow the ideas.**

Leilani placed her topic sentence in her report's introduction. The scoring guide also tells you to stick to the topic so the reader can easily follow your ideas. In the body of her report, Leilani stays focused on the topic and tells about the history of Navy ships. A good example can be seen in the opening sentences of the body of her report.

> Work began on the first ships in 1794. These ships were called "frigates." Frigates protected American ships from pirates and attack by other countries.

Content/ Ideas

- The report includes examples or explanations that relate to the topic.

In her report, Leilani talks about the first ships in the United States Navy called "frigates." As an example, she tells the reader about the most famous of those frigates: the *U.S.S. Constitution*.

> One of the frigates was built in Boston, Massachusetts. Its name is the *U.S.S. Constitution*, but most people know it as "Old Ironsides." The *Constitution* was used as a warship for more than 60 years. Then for about 40 years it was used to train sailors.

Word Choice/ Clarity

- The report is written using to-the-point language.

In her report, Leilani follows the scoring guide—her writing is clear and direct. In this example, she describes the major changes in warships over the years.

> America's warships kept getting bigger and better. Steam engines replaced sails in the late 1800s. Submarines became an important part of the Navy after 1914 and the start of World War I. When planes needed a safe place to land, the Navy built aircraft carriers. Aircraft carriers helped America win World War II in the 1940s.

Using the Scoring Guide to Study the Model

- **The report includes a variety of lively, energetic sentences.**

The scoring guide tells you to include a variety of lively, energetic sentences. This will make your writing more interesting and keep your reader's attention. In this example, notice how Leilani varies her sentences to make them more energetic.

Aircraft carriers are truly "mighty ships." These vessels are like a floating city with a runway area for launching and landing planes. They use nuclear energy for power. About 3,200 crew members can live on one aircraft carrier. Their jobs might be in the post office, a television or radio station, stores, a hospital, or a library.

- **The report has correct grammar, spelling, capitalization, and punctuation.**

Usually the scoring guide will remind you to check your grammar, spelling, capitalization, and punctuation. Look for mistakes you made and correct them. Watch especially for mistakes that you make often, such as using pronouns or homophones incorrectly. Leilani has done a good job in her report. Her final draft doesn't have any errors.

Planning My Time

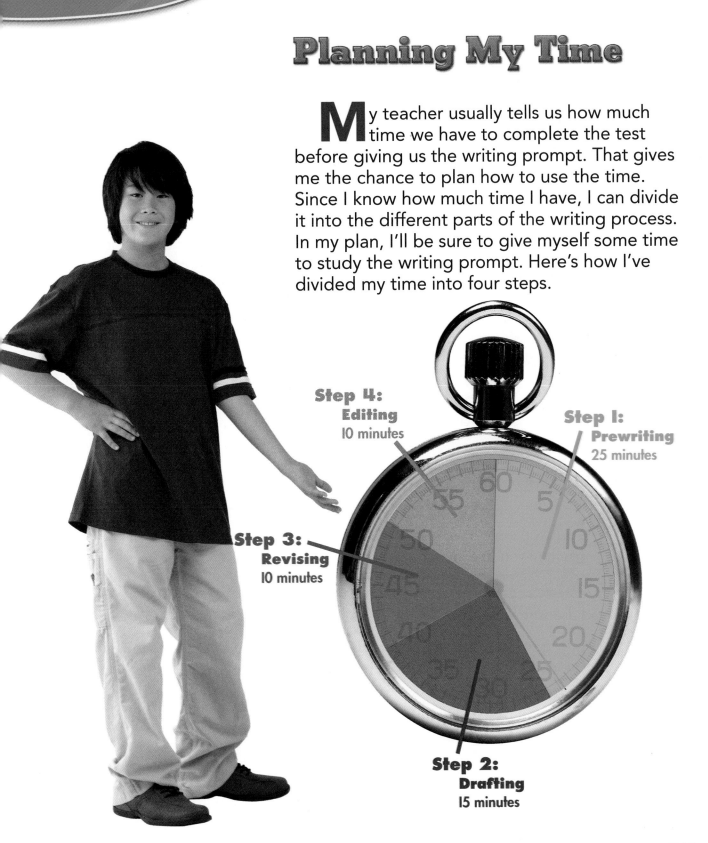

My teacher usually tells us how much time we have to complete the test before giving us the writing prompt. That gives me the chance to plan how to use the time. Since I know how much time I have, I can divide it into the different parts of the writing process. In my plan, I'll be sure to give myself some time to study the writing prompt. Here's how I've divided my time into four steps.

Step 4:
Editing
10 minutes

Step 1:
Prewriting
25 minutes

Step 3:
Revising
10 minutes

Step 2:
Drafting
15 minutes

Prewriting Study the Writing Prompt

Information/Organization

Writing Strategy Study the writing prompt to be sure I know what to do.

When my teacher gives us the writing prompt, I study it to be sure I know exactly what I'm supposed to do. I find each of the parts and label them: the setup, the task, and the scoring guide. Then I circle key words in the writing prompt that tell what kind of writing to do. You should do the same thing when you take a writing test.

I circled **Write a report** because this tells what kind of writing I'll be doing. I also circled **a place you know about** because that is the topic of my report—what I'll be writing about.

My Writing Test Prompt

Setup — Most people have places that they like. These places can be near where you live, in another state, or anywhere!

Task — Write a report about a place you know about

Scoring Guide —
Be sure your report

- provides interesting information on a topic and is well organized with a clear introduction, body, and conclusion.
- begins with a topic sentence and sticks to the topic so the reader can easily follow the ideas.
- includes examples or explanations that relate to the topic.
- is written using to-the-point language.
- includes a variety of lively, energetic sentences.
- has correct grammar, spelling, capitalization, and punctuation.

I've studied the writing prompt. Next I'll think about how the scoring guide relates to the six writing traits I've studied in the rubrics. All of the traits might not be included in every scoring guide. Even so, I need to remember them all to write a good report.

- **Be sure your report provides interesting information on a topic and is well organized with a clear introduction, body, and conclusion.**

I'll use a graphic organizer to organize my report. That way I'll know that my report is complete.

- **Be sure your report begins with a topic sentence and sticks to the topic so the reader can easily follow the ideas.**

My topic sentence will be the most important part of the first paragraph. It will tell the reader what the report is about. It's important that I stick to the topic throughout my report.

- **Be sure your report includes examples or explanations that relate to the topic.**

Examples and explanations are an important part of the body of my report.

- **Be sure your report is written using to-the-point language.**

When I begin drafting my report, using to-the-point language will make my writing easy to read and understand.

- **Be sure your report includes a variety of lively, energetic sentences.**

Including a variety of lively, energetic sentences will make my writing more interesting. It will also keep the reader's attention.

- **Be sure your report has correct grammar, spelling, capitalization, and punctuation.**

Carefully proofreading my writing is an important step. I'll do this after I write my first draft.

Prewriting **Gather Information**

Information/Organization   **Writing Strategy** Respond to the task.

I've learned that writers first gather information to help them write. This is a key step when writing a report. It's even more important when you are writing for a test and don't have much time.

I'll start by looking again at the task in the writing prompt. The task explains what I'm supposed to write about. It tells me that I need to write a report about a place I know about. So first I'll make a list of places to write about. Then I'll decide which place I have the most information about.

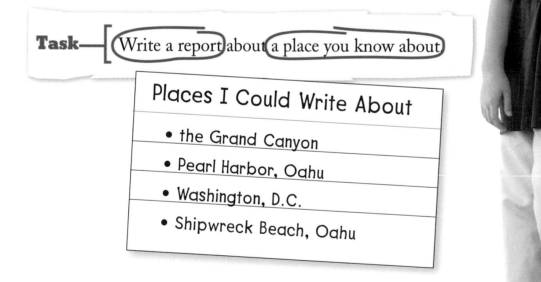

Task—[(Write a report) about (a place you know about)]

Places I Could Write About

- the Grand Canyon
- Pearl Harbor, Oahu
- Washington, D.C.
- Shipwreck Beach, Oahu

Remember! Take time to think about how you'll respond to the task part of the prompt before you write. To gather information, jot down notes or make a short list.

Prewriting Organize Ideas

Writing Strategy Choose a graphic organizer.

I need to start organizing my ideas. I've decided to write my report about Pearl Harbor since I know the most about it. A good graphic organizer for a report is a Web. It will help me organize my information around the main topic.

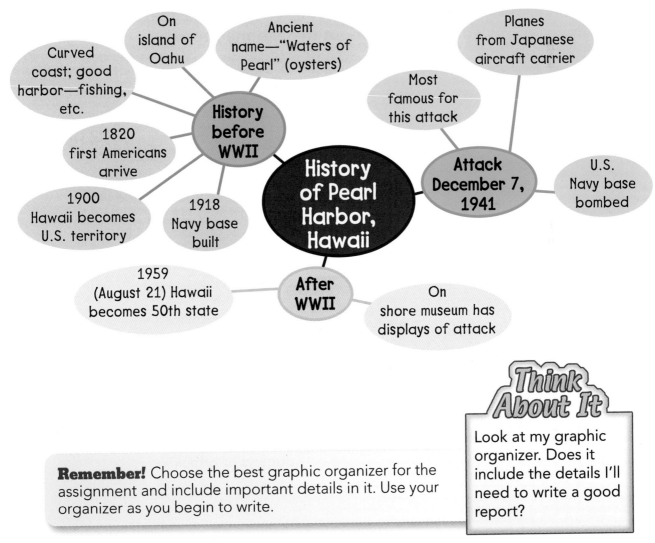

Remember! Choose the best graphic organizer for the assignment and include important details in it. Use your organizer as you begin to write.

Think About It
Look at my graphic organizer. Does it include the details I'll need to write a good report?

Prewriting Check the Scoring Guide

Information/Organization

Writing Strategy Check my graphic organizer against the scoring guide.

When you are writing for a test, you don't have much time to revise. So, prewriting is more important than ever! Before I start drafting, I'll check my Web against the scoring guide in the writing prompt. Then I'll know for sure that I'm writing about the assigned topic.

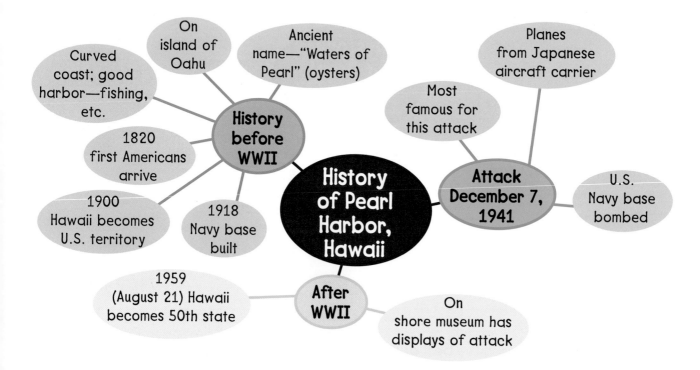

- Curved coast; good harbor—fishing, etc.
- On island of Oahu
- Ancient name—"Waters of Pearl" (oysters)
- **History before WWII**
- 1820 first Americans arrive
- 1900 Hawaii becomes U.S. territory
- 1918 Navy base built
- 1959 (August 21) Hawaii becomes 50th state
- **History of Pearl Harbor, Hawaii**
- **After WWII**
- On shore museum has displays of attack
- Most famous for this attack
- Planes from Japanese aircraft carrier
- **Attack December 7, 1941**
- U.S. Navy base bombed

Information/Organization

• provides interesting information on a topic and is well organized with a clear introduction, body, and conclusion.

The topic and the information about it are all included in my Web. I'll use it to write a clear introduction, body, and conclusion.

Voice/Audience

• begins with a topic sentence and sticks to the topic so the reader can easily follow the ideas.

I haven't written my topic sentence yet, but I know that the information is in the center of my Web. As I write my report, I'll stay focused on the topic.

Content/Ideas

• includes examples or explanations that relate to the topic.

There are examples and explanations in my notes and Web. As I write my draft, I'll use them to develop my ideas.

Word Choice/Clarity

• is written using to-the-point language.

Using to-the-point language will make my writing easy to read and understand. I'll keep this in mind as I write and edit my draft.

Sentence Fluency

• includes a variety of lively, energetic sentences.

I want to keep my reader's attention. I'll be sure to write a variety of sentences that are lively and full of energy.

Grammar/Mechanics

• has correct grammar, spelling, capitalization, and punctuation.

I need to check my grammar, spelling, capitalization, and punctuation when I edit my draft.

Remember! Before you begin writing your draft, look back at the scoring guide in the writing prompt. Make sure that you understand everything you need to do.

Think About It

Does my graphic organizer cover all the points in the scoring guide? What else do I need to include before I begin writing?

Drafting Write a Draft

Voice/Audience

Writing Strategy Begin with a topic sentence and stick to the topic so the reader can easily follow my ideas.

N ow it's time to start drafting. The scoring guide tells me to begin with a topic sentence. This will be the most important part of the introduction. As I write the rest of my report, I'll stay focused on the topic so I won't confuse my reader.

[DRAFT]

Pearl Harbor, Hawaii
by Alika

Pearl Harbor is a place with a lot of history. Most people only think of World War II when they hear "Pearl Harbor." **A visit to Pearl Harbor, though, will show their are many interesting things about this place.**

topic sentence

On December 7, 1941, planes from a Japanese aircraft carrier flew over Hawaii and bombed the United States Navy base at Pearl Harbor. After that, the United States and Japan were at war and because of this Americans will always remember the bombing of Pearl Harbor.

Pearl Harbor is not just a battle in World War II. Its also a beautiful place with an interesting history. Pearl Harbor is on the island of Oahu in Hawaii. The Ancient People of Hawaii named Pearl Harbor. The coast is curved. That makes the harbor a terrific place to go fishing, swimming, and sailing. The first Americans to live in Hawaii arrived in 1820. In 1900, Hawaii became a territory of the United States. In 1918, the navy base was built in Pearl Harbor. In 1959, Hawaii became the 50th state.

Pearl Harbor, Hawaii, is a great place to visit. It is famous for the terrible battle that took place their in 1941. A museum displays what the attack was like. Today, Pearl Harbor is a place with a long history and beautiful scenery.

Think About It

Read my draft. Does my report begin with a good topic sentence? Did I stick to the topic? Can you easily follow my ideas?

Remember! A good topic sentence is the most important part of the introduction to your report. As you write the body of your report, stay focused on the topic so the reader will be able to follow your ideas easily.

Revising Extend Writing

Content/ Ideas

Writing Strategy Add examples or explanations.

Now that my first draft is complete, the next step is to check it against the scoring guide. I want to be sure I've covered all the points that I'll be graded on. I'll read over my draft to see if I've missed anything.

While reading my draft, I discovered that I didn't explain some facts about Pearl Harbor's history very clearly. I checked my notes and Web and found some good details that I can add to better explain what I mean. I'll add these now.

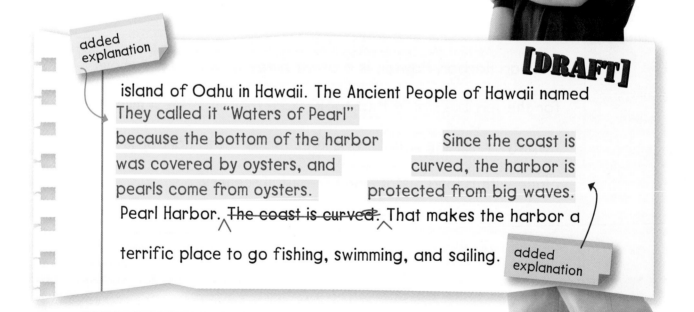

[DRAFT]

added explanation

island of Oahu in Hawaii. The Ancient People of Hawaii named They called it "Waters of Pearl" because the bottom of the harbor was covered by oysters, and pearls come from oysters.

Since the coast is curved, the harbor is protected from big waves.

Pearl Harbor. ~~The coast is curved.~~ That makes the harbor a terrific place to go fishing, swimming, and sailing.

added explanation

Remember! Read your draft, then check your graphic organizer to be sure that all important facts and details are in your report. Add examples and explanations that further develop and clarify your ideas.

Revising Clarify Writing

Word Choice/Clarity

Writing Strategy Replace wordy phrases with to-the-point language.

The scoring guide reminds me to use to-the-point language in my report. This will make my report easy to read and understand. I'll read my draft again. This time, I'll check for any long, wordy phrases. If I find any, I'll either shorten the phrase or get rid of it, if it isn't necessary.

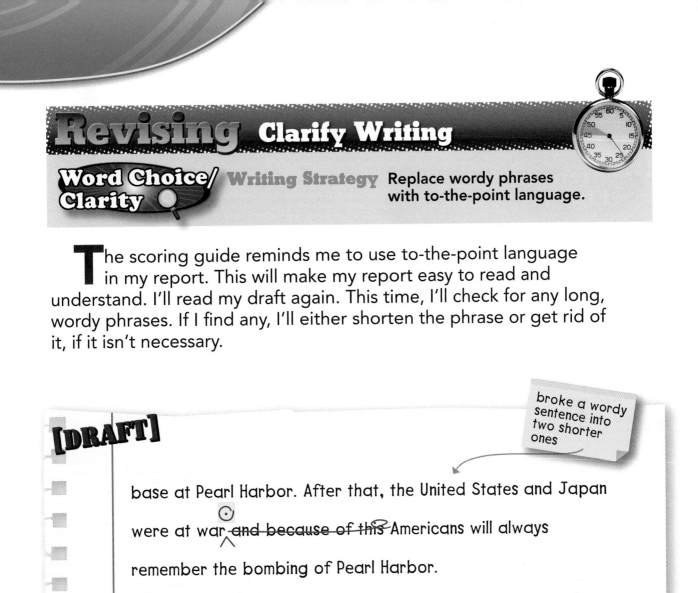

[DRAFT]

broke a wordy sentence into two shorter ones

base at Pearl Harbor. After that, the United States and Japan

were at war. ~~and because of this~~ Americans will always

remember the bombing of Pearl Harbor.

Remember! Use to-the-point language in your report. Replace long, wordy phrases. Using language that is clear and direct will make your writing easier to read and understand.

Think About It

Look at my revisions. Do the added explanations develop and clarify my ideas? Did I replace long, wordy phrases with to-the-point language?

Editing Check Sentences

Sentence Fluency

Writing Strategy Use a variety of lively, energetic sentences.

The scoring guide tells me to include a variety of lively, energetic sentences. This will make my writing more interesting and keep the reader's attention. While reading my draft, I noticed a group of sentences near the end that had pretty much the same length and structure. Even though the information is important, it seems boring. I'll add some variety that will make the sentences livelier and more interesting.

Americans to live in Hawaii arrived in 1820. In 1900, Hawaii became a territory of the United States. ~~In 1918,~~ the navy base

It wasn't until

eighteen years later   August 21, 1959, that
was built in Pearl Harbor. ~~In 1959,~~ Hawaii became the 50th state.

[DRAFT]

lively, energetic sentences

Remember! A variety of lively, energetic sentences will keep your reader interested in what you have to say!

Editing Proofread Writing

Grammar/Mechanics

Writing Strategy Check the grammar, spelling, capitalization, and punctuation.

The scoring guide reminds me to check my grammar, spelling, capitalization, and punctuation. It's a good thing that I planned how to use my time. Now I have plenty of time to check for errors. I'll carefully read my draft once more.

Pearl Harbor, Hawaii
by Alika

Pearl Harbor is a place with a lot of history. Most people only think of World War II when they hear "Pearl Harbor." A visit to Pearl Harbor, though, will show ~~their~~ ^there^ are many interesting things about this place.

On December 7, 1941, planes from a Japanese aircraft carrier flew over Hawaii and bombed the United States Navy base at Pearl Harbor. After that, the United States and Japan were at war⊙ ~~and because of this~~ Americans will always remember the bombing of Pearl Harbor.

Remember! Every time you write for a test, you need to check your grammar, spelling, capitalization, and punctuation.

[FINAL DRAFT]

Pearl Harbor is not just a battle in World War II. ~~Its~~ It's also a beautiful place with an interesting history. Pearl Harbor is on the island of Oahu in Hawaii. The Ancient People of Hawaii named

They called it "Waters of Pearl" because the bottom of the harbor was covered by oysters, and pearls come from oysters.

Since the coast is curved, the harbor is protected from big waves.

Pearl Harbor. ~~The coast is curved.~~ That makes the harbor a terrific place to go fishing, swimming, and sailing. The first Americans to live in Hawaii arrived in 1820. In 1900, Hawaii became a territory of the United States. ~~In 1918,~~ the navy base

It wasn't until

eighteen years later August 21, 1959, that

was built in Pearl Harbor. ~~In 1959,~~ Hawaii became the 50th state.

Pearl Harbor, Hawaii, is a great place to visit. It is famous

there

for the terrible battle that took place ~~their~~ in 1941. A museum displays what the attack was like. Today, Pearl Harbor is a place with a long history and beautiful scenery.

Check my report against the scoring guide. Did I include everything I will be graded on?

Can you believe it? We're finished! We used the writing prompt and scoring guide to write an interesting report. Remember these important tips when you write for a test.

TEST TIPS

1. **Study the writing prompt before you begin to write.** Remember that most writing prompts have three parts: the setup, the task, and the scoring guide. They won't be labeled. You'll have to figure them out for yourself.

2. **Make sure you understand the task before you begin to write.**
   - Read the three parts of the writing prompt. Then label them.
   - Circle key words in the task. These tell you what kind of writing you need to do. The task might also identify your audience.
   - Read the scoring guide. Make sure you know how you'll be graded.
   - Say the assignment in your own words to yourself.

3. **Plan your time. Then keep an eye on the clock.** Decide how much time you'll spend on each part of the writing process. Stick to your plan as closely as possible. You want to have plenty of time to revise and edit your draft.

4. **Use the scoring guide to check your draft.** The scoring guide is a valuable tool. Like the rubrics you've used on other papers, it reminds you of what is important. Reread your draft at least twice. Make sure that it does what the scoring guide says it should do.

5. **Plan your report well because you won't have much time for revising.** Make notes and use a graphic organizer before you write a draft.

6. **Write neatly.** Remember, the people who score your test must be able to read it!

PERSUASIVE writing

tries to persuade the reader to take action or to have or change an opinion.

Hi, my name is Shamari, and I'm learning all about persuasive writing! I love drawing pictures and visiting art museums. When I see art that I like, I write about it to tell others why they would love it, too. Learning about persuasive writing will help me do this.

IN THIS UNIT

1. **Persuasive Essay**
2. **Editorial**
3. **Friendly Letter**
4. **Writing for a Test**

Name: Shamari

Home: North Carolina

Favorite Activities: camping and canoeing with the family, drawing pictures, and visiting art museums

Favorite Food: barbecued anything

Favorite Subjects in School: social studies and art

Favorite Sport: volleyball

Favorite Author: Virginia Hamilton

What's a Persuasive Essay?

A persuasive essay states my opinion and tries to persuade readers to agree.

What's in a Persuasive Essay?

Opinion
That's what I think about my topic. I can't prove that my opinion is right, but I can explain it and support it. I can persuade others to agree with me. For instance, I think my class should take a trip to the university art museum. It's full of beautiful paintings and sculptures!

Argument
That's the support I give for my opinion. I want to persuade my audience to agree with me, so my argument will have reasons and facts.

Introduction
The first paragraph of my essay will be my introduction. I'll get my reader interested in my topic and state my opinion.

Conclusion
That's my last paragraph. In my conclusion, I'll restate my opinion and sum up my argument.

Why write a Persuasive Essay?

There are many reasons to write a persuasive essay. Here are several.

Persuasion

I might write a persuasive essay to members of the parent-teacher organization to persuade them to sponsor a class trip.

A librarian might post a persuasive essay for people who visit the library. He may want to persuade them to come listen to an author read from her book.

An applicant to a special program sometimes writes a persuasive essay to persuade the program to accept him or her.

Persuasive Essay
Writing Traits

What makes a good persuasive essay? A persuasive essay should have a convincing argument. Here are traits of a persuasive essay.

Information/ Organization	The essay has an opinion and reasons. It is organized from the strongest reason to the weakest.
Voice/ Audience	The writer uses a sincere voice throughout the four-paragraph essay.
Content/ Ideas	Details make the argument strong.
Word Choice/ Clarity	There are no loaded words.
Sentence Fluency	A variety of sentence patterns makes the essay flow.
Grammar/ Mechanics	Spelling, punctuation, and capitalization are correct. Adverbs are used correctly.

Let's read Bob West's persuasive essay, "Help Keep Our Town Clean!" on the next page. Did he follow all of the writing traits?

by Bob West

introduction

The annual spring cleanup will take place next Saturday. We will pick up litter in our town's parks and public places. We also need to pick up the trash along the highway. Everyone in town should plan to help out.

opinion

The main reason for needing so many people is that the town has a huge amount of litter. Paper, bags, and bottles need to be picked up along the roads. The public boat landing needs to be cleaned up. The litter around Swan Pond is destroying the beauty of the woods and water. The small parks department cannot do all of this work. To do a good job, many people are needed. Teams of four people will be assigned to small sections of highways, parks, and other sites. The cleanup committee is hoping to have a hundred cleanup teams. If we all help, the town won't have to raise extra money for cleanup.

argument

Another reason why everyone should join in is to build community spirit. Teams of people who work together will get to know each other. They will feel needed in their town. Some people will become more aware of the litter problem. Once they know about it, they will discourage littering. They may want to talk about the problem with others. Our town will become a clean place. People who have worked hard to clean up won't want to see litter in their beautiful town again.

We should all gladly help out next Saturday. We have a huge litter problem, and it is up to us to solve it. The people who do the work will also benefit by building community spirit. As Mayor Willis has said, "When we take care of our town, we take care of ourselves."

conclusion

Persuasive Essay Rubric

The rubric below was made using the traits of a persuasive essay on page 284. To score a persuasive essay, assign one to four stars for each trait. Four stars mean that trait is excellent! Three stars mean it is very good. Two stars or one star means that trait needs more work.

	Excelling ★★★★	Achieving ★★★	Developing ★★	Beginning ★
Information/ Organization	The essay has an opinion and reasons. It is organized from the strongest reason to the weakest.	The essay has an opinion and reasons. It is organized from the strongest reason to the weakest most of the time.	The essay has an opinion but few reasons. Some of it is organized from the strongest reason to the weakest.	The essay needs an opinion and reasons. It needs to be organized from the strongest reason to the weakest.
Voice/ Audience	The writer uses a sincere voice throughout the four-paragraph essay.	The writer uses a sincere voice in most of the four-paragraph essay.	The writer does not use a sincere voice. Or, one paragraph is missing.	The writer does not use a sincere voice, and one or more paragraphs are missing.
Content/ Ideas	Excellent details make the argument very strong.	Details make the argument strong.	A few details make the argument strong.	More details are needed to make the argument strong.
Word Choice/ Clarity	There are no loaded words.	There are few loaded words.	There are some loaded words.	There are many loaded words.
Sentence Fluency	A great variety of sentence patterns makes the essay flow.	A variety of sentence patterns makes the essay flow most of the time.	Some variety of sentence patterns makes the essay flow sometimes.	A variety of sentence patterns is needed to make the essay flow.
Grammar/ Mechanics	Spelling, punctuation, and capitalization are correct. Adverbs are used correctly.	There are few errors in spelling, punctuation, capitalization, or use of adverbs.	There are some errors in spelling, punctuation, capitalization, and use of adverbs.	There are many errors in spelling, punctuation, capitalization, and use of adverbs.

Persuasive Essay
Using the Rubric to Study the Model

Now, let's use the rubric to check Bob West's persuasive essay, "Help Keep Our Town Clean!" What score would you give Bob for each category in the rubric?

- **The essay has an opinion and reasons.**
- **It is organized from the strongest reason to the weakest.**

Bob does a good job of clearly stating his opinion in the essay's introduction: everyone in town should help out with the spring cleanup. Then, in the next two paragraphs—the argument—he presents two important reasons for his opinion.

The main reason for needing so many people is that the town has a huge amount of litter.

Another reason why everyone should join in is to build community spirit.

- **The writer uses a sincere voice throughout the four-paragraph essay.**

Look at the conclusion. Notice that the voice Bob uses in this final paragraph matches the sincerity of the beginning paragraph.

We should all gladly help out next Saturday. We have a huge litter problem, and it is up to us to solve it. The people who do the work will also benefit by building community spirit. As Mayor Willis has said, "When we take care of our town, we take care of ourselves."

Content/Ideas

- Details make the argument strong.

Bob presents a strong argument for people to get involved in the annual cleanup. He explains how much help is needed to do the job. He makes it clear how the people and the town will benefit. In this example, Bob provides details that make it clear why so many people are needed for the spring cleanup.

The main reason for needing so many people is that the town has a huge amount of litter. Paper, bags, and bottles need to be picked up along the roads. The public boat landing needs to be cleaned up. The litter around Swan Pond is destroying the beauty of the woods and water. The small parks department cannot do all of this work. To do a good job, many people are needed.

Word Choice/Clarity

- There are no loaded words.

Litterbug, slob, and **trashed** are all examples of loaded words, or words with extra meanings. Bob doesn't use loaded words. He doesn't blame people. In this section of the essay, he doesn't call anyone a **litterbug** or a **slob**. He doesn't say that people have **trashed** the town. Instead, he just explains how the cleanup can help people.

Some people will become more aware of the litter problem. Once they know about it, they will discourage littering. They may want to talk about the problem with others.

Using the Rubric to Study the Model

Persuasive Essay

Sentence Fluency

• A variety of sentence patterns makes the essay flow.

Bob uses a variety of long and short, simple and complex sentences throughout his essay. This made his essay flow and helped me to easily follow his thinking.

> The small parks department cannot do all of this work. To do a good job, many people are needed. Teams of four people will be assigned to small sections of highways, parks, and other sites. The cleanup committee is hoping to have a hundred cleanup teams. If we all help, the town won't have to raise extra money for cleanup.

Grammar/Mechanics

• Spelling, punctuation, and capitalization are correct. Adverbs are used correctly.

I looked through the essay again, and every word is spelled correctly. The sentences begin with a capital letter and end with correct punctuation. Bob also uses adverbs correctly. In these sentences, the adverbs **hard** and **gladly** describe verbs.

> People who have <u>worked hard</u> to clean up won't want to see litter in their beautiful town again.

> We should all <u>gladly help</u> out next Saturday.

My Turn!

Now it's my turn to write a persuasive essay. Follow along to see how I use the rubric and good writing strategies to help me.

Prewriting Gather Information

Information/Organization The essay has an opinion and reasons.

Writing Strategy Decide on an opinion. List reasons for my opinion.

My teacher gave us a list of possible topics for a persuasive essay. The topic I'm most interested in is whether our school should stay open until 6:00 P.M. I've always wanted the school to stay open later.

I listed all the reasons I could think of for keeping the school open later. That was my strategy for getting started.

> **Writer's Term**
>
> **Opinion**
> An **opinion** is a belief that is based on reasons. Unlike a fact, an opinion cannot be proven to be true.

My Opinion: The school building should stay open until 6:00 P.M.

Reasons to Support My Opinion

1. There could be more after-school activities and clubs.
2. Students can wait inside for a ride home.
3. Activities can last longer, and students can get back into the building after outdoor activities.
4. The band and other groups could meet later.

Practice!

Choose a topic that you find interesting for a persuasive essay. Decide what your opinion is, and then brainstorm a list of reasons that support your opinion.

Prewriting Organize Ideas

Information/Organization
The essay is organized from the strongest reason to the weakest.

Writing Strategy
Use an Order-of-Importance Organizer to list my reasons from strongest to weakest.

The rubric reminds me to use strong reasons to support my opinion. An Order-of-Importance Organizer will help me put my reasons in order from most important to least important.

Writer's Term

Order-of-Importance Organizer
An **Order-of-Importance Organizer** shows reasons in order of their importance. The most important reason goes first, and the least important reason goes last.

Order-of-Importance Organizer

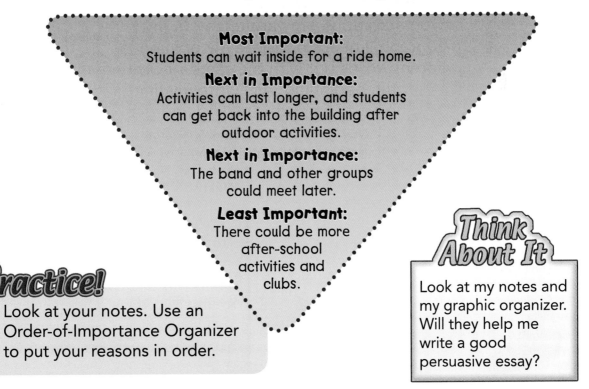

Most Important:
Students can wait inside for a ride home.

Next in Importance:
Activities can last longer, and students can get back into the building after outdoor activities.

Next in Importance:
The band and other groups could meet later.

Least Important:
There could be more after-school activities and clubs.

Practice!
Look at your notes. Use an Order-of-Importance Organizer to put your reasons in order.

Think About It
Look at my notes and my graphic organizer. Will they help me write a good persuasive essay?

Drafting Write a Draft

Voice/Audience The writer uses a sincere voice throughout the four-paragraph essay.

Writing Strategy Use a sincere voice to state my opinion in the first paragraph, explain my reasons in the next two paragraphs, and restate my opinion in the last paragraph.

Now I can start writing. I know from the rubric that I should use a sincere voice throughout my essay. The reader needs to know what I honestly think about this topic and why I think that way. That means I should state my opinion clearly and openly in the first paragraph. Then I should support my belief with my two most important reasons in the next two paragraphs—my argument. In my final paragraph, I need to restate my opinion in different words but with the same sincerity that I had at the beginning. As I write my first draft, I'll do the best I can with spelling and grammar, but I won't worry about mistakes right now. I'll have a chance to fix them later. My draft starts on page 294.

Writer's Term

Argument

An **argument** is a set of reasons to support an opinion. The argument shows why the writer is for or against something. The argument should persuade the reader to agree with the writer's opinion.

My Opinion (first paragraph):

The school building should stay open until 6:00 P.M.

My Argument

Reason 1 (next paragraph):

Students can wait inside for a ride home.

Reason 2 (next paragraph):

Activities can last longer, and students can get back into the building after outdoor activities.

My Restatement (final paragraph):

Adams School should keep its doors open until 6:00 P.M.

[DRAFT]

Keep the Doors Open

Adams School is a busy place. The first teachers arrive very early in the morning. There is activity all day long. The problem is that the day ends too erly. The doors are locked at 4:30 P.M. Everybody must leave before the doors are locked. Because many people need to use the building after that, the school should stay open until 6:00 P.M.

sincere voice

opinion stated in first paragraph

The most important reason is that sometimes students have to wait for a ride home. Often students have school clubs and activities. They might have sports or band practice. It's stupid to think that all parents get out of work before 5:00 P.M. Miserable, over-tired kids who need to wait for a ride should not have to stand outside the building, especially when it is cold, rainy, or dark. If students could wait inside, they could use their time good. They could have do homework or read quietly in the school liberry. They could also just sit comfortable and talk softly with their friends in a warm place.

strongest reason in first argument paragraph

[DRAFT]

next strongest reason in second argument paragraph

The second reason why the doors should be open is for students who have activities there. After school ends, many activities take place in and around the school building. Some go on after 4:30 P.M. For example, many sports teams practice on the school fields. Some practices end after 5:00 P.M. Sometimes, students need to go back into the school after practice. Right now, they can't do that. Also, some activities that take place inside the school are cut short because the building closes so early.

restates opinion in last paragraph

Adams School should keep its doors open until 6:00 P.M. Many students are still using the school building or grounds at 4:30 P.M. keeping the school open an hour and a half later would make life easier for them and sometimes for the adults in their lifes, too.

Practice!

Use your Order-of-Importance Organizer to write a draft of your persuasive essay. Remember to use a sincere voice throughout your writing.

Think About It

Read my draft. Did I use a sincere voice and give reasons for my opinion?

Revising Extend Writing

Content/Ideas Details make the argument strong.

Writing Strategy Add details to make my argument strong.

Kristen read my draft. She didn't agree with me on some points. She couldn't think of any reasons for students to need to go back into the school after sports practice.

The rubric reminds me that details will make an argument strong. I know just what details I need to add to strengthen my argument.

[DRAFT]

the school fields. Some practices end after 5:00 P.M.

Sometimes, students need to go back into the school after

practice. Right now, they can't do that.

to get their books, make a phone call, get
a drink of water, or use the bathroom

 added details

 **Practice!**

Read your draft. Look for places to add details to make your argument strong. Add these details to your draft.

Revising   Clarify Writing

Word Choice/ Clarity

There are no loaded words.

Writing Strategy   Replace loaded words with neutral words.

When I reread the rubric, I realized I had to check my persuasive essay for loaded words. I want to persuade my readers with my argument. I don't want to trick them by using words with added meanings. I'll replace loaded words with words that are more neutral.

Writer's Term

Loaded Words

Loaded words carry extra meaning. For example, a shack and a house are both places in which to live, but the word **shack** makes the place seem shabby. It creates a different feeling in the reader than the word **house** does.

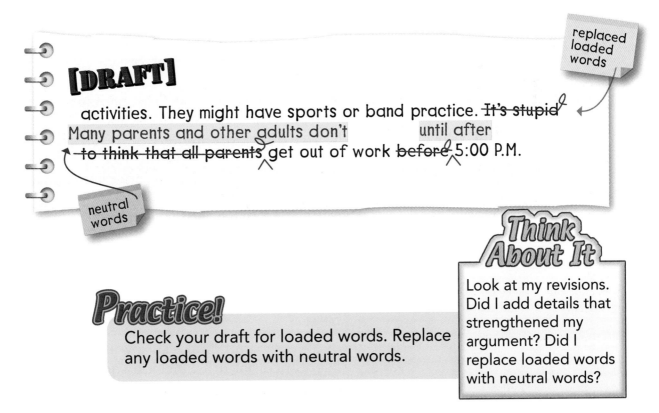

replaced loaded words

[DRAFT]

activities. They might have sports or band practice. ~~It's stupid~~
Many parents and other adults don't   until after
~~to think that all parents~~ get out of work ~~before~~ 5:00 P.M.

neutral words

Practice!

Check your draft for loaded words. Replace any loaded words with neutral words.

Think About It

Look at my revisions. Did I add details that strengthened my argument? Did I replace loaded words with neutral words?

Editing · Check Sentences

Sentence Fluency

A variety of sentence patterns makes the essay flow.

Writing Strategy Use a variety of sentence patterns.

The rubric reminds me that using a variety of sentence patterns will make my writing flow. I checked my essay and noticed that my opinion paragraph has quite a few sentences with the same pattern. This created a lot of stops and starts that break the flow and make the writing dull. Here's how I added some variety.

[DRAFT]

Adams School is a busy place. The first teachers arrive very

early in the morning. ~~,and~~ There is activity all day long. The problem

is that the day ends too erly. ~~The doors are locked at 4:30 P.M.~~

at 4:30 P.M.

Everybody must leave before the doors are locked. Because

many people need to use the building after that, the school

should stay open until 6:00 P.M.

created a variety of sentence patterns

Practice!

Read through your draft. Make sure you have a variety of sentence patterns. Include short and long, as well as simple and complex sentences.

Grammar/ Mechanics

Spelling, punctuation, and capitalization are correct.
Adverbs are used correctly.

Writing Strategy Check that adverbs are used correctly.

I know from the rubric that I need to check my essay for errors. First, I'll check spelling, punctuation, and capitalization. Next I'll check to see that I used each adverb correctly.

Writer's Term

Adverbs

Adverbs are words that describe verbs. Many adverbs end in **-ly**. However, some common adverbs, including **fast, later, well,** and **once,** do not.

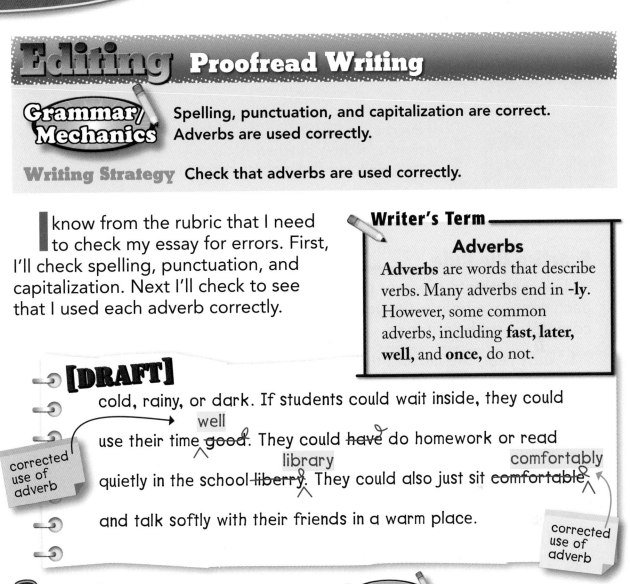

[DRAFT]

cold, rainy, or dark. If students could wait inside, they could

use their time ~~good~~. They could ~~have~~ do homework or read

(well)

corrected use of adverb

quietly in the school ~~liberry~~. They could also just sit ~~comfortable~~

(library)

(comfortably)

and talk softly with their friends in a warm place.

corrected use of adverb

Practice!

Edit your draft for spelling, punctuation, and capitalization. Check that you have used all adverbs correctly.

Grammar/ Mechanics

For more practice using adverbs correctly, use the exercises on the next two pages.

Think About It

Look at my editing. Have I used a variety of sentence patterns? Did I proofread my writing and use adverbs correctly?

Adverbs

 **Adverbs** are describing words. An adverb describes a verb. Adverbs tell how or when. Many adverbs end in **-ly**. The words **well** and **fast** are also adverbs.

Practice the Rule

Use a separate piece of paper. Number your paper 1–12. Read each sentence below. On your paper, write the word that correctly completes each sentence.

1. Last year, the closing time for the school was (usual/usually) three o'clock.
2. This year, those hours were (quiet/quietly) changed.
3. The officials looked (careful/carefully) at many things.
4. They wanted to use the school building (intelligent/intelligently).
5. (Late/Lately) one afternoon, a meeting was held.
6. Most people behaved (good/well) at the meeting.
7. They listened (polite/politely) to each speaker.
8. The officials (surprising/surprisingly) discovered some interesting facts.
9. Workers (regular/regularly) clean the building each night.
10. Many teachers would (happy/happily) stay after school to oversee activities.
11. The town officials (final/finally) decided to let local groups use the building after school hours.
12. Our teacher (excited/excitedly) told us the news the next day.

Apply the Rule

Read the following paragraphs. Correct any errors in the use of adverbs. Write the paragraphs correctly on a separate sheet of paper.

Many students do not eat good at school. The lunchroom offers good food. However, students do not always choose sensible. They general forget what they learned about a healthful diet. Some well-placed reminders could help students to choose their food more wise.

A chart of the food pyramid would quick show the most nutritious foods to eat. Also, students easy could see what foods to eat in smaller amounts. It would be a quiet reminder of the importance of proper nutrition. The cafeteria wall would be a good place for this chart.

Another helpful reminder would be a poster with tips for eating healthful. The title could be "You are What You Eat: Ten Tips for Eating Good." It would include information on smart making food choices.

Publishing Share Writing

Give my essay as a speech on "Sound Off Day."

My persuasive essay is done! Now it's time to publish. My classmates and I realized that everyone in our class wrote a persuasive essay on a different topic. We thought it would be good if everyone could hear all the opinions. That's why we decided to have a "Sound Off Day" where all the students could give their essays as speeches. Before I read my essay to the class, I'll read through it once more. I'll use this final checklist.

My Checklist

✔ The title of my essay and my name are at the top of the first page.

✔ My essay has an opinion and reasons.

✔ I've used a sincere voice.

✔ Details make my argument strong.

✔ There are no loaded words.

✔ Spelling, grammar, and punctuation are all correct. Adverbs are used correctly.

Practice!

Make a checklist to check your persuasive essay. Then make a final draft. Practice reading your essay aloud before presenting it to your classmates.

SOUND OFF DAY

Keep the Doors Open
by Shamari

Adams School is a busy place. The first teachers arrive very early in the morning, and there is activity all day long. The problem is that the day ends too early. Everybody must leave before the doors are locked at 4:30 P.M. Because many people need to use the building after that, the school should stay open until 6:00 P.M.

The most important reason is that sometimes students have to wait for a ride home. Often students have school clubs and activities. They might have sports or band practice. Many parents and other adults don't get out of work until after 5:00 P.M. Students who need to wait for a ride should not have to stand outside the building, especially when it is cold, rainy, or dark. If students could wait inside, they could use their time well. They could do homework or read quietly in the school library. They could also just sit comfortably and talk softly with their friends in a warm place.

The second reason why the doors should be open is for students who have activities there. After school ends, many activities take place in and around the school building. Some go on after 4:30 P.M. For example, many sports teams practice on the school fields. Some practices end after 5:00 P.M. Sometimes, students need to go back into the school after practice to get their books, make a phone call, get a drink of water, or use the bathroom. Right now, they can't do that. Also, some activities that take place inside the school are cut short because the building closes so early. This happened just last week. Mr. Azar's class was practicing for the holiday play. The cast needed more practice time, but everyone had to leave by 4:30 P.M.

Adams School should keep its doors open until 6:00 P.M. Many students are still using the school building or grounds at 4:30 P.M. Keeping the school open an hour and a half later would make life easier for them and sometimes for the adults in their lives, too.

Use the rubric to check my essay. Are all the traits of a good persuasive essay there? How does your persuasive essay compare against the rubric?

Ways to Publish a Persuasive Essay

Persuasive essays are a great way to share your opinions on a topic. There are lots of ways to publish a persuasive essay. Keep these ideas in mind as you think about where to publish your essay.

✓ Post your persuasive essay on the class or school Web site. Include photographs or graphics that support your opinion.

✓ **Submit your persuasive essay to your school newspaper.**

✓ Use your essay as the basis for a debate. Ask a fellow student to take the opposing viewpoint and plan his or her argument.

✓ **Send a copy of your essay to the individual or organization you would like to persuade. Request a response to your ideas.**

✓ Use your essay as the basis for a videotaped commercial promoting your ideas.

Writing Across the Content Areas
Persuasive Essay

Good topics for a persuasive essay are all around you. Lots of school subjects can give you the opportunity to write a persuasive essay. Here are some ideas.

Social Studies

- Write an essay to persuade your classmates that studying history is important.
- Persuade a historic figure to take some action. For example, encourage George Washington to become our new nation's first president.

Language Arts

- Read about an American folk hero. Then write an essay to persuade town leaders to put up a statue to honor him or her.
- Write an essay to persuade your teacher to help the class put on a play.

Art and/or Music

- Persuade your teacher or principal to arrange a class trip to a local art museum.
- Write an essay to persuade your parents to enroll you in an art, music, or dance class.

What's an Editorial?

It's an article I write for a newspaper or magazine that expresses my opinion about a topic. My topic should interest readers of that publication.

What's in an Editorial?

Introduction
That's my first paragraph. I'll get the reader interested in my topic. Then, I'll state my opinion. One thing I feel strongly about is that my school needs a student newspaper! My friends and I want to take photographs and write articles about life at school.

Body
The body is where I convince the reader that my opinion is correct. I'll give reasons for my opinion and offer examples that support it. I'll also give facts and information that support my reasons.

Conclusion
That's my last paragraph. I'll restate my opinion and summarize my reasons and facts.

Why write an Editorial?

There are many reasons to write an editorial. Here are some reasons I thought of.

Persuasion

Citizens write editorials about articles in newspapers. They may agree or disagree with the article, or they may state an opinion about a current event.

Entertainment

Some people write editorials to share an idea or view that they think is interesting. Sometimes editorials are written to be funny or sarcastic.

Information

Some editorials are written to give information about a topic. The writer may express an opinion, but the main purpose is to call attention to the issue.

Editorial
Writing Traits

What makes a good editorial? An editorial should challenge the reader to think about the issue and to consider the writer's opinion. Here are traits of an editorial.

Information/ Organization	The editorial states an opinion on one issue. It is well organized around a main idea.
Voice/ Audience	The writer connects with the audience by using a persuasive tone.
Content/ Ideas	Examples help to clarify and support the opinion.
Word Choice/ Clarity	All word choices support the writer's opinion.
Sentence Fluency	Sentences flow naturally.
Grammar/ Mechanics	Spelling, punctuation, and capitalization are correct. Past tense verbs are used correctly.

Let's read Joaquin Dasilva's editorial on the next page. Did he follow all of the writing traits?

Help Students to Be Healthy

by Joaquin Dasilva

Just eat right. This sounds simple, but it's not always as easy as it sounds, especially when we're in school. As students, what can we do to help ourselves develop healthy eating habits? First, we need to remove vending machines that sell junk food and change soda machine choices to water and low-sugar juices. Then we need to work with teachers, staff, and parents to develop a healthy eating program at school.

Why are good eating habits so important? What we eat affects our health now and will continue to affect us in the future. When we eat snack foods and sugary sodas too often, we eat too much fat, sugar, and salt. This type of diet causes many students to gain weight. Children who have poor eating habits tend to have less energy and to get tired quickly. They don't exercise enough and may have trouble paying attention in class.

Vending machines encourage students to eat junk. Most of the foods sold in vending machines are candy, chips, baked goods, and sodas. These are bad for our health. At lunchtime, we should be eating fresh foods such as fruits, juices, and vegetables that are served in the cafeteria. Vending machines make unhealthy snack foods and high-sugar sodas easily available to us. Many kids are in a hurry to eat because they are hungry or they have a short lunch period. Often students would rather buy junk food than wait in a long cafeteria line for healthier choices. We need to get rid of these snack vending machines and fill soda machines with low-sugar juices and water. It also would help to organize lunch lines in the cafeteria so they are shorter and move more quickly.

Students, teachers, staff, and parents should work together to plan a healthy eating program. The program would eliminate unhealthy foods and give us more healthy choices. We need more fresh fruits, vegetables, and salads. We should have sandwiches on whole grain breads with lean meats like turkey, chicken, ham, and tuna fish. We should also have low-fat dairy products like yogurt and low-fat cheeses. Fried foods such as French fries, fried chicken, and fish sticks should be replaced with baked potatoes, chicken, or fish.

Eating right in school may not always be simple, but it's a challenge we can meet!

Editorial Rubric

The rubric below was made using the traits of a good editorial on page 310. To check an editorial, assign one to four stars for each trait. Four stars mean that trait is excellent! Three stars mean it is very good. One or two stars mean that trait needs more work.

	Excelling	Achieving	Developing	Beginning
Information/Organization	The editorial states an opinion on one issue. It is well organized around a main idea.	The editorial states an opinion on one issue. It is organized around a main idea most of the time.	The editorial states an opinion on more than one issue. It is organized around a main idea some of the time.	The editorial needs to state an opinion on an issue. It needs to be organized around a main idea.
Voice/Audience	The writer connects with the audience by using a persuasive tone.	The writer connects with the audience by using a persuasive tone most of the time.	The writer connects with the audience by using a persuasive tone some of the time.	The writer needs to connect with the audience by using a persuasive tone.
Content/Ideas	Many excellent examples help to clarify and support the opinion.	Some good examples help to clarify and support the opinion.	One or two examples help to clarify and support the opinion.	Examples to help clarify and support the opinion are needed.
Word Choice/Clarity	All word choices support the writer's opinion.	Most word choices support the writer's opinion.	Some word choices support the writer's opinion.	Few word choices support the writer's opinion.
Sentence Fluency	Sentences flow naturally from beginning to end.	Sentences flow naturally most of the time.	Sentences flow naturally some of the time.	Few sentences flow naturally.
Grammar/Mechanics	Spelling, punctuation, and capitalization are correct. Past tense verbs are used correctly.	There are few errors in spelling, punctuation, or capitalization. Past tense verbs are used correctly.	There are some errors in spelling, punctuation, capitalization, and past tense verbs.	There are many errors in spelling, punctuation, capitalization, and past tense verbs.

Using the Editorial Rubric to Study the Model

Now, let's use the rubric to check Joaquin Dasilva's editorial, "Help Students to Be Healthy." What score would you give Joaquin for each category in the rubric?

Information/Organization

- **The editorial states an opinion on one issue.**
- **It is well organized around a main idea.**

Joaquin clearly states his opinion in the editorial's introduction. The body of his editorial is well organized around a main idea. Look at how Joaquin's introduction prepares the reader for the rest of the editorial.

As students, what can we do to help ourselves develop healthy eating habits? First, we need to remove vending machines that sell junk food and change soda machine choices to water and low-sugar juices. Then we need to work with teachers, staff, and parents to develop a healthy eating program at school.

Voice/Audience

- **The writer connects with the audience by using a persuasive tone.**

Joaquin uses words like "we" and "our health" to connect with his audience—other students. His choice of words creates a persuasive tone. Here's a good example.

Vending machines encourage students to eat junk. Most of the foods sold in vending machines are candy, chips, baked goods, and sodas. These are bad for our health. At lunchtime, we should be eating fresh foods such as fruits, juices, and vegetables that are served in the cafeteria. Vending machines make unhealthy snack foods and high-sugar sodas easily available to us.

Content/Ideas

- Examples help to clarify and support the opinion.

Joaquin doesn't just state his opinion. He provides lots of examples that support and clarify it. Look at his paragraph about planning a healthy eating program. Joaquin provides a lot of good examples for his readers to think about.

Students, teachers, staff, and parents should work together to plan a healthy eating program. The program would eliminate unhealthy foods and give us more healthy choices. We need more fresh fruits, vegetables, and salads. We should have sandwiches on whole grain breads with lean meats like turkey, chicken, ham, and tuna fish.

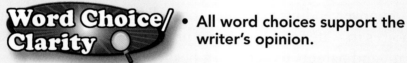

Word Choice/Clarity

- All word choices support the writer's opinion.

Joaquin phrases everything in a way that supports his opinion. In the second paragraph, he explains why eating right is an issue that students should be concerned about. His choice of words supports his opinion that steps should be taken to help students eat better when they are in school. Look at the words I underlined.

What we eat <u>affects our health</u> now and will continue to affect us in the future. When we eat snack foods and <u>sugary sodas</u> too often, we eat too much fat, sugar, and salt. This type of diet causes many students to gain weight. Children who have <u>poor eating habits</u> tend to have less energy and to get tired quickly. They don't exercise enough and may have <u>trouble paying attention in class</u>.

Using the Editorial Rubric to Study the Model

Sentence Fluency

• Sentences flow naturally.

Each sentence should lead smoothly and naturally into the next one. Joaquin does a good job of creating flow. Each sentence leads easily to the next. For example, after he explains why vending machines are a problem in school, he follows with a solution to the problem.

Many kids are in a hurry to eat because they are hungry or they have a short lunch period. Often students would rather buy junk food than wait in a long cafeteria line for healthier choices. We need to get rid of these snack vending machines and fill soda machines with low-sugar juices and water. It also would help to organize lunch lines in the cafeteria so they are shorter and move more quickly.

Grammar/ Mechanics

• Spelling, punctuation, and capitalization are correct. Past tense verbs are used correctly.

Every word is spelled correctly, and the sentences begin with a capital letter and end with correct punctuation. When Joaquin uses a past tense verb, he uses it correctly.

Most of the foods sold in vending machines are candy, chips, baked goods, and sodas.

My Turn!

Now it's my turn to write an editorial. Follow along to see how I use the rubric and good writing strategies to help me.

Prewriting Gather Information

Information/Organization The editorial states an opinion on one issue.

Writing Strategy Write my opinion on an issue. List reasons for my opinion.

My teacher asked us to imagine that we have been hired to write an editorial for a travel magazine. Our job will be to persuade people to visit a special place for vacation. In my opinion, North Carolina is the best place for a vacation!

I'll write down my opinion and a list of the best reasons I know for visiting North Carolina.

Writer's Term

Reason

A **reason** is the explanation behind an act, idea, or opinion.

My Opinion: North Carolina is the perfect place for a vacation.

Reasons That Support My Opinion

the Great Smoky Mountains

the Piedmont Region; historic Stagville

the people are great, too

Things to do: camping, hiking, horseback riding, white-water rafting, swimming, fishing, sailing, shopping, golf, go to a theme park

Practice!

Choose a topic for an editorial. Write down your opinion about the topic. Then, jot down a list of reasons that support your opinion.

Information/Organization The editorial is well organized around a main idea.

Writing Strategy Use a Main-Idea Table to organize my opinion and reasons.

Now I need to organize my notes. The rubric reminds me that a well-written editorial is organized around a main idea. I'll use a Main-Idea Table to organize my notes.

Writer's Term

Main-Idea Table

A **Main-Idea Table** shows how a main idea is supported by details. It helps you organize information by showing how supporting details hold up the main idea.

Main-Idea Table

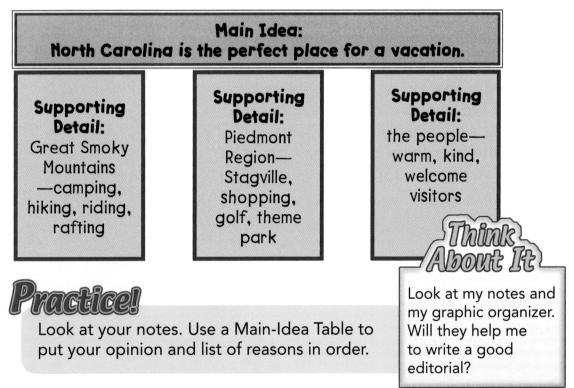

Main Idea:
North Carolina is the perfect place for a vacation.

Supporting Detail:	Supporting Detail:	Supporting Detail:
Great Smoky Mountains —camping, hiking, riding, rafting	Piedmont Region— Stagville, shopping, golf, theme park	the people— warm, kind, welcome visitors

Practice!

Look at your notes. Use a Main-Idea Table to put your opinion and list of reasons in order.

Think About It

Look at my notes and my graphic organizer. Will they help me to write a good editorial?

Drafting Write a Draft

Voice/Audience The writer connects with the audience by using a persuasive tone.

Writing Strategy Use a persuasive tone to state my opinion and reasons.

It's time to start writing! I'm going to use my Main-Idea Table to write a draft. The rubric reminds me that I should connect with my readers and persuade them to accept my opinion. The best way to do that is with the words I choose to express my opinion. If the tone of my editorial is sincere and believable, the reader will probably accept my point of view. I want people to feel as enthusiastic about North Carolina as I do!

As I write my draft, I'll do the best I can with spelling and grammar, but I won't worry about mistakes right now. I'll have a chance to fix them later. Read the beginning of my draft on the next page.

Writer's Term

Tone

Tone is the way writing sounds. It shows the writer's attitude toward the subject of his or her writing. A writer's tone can be serious, funny, objective, personal, etc.

[DRAFT]

opinion

North Carolina is a perfect place for a vacation! I should   the issue

know—I live in this magnifisent state! During school vacations

my family looks for adventure, and we don't have to travel far.

I'm going to share with you some of the exciting things we

have done.   persuasive tone

My very favorite place in North Carolina is the Great Smoky

Mountains in the western part of the state. my family goes

camping at Great Smoky Mountains National Park. Everyone

in the family can enjoy the outdoor activities.   reasons

Practice!

Use your Main-Idea Table to write a draft of your editorial. Remember your audience as you write, and use a persuasive tone.

Think About It

Read my draft. Did I use a persuasive tone to state my opinion and reasons?

Revising **Extend Writing**

Content/Ideas Examples help to clarify and support the opinion.

Writing Strategy Add examples to support my opinion.

The rubric reminds me that it's not enough just to state my opinion. I need to provide examples that support it and make my meaning clear. I'll add some examples to my second paragraph so the reader knows exactly what I'm talking about.

[DRAFT]

camping at Great Smoky Mountains National Park. Everyone

in the family ~~can~~ enjoys ~~outdoor activities.~~

hiking parts of the Appalachian Trail. There's horseback riding in the mountain forests and white-water rafting on the Nantahala River.

added examples

Practice!

Read your draft. Look for places where you can add examples to help clarify and support your opinion. Add these examples to your draft.

Word Choice/ Clarity

All word choices support the writer's opinion.

Writing Strategy Take out anything that doesn't support my opinion.

The rubric says that all the words in my editorial should support my opinion. I read through my draft again. In my last paragraph, I found some information that has nothing to do with the idea that North Carolina is the perfect vacation spot. I'll take that out now. I'll also fix an adverb that I used incorrectly.

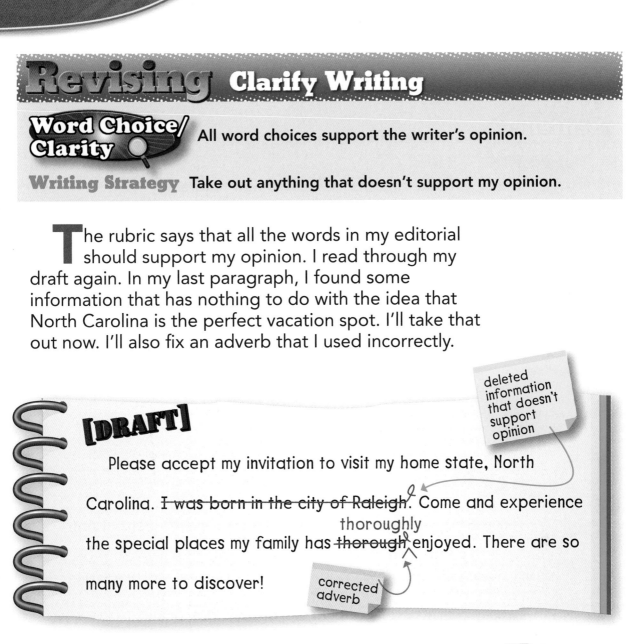

deleted information that doesn't support opinion

[DRAFT]

Please accept my invitation to visit my home state, North

Carolina. ~~I was born in the city of Raleigh.~~ Come and experience

the special places my family has ~~thorough~~ thoroughly enjoyed. There are so

many more to discover!

corrected adverb

Think About It

Read my revisions. Did I add examples to support my opinion? Do all my word choices support my opinion now?

Practice!

Read your draft again. Take out any information that doesn't support your opinion.

Editing Check Sentences

Sentence Fluency Sentences flow naturally.

Writing Strategy Make sure that sentences flow naturally.

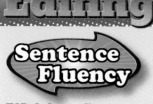

When I write, each sentence should lead smoothly and naturally to the next. The paragraph about the people of North Carolina seems difficult to read. The ideas are mixed up. I'll do some editing to fix it.

[DRAFT]

~~You get to meet wonderful people here. That's~~ last but not
, , you get to meet wonderful people like my family and me
least when you take a vacation in North Carolina. ~~For example~~

~~there's my family and me.~~ North Carolinians are proud to live in
We
such a beautiful state. ~~North Carolinians~~ are warm and kind,
always
and we ~~all times~~ welcome visitors.

rewrote so sentences flow naturally

Practice!

Read your draft. Make sure each sentence flows smoothly into the next.

Editing   Proofread Writing

Grammar/Mechanics
Spelling, punctuation, and capitalization are correct.
Past tense verbs are used correctly.

Writing Strategy   Make sure that past tense verbs are used correctly.

The rubric reminds me that I need to check my editorial for errors. I'll begin by checking my spelling, punctuation, and capitalization. Next, I'll look over my draft to make sure that I used past tense verbs correctly.

Writer's Term

Past Tense Verbs

Past tense verbs show that an action happened in the past. For example: While we stayed on the Outer Banks, we swam in the ocean. The verbs **stayed** and **swam** are past tense verbs.

[DRAFT]

than one hundred and fifty years ago. It ~~is~~ **was** very interesting to

see how people ~~have~~ **had** to make so many of the things they used.

It was also very sad to see how enslaved people ~~live~~ **lived**.

corrected verb tense

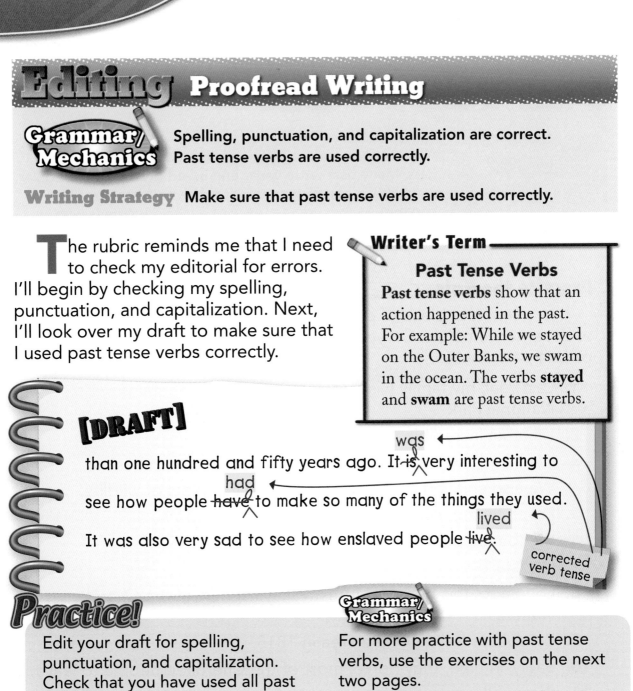

Practice!

Edit your draft for spelling, punctuation, and capitalization. Check that you have used all past tense verbs correctly.

Grammar/Mechanics

For more practice with past tense verbs, use the exercises on the next two pages.

Think About It

Look at my editing. Do all my sentences flow naturally? Did I proofread my writing and use past tense verbs correctly?

Past Tense Verbs

A **past tense verb** shows an action that happened in the past. Many past tense verbs end in **-ed (live/lived)**. Irregular verbs change spelling in their past tense form **(speak/ spoken)**. Make sure the tense of each verb agrees with the time in which the action takes place.

Practice the Rule

Use a separate piece of paper. Number your paper 1–12. Read each sentence below. On your paper, write the correct form of the verb in parentheses.

1. Last year, my family (visit) the Great Smoky Mountains National Park.
2. What an incredible vacation we (has)!
3. We hiked, (swim), had picnics, and visited historic sites.
4. We also enjoyed beautiful scenery and (see) lots of wildlife.
5. I even (learn) a little about the history of the park.
6. We (begin) our day with a visit to Cades Cove.
7. We (start) out early in the morning.
8. Long ago, this beautiful forest valley (is) part of the Cherokee Nation.
9. Europeans (settle) in the area in 1818.
10. Sadly, in time, they (force) most of the Cherokee people to leave.
11. Bison, elk, mountain lions, and wolves once (live) in the valley, too, but now are gone.
12. However, when we visited, we (see) whitetail deer, a young black bear, and some wild turkeys.

Apply the Rule

The following paragraphs are written using only present tense verbs. However, the events described happened in the past. Rewrite the paragraphs correctly in the past tense on a separate sheet of paper.

After lunch, we drive to Clingmans Dome, the highest peak in the park. We park the car and walk the last half mile to the top. Then we climb the 54-foot observation tower. The view is spectacular! We can see for miles and miles! Everyone is enjoying the view when suddenly clouds roll in. The next thing we know, it is raining! We all scramble down from the tower and hurry to the car.

By the time we drive back to our campsite, the rain is over. The air smells fresh, and everything glistens with water drops. The sun is going down and paints the clouds with color. It is the perfect end to our first day at the Great Smoky Mountains National Park.

Publishing Share Writing

Publish my editorial in the class newspaper.

My editorial is finished! It's time to think about ways of publishing it. There are lots of ways to publish an editorial: in newspapers, magazines, and online, to name a few. Since I'd like to give everyone in my class a chance to read my editorial, I'll publish it in the first issue of our class newspaper. Before publishing it, though, I need to read through it one last time. Here's the final checklist I'll use.

My Checklist

✔ The title of my editorial and my name are at the top of the page.

✔ My editorial states an opinion on one issue.

✔ I use a persuasive tone.

✔ Examples support my opinion.

✔ All my words support my opinion.

✔ Spelling, grammar, and punctuation are all correct. Past tense verbs are used correctly.

Practice!

Make a checklist. Check your editorial against it. Then make a final draft. Submit your editorial to the editor of your class newspaper for publication.

Welcome to North Carolina!

by Shamari

North Carolina is a perfect place for a vacation! I should know— I live in this magnificent state! During school vacations my family looks for adventure, and we don't have to travel far. I'm going to share with you some of the exciting things we have done. I hope you will be persuaded to discover North Carolina on your next vacation!

My favorite place in North Carolina is the Great Smoky Mountains in the western part of the state. My family goes camping at Great Smoky Mountains National Park. Everyone in the family enjoys hiking parts of the Appalachian Trail. There's horseback riding in the mountain forests and white-water rafting on the Nantahala River.

The Piedmont Region in central North Carolina is where most of our cities are located. There's a fun theme park, great shopping, and nice golf courses. There are fascinating historic sites like the plantation in Stagville. On our visit, we learned about life on a plantation more than one hundred and fifty years ago. It was very interesting to see how people had to make so many of the things they used. It was also very sad to see how enslaved people lived. I'm sure glad life is very different in North Carolina now!

Last but not least, when you take a vacation in North Carolina, you get to meet wonderful people like my family and me. North Carolinians are proud to live in such a beautiful state. We are warm and kind, and we always welcome visitors.

Please accept my invitation to visit my home state, North Carolina. Come and experience the special places my family has thoroughly enjoyed. There are many more to discover!

Use the rubric to check my editorial. Are all the traits of a good editorial there? How does your editorial compare against the rubric?

Ways to Publish an Editorial

An editorial is an excellent way to get people interested in a problem or issue. By sharing your opinion, you can provide others with information on a topic and get them to think about it, too. Let's take a look at a few ways to publish an editorial.

✓ **Read your editorial to your classmates. Encourage questions and comments in response.**

✓ **Submit your editorial to a magazine that publishes student editorials.**

✓ **Create a classroom display featuring your editorial.**

✓ **Post your editorial on the class or school Web site. Include photographs or graphics that support your opinion.**

✓ **Submit your editorial to an online publisher of student work about topics like yours.**

Writing Across the Content Areas
Editorial

Think of how many times each day you express an opinion about something. You can write an editorial about so many topics! School subjects can be a great source of editorial topics. Here are some examples.

Math

- Write about whether calculators should be used during math tests.
- Write an editorial on whether you think that computer math games are a good way to learn math.

Art and/or Music

- Share information about an art museum that you visited and enjoyed.
- Write about whether classes in music and art are an important part of a student's education.

Science

- Write an editorial to call attention to an environmental issue that concerns you.
- Write about whether schools should provide science labs for hands-on student experiments and projects.

What's a Friendly Letter?

I write a friendly letter to someone I know well—like a family member or a friend. I write a persuasive friendly letter when I want to persuade my reader to agree with me about something.

What's in a Friendly Letter?

Personal Tone
In a friendly letter, I want to use a personal tone. I wrote a letter to my cousin when I was on vacation with my family. I used a personal tone because she's my cousin and my best friend.

Organization
I want to be organized and convincing. I'll state my opinion in an introduction, support it with facts and reasons in the body, and restate it in a conclusion.

Five Parts
A friendly letter has certain words and pieces of information in a particular place on the page. The five parts of a friendly letter are the heading, greeting, body, closing, and signature.

Why write a Friendly Letter?

There are a lot of reasons to write a friendly letter. Here are some I thought of.

Persuasion
I may write a friendly letter to persuade a friend or family member to come visit me or to watch a movie I saw.

Resolution
If a friend and I disagree about something, a friendly letter can help resolve the issue.

Entertainment
Sometimes, it's fun to debate about something. I can carry on a debate long distance by writing my arguments out in a friendly letter.

Friendly Letter
Writing Traits

What makes a good persuasive friendly letter? A persuasive friendly letter should have a personal tone and a convincing message. Here are traits of a persuasive friendly letter.

Information/Organization	The letter states an opinion. It has an introduction, body, and conclusion.
Voice/Audience	The writer uses a personal tone to show respect for the reader.
Content/Ideas	Facts provide convincing support for reasons.
Word Choice/Clarity	Signal words connect ideas.
Sentence Fluency	A variety of sentence structures makes the writing flow.
Grammar/Mechanics	Spelling, punctuation, capitalization, and all five parts of a friendly letter are correct.

Let's read Samuel Taylor's persuasive friendly letter on the next page. Did he follow all of the writing traits?

100 West Street
Rivertown, MN 52045
October 3, 20—

heading

greeting

Dear Chase,

personal tone

I am very happy that you are coming to visit me next summer. It will be fun to spend a whole week together. My parents said that we can either go to our campsite or stay here. I think we'll have more fun if we go to my family's campsite than if we stay at my house the whole time.

introduction

First, there's a lot to do at the campsite. There is a lake, so we can go swimming any time we want to. We can also go fishing or hike up Overlook Hill. There are bike paths, so we can ride our bikes. At night, we can have bonfires and roast marshmallows. At home there's nothing to do except watch TV. We don't have a pool, and there aren't any hills to go hiking. Of course, there's no place to fish, either. So, we wouldn't have as much fun at home.

Camping would be good for us, too. We can get a bunch of exercise. At my house, we would just sit around. If we go camping, we would get to spend a lot of time outdoors, so we'd get lots of fresh air. As a result, we would both feel great! At home, we would probably stay indoors most of the time. Because of that, we wouldn't feel as good.

body of the letter

When you come to visit, I hope that you will want to go to my family's campsite. I know we'll have lots of fun there, and it will be good for us, too.

conclusion

closing

Your friend,

signature

Samuel

Friendly Letter Rubric

The rubric below was made using the traits of a persuasive friendly letter on page 332. To score a piece of writing, assign one to four stars for each trait. Four stars mean that trait is excellent! Three stars mean it is very good. One or two stars mean that trait needs some more work.

	Excelling	Achieving	Developing	Beginning
Information/ Organization	The letter states an opinion. It has an excellent introduction, body, and conclusion.	The letter states an opinion. It has an introduction, a body, and a conclusion.	The letter states an opinion. The introduction, body, or conclusion is missing.	The letter needs to state an opinion. It needs an introduction, body, and conclusion.
Voice/ Audience	The writer uses a personal tone to show respect for the reader throughout the letter.	The writer uses a personal tone to show respect for the reader most of the time.	The writer uses a personal tone to show respect for the reader some of the time.	The writer needs to use a personal tone to show respect for the reader.
Content/ Ideas	All facts provide convincing support for reasons.	Facts provide convincing support for reasons most of the time.	Facts provide convincing support for reasons some of the time.	Facts are needed to provide convincing support for reasons.
Word Choice/ Clarity	Many signal words connect ideas.	Some signal words connect ideas.	A few signal words connect ideas.	Signal words are needed to connect ideas.
Sentence Fluency	A great variety of sentence structures makes the writing flow.	A variety of sentence structures makes the writing flow most of the time.	A variety of sentence structures makes the writing flow some of the time.	The letter needs a variety of sentence structures to help it flow.
Grammar/ Mechanics	Spelling, punctuation, capitalization, and all five parts of a friendly letter are correct.	There are few errors in spelling, punctuation, capitalization, or the five parts of a friendly letter.	There are some errors in spelling, punctuation, capitalization, and the five parts of a friendly letter.	There are many errors in spelling, punctuation, capitalization, and the five parts of a friendly letter.

Using the Rubric to Study the Model

Friendly Letter

Now, let's use the rubric to check Samuel Taylor's persuasive friendly letter. What score would you give Samuel for each category in the rubric?

Information/ Organization

- **The letter states an opinion.**
- **It has an introduction, body, and conclusion.**

Samuel states his opinion clearly in the introduction—the first paragraph of his letter. In the two body paragraphs, Samuel presents reasons for his opinion and lots of supporting facts and details. The final paragraph of his letter is the conclusion. Look at how Samuel states his opinion in the introduction.

> I think we'll have more fun if we go to my family's campsite than if we stay at my house the whole time.

Voice/ Audience

- **The writer uses a personal tone to show respect for the reader.**

In writing, I know that tone reveals your attitude towards your topic and your reader. Samuel chose just the right words for his letter. I could tell that he was writing to a friend. His language was casual and friendly and set a personal tone that showed respect for his friend Chase.

> I am very happy that you are coming to visit me next summer. It will be fun to spend a whole week together. My parents said that we can either go to our campsite or stay here.

Content/Ideas

- Facts provide convincing support for reasons.

Samuel doesn't just tell Chase that staying at the campsite would be more fun than staying at home. He gives Chase a lot of good reasons why he thinks this is true. Here's an example.

First, there's a lot to do at the campsite. There is a lake, so we can go swimming any time we want to. We can also go fishing or hike up Overlook Hill. There are bike paths, so we can ride our bikes. At night, we can have bonfires and roast marshmallows.

Word Choice/Clarity

- Signal words connect ideas.

I've learned that signal words help tie ideas together. Samuel uses signal words like **so, as a result,** and **because of that** to show the connections between his ideas.

If we go camping, we would get to spend a lot of time outdoors, so we'd get lots of fresh air. As a result, we would both feel great! At home, we would probably stay indoors most of the time. Because of that, we wouldn't feel as good.

Using the Rubric to Study the Model
Friendly Letter

Sentence Fluency

- **A variety of sentence structures makes the writing flow.**

In his letter, Samuel uses a variety of long and short, simple and complex sentences. Each sentence begins differently, too. This made his writing flow and his letter interesting to read.

> At home there's nothing to do except watch TV. We don't have a pool, and there aren't any hills to go hiking. Of course, there's no place to fish, either. So, we wouldn't have as much fun at home.

Grammar/ Mechanics

- **Spelling, punctuation, capitalization, and all five parts of a friendly letter are correct.**

If you look again at the letter on page 333, you'll see that the parts of Samuel's letter have been labeled. He included all five parts of a friendly letter: the heading, the greeting, the body of the letter, the closing, and the signature. Also, he was careful to use capital letters and commas correctly in all the parts and to end each sentence with correct punctuation.

My Turn!

Now it's my turn to write a persuasive friendly letter. I'll use what I've learned from studying the model. Follow along as I use the rubric and good writing strategies to help me.

Prewriting Gather Information

Information/Organization The letter states an opinion.

Writing Strategy Decide what I want to write about, and research facts about the issue.

My teacher asked us to write a letter to persuade someone about something. I have the perfect topic. My parents said we could have a pet. My grandparents are going to get it for us, but they haven't decided on a puppy or a kitten. My dad helped me find information about cats and dogs on the Internet, and I took notes.

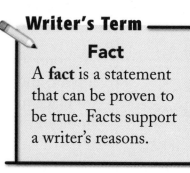

Writer's Term

Fact
A **fact** is a statement that can be proven to be true. Facts support a writer's reasons.

Dogs	Cats
loving	loving, but also independent
playful	playful, but mostly as kittens
can learn tricks	don't learn tricks easily
can help people	don't help people
can protect their owners	don't protect their owners

Practice!

Choose a topic for a persuasive friendly letter. Use print or Internet resources to research facts about the issue. Make a list of important things to remember about the topic.

Information/Organization The letter has an introduction, body, and conclusion.

Writing Strategy Use a Network Tree to organize facts and reasons.

I know from the rubric that my letter must have an introduction, body paragraphs, and a conclusion. I think a puppy would be better for us than a kitten. I'll use a Network Tree to organize my notes and plan my letter.

Writer's Term

Network Tree

A **Network Tree** organizes information. The writer's opinion goes at the top of the tree. Reasons for the opinion go on the next level. Facts and other details go on the lowest level.

Network Tree

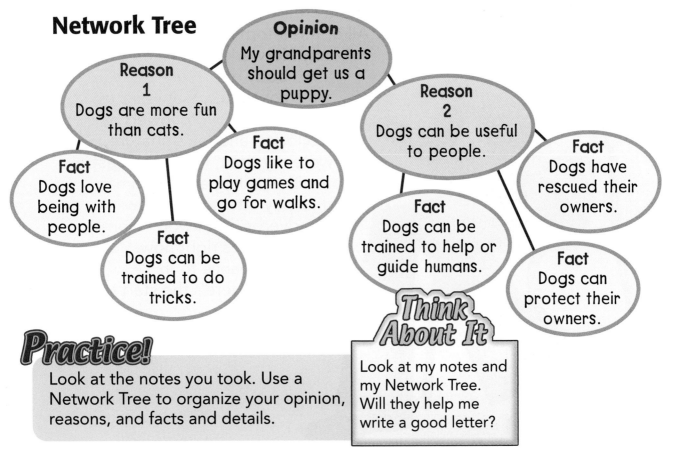

Opinion
My grandparents should get us a puppy.

Reason 1
Dogs are more fun than cats.

Fact
Dogs love being with people.

Fact
Dogs can be trained to do tricks.

Fact
Dogs like to play games and go for walks.

Reason 2
Dogs can be useful to people.

Fact
Dogs can be trained to help or guide humans.

Fact
Dogs have rescued their owners.

Fact
Dogs can protect their owners.

Practice!

Look at the notes you took. Use a Network Tree to organize your opinion, reasons, and facts and details.

Think About It

Look at my notes and my Network Tree. Will they help me write a good letter?

Drafting Write a Draft

Voice/Audience The writer uses a personal tone to show respect for the reader.

Writing Strategy Use a personal tone to show respect for my reader.

It's time to write my letter. I want to set the right tone. Since this will be a letter to my grandparents, I'll choose the right greeting and closing and keep my language casual and friendly.

I'll begin the body of my letter with an introduction that states my opinion. Then I'll support my opinion with two reasons. I'll support my reasons with facts and details. All of this information is organized in my Network Tree. I'll end the body of my letter with a conclusion that restates my opinion, followed by the closing and my signature. As I write my draft, I'll do the best I can with spelling and grammar, and I'll pay attention to how I use adverbs, but I won't worry about mistakes right now. I'll have a chance to fix them later. Here's the start of my letter.

[DRAFT]

Proofreading Marks

⌐ Indent   ℓ Take out something
≡ Make a capital   ⊙ Add a period
/ Make a small letter   ⌗ New paragraph
∧ Add something   ⓈⓅ Spelling error

1000 martin st
Raleigh, Nc 27601
march 16, 20—

Dear Grandma and Grandpa

personal tone

I am very grateful that you are going to get a pet for our family. Mom and dad said we could have either a puppy or a kitten. I think you should get us a puppy. Dogs are much more fun than cats. They are also more useful than cats.

opinion

Dogs have always make better pets than cats because dogs are more fun. Dogs go on walks with people and play games like fetch. They can lern tricks like lying down and rolling over. A dog will wag its tail, bark, and jump around. Dogs are very loving animals. A dog will put its head on your lap or nuzzle you to be petted. Cats are very different. Cats do not go for walks. They don't play games. They don't learn tricks very easily. They don't jump around. They don't join in the fun. Cats can be loving, but a cat has to be in the mood to be stroked or petted.

reason 1

correct use of adverb

Practice!

Use your Network Tree to write a draft of your persuasive friendly letter. Set the right tone by choosing your words thoughtfully.

Think About It

Read my draft. Did I use a personal tone that shows respect for my reader?

Revising Extend Writing

Content/Ideas Facts provide convincing support for reasons.

Writing Strategy Add facts to support my reasons.

When I write, I always look back at the rubric. It reminds me that I should have facts to support my opinion. When I read the third paragraph of my letter, I noticed that I didn't have enough facts to support my opinion. I'll add some facts to that paragraph.

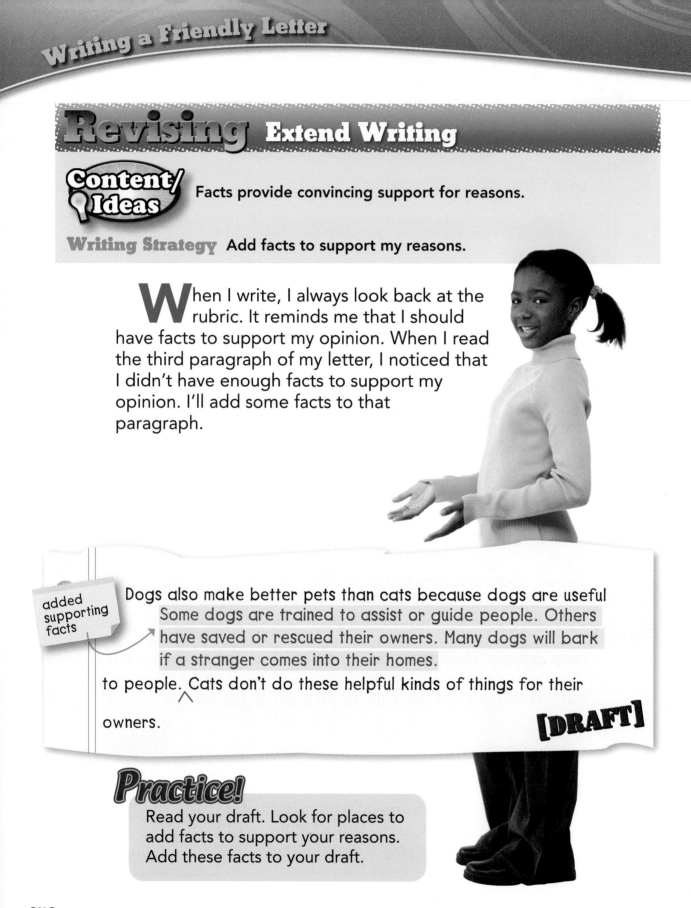

added supporting facts

Dogs also make better pets than cats because dogs are useful Some dogs are trained to assist or guide people. Others have saved or rescued their owners. Many dogs will bark if a stranger comes into their homes.
to people. Cats don't do these helpful kinds of things for their
owners.

[DRAFT]

Practice!

Read your draft. Look for places to add facts to support your reasons. Add these facts to your draft.

Revising Clarify Writing

The rubric reminds me to use signal words. I want my grandparents to see how my ideas are connected. I found some places where signal words can help! I'll also correct a past tense verb that I used incorrectly.

Writer's Term

Signal Words

Signal words help tie ideas and sentences together. Signal words help the reader follow as the writer moves from one idea to the next. Signal words are usually separated from the rest of the sentence with a comma. Here are some signal words:

also	however	so	as a result
in addition	therefore	because	first

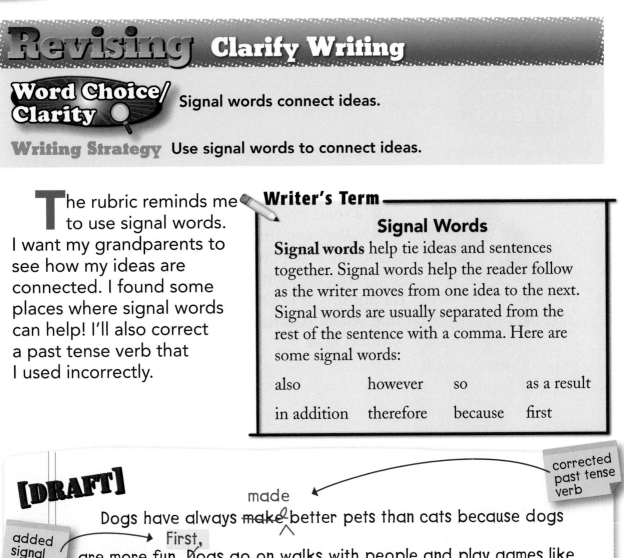

[DRAFT]

corrected past tense verb

made

Dogs have always ~~make~~ better pets than cats because dogs

added signal words

First,

are more fun. Dogs go on walks with people and play games like

Also,

fetch. They can lern tricks like lying down and rolling over.

Practice!

Read your draft again. Add signal words to show your reader how important ideas are linked.

Think About It

Look at my revisions. Did I add facts that support my reasons? Have I used signal words to connect my ideas?

Editing Check Sentences

Sentence Fluency A variety of sentence structures makes the writing flow.

Writing Strategy Combine short, choppy sentences to make the writing flow.

I'll read my draft again, this time to make sure that I've used a variety of sentence structures. I found a lot of short, choppy sentences in my second paragraph. If I combine some of them, that will add variation and make my writing flow.

[DRAFT]

petted. Cats are very different. Cats do not go for walks. They

don't play games. ~~They don't~~ **or** learn tricks very easily. They don't

jump around. ~~They don't~~ **and** join in the fun.

combined short, choppy sentences

Practice!

Read through your draft. Combine short, choppy sentences to make your writing flow.

Editing Proofread Writing

Grammar/Mechanics
Spelling, punctuation, capitalization, and all five parts of a friendly letter are correct.

Writing Strategy Be sure I've used all five parts of a friendly letter correctly.

I'll check my spelling, capitalization, and punctuation. Then I'll check that my letter has all five parts. I'll also make sure that I've used capital letters and commas correctly. Here's my heading.

Writer's Term

Punctuating a Friendly Letter

Capitalize	Use Commas
• street	• between day and year
• city	
• state	• between city and state
• month	
• words in greeting	• after greeting
• closing	• after closing
• signature	

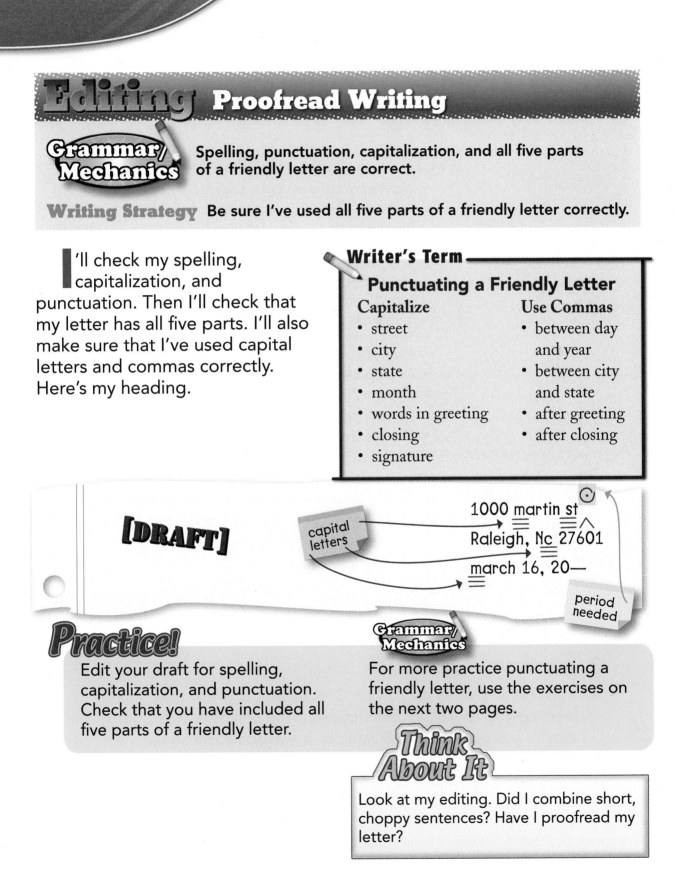

[DRAFT]

capital letters

1000 martin st
Raleigh, Nc 27601
march 16, 20—

period needed

Practice!
Edit your draft for spelling, capitalization, and punctuation. Check that you have included all five parts of a friendly letter.

Grammar/Mechanics
For more practice punctuating a friendly letter, use the exercises on the next two pages.

Think About It
Look at my editing. Did I combine short, choppy sentences? Have I proofread my letter?

Punctuating a Friendly Letter

A friendly letter has five parts.
- The **heading** gives your address and the date. Use a comma to separate the name of a city or town from the name of a state. Use another comma to separate the month and the day from the year.
- The **greeting** includes the name of the person you are writing to. It begins with a capital letter and ends with a comma.
- The **body** of the letter is your message.
- The **closing** is a friendly way to say good-bye. It begins with a capital letter and ends with a comma.
- The **signature** is your name.

A letter's envelope has two parts.
- The **address** of the person receiving the letter.
- The **return address** of the person sending the letter.

Practice the Rule

Use a separate piece of paper. Number your paper 1–7. Read the letter and envelope below and on the next page. Write the name of each numbered part of this friendly letter.

1. 32 Lake St.
Duluth, MN 50800
November 12, 20—

2. Dear Samuel,

3. Thanks for inviting me to visit. I really had a great time. I liked meeting your parents, and staying at the campsite was a lot of fun. Maybe you can come to Duluth for a visit sometime soon.

4. Your friend,

5. Chase

6. Chase Simons
32 Lake St.
Duluth, MN 50800

U.S.
POSTAGE

7. Samuel Taylor
100 West Street
Rivertown, MN 52045

Apply the Rule

Look at the following friendly letter. Nothing is in the right place! Rewrite the letter correctly on your paper. Be sure to rearrange the paragraphs so that the letter has an introduction, body, and conclusion that make sense. Don't forget to check that capital letters, commas, and punctuation are used correctly.

april 03. 20— greenville NC 27835

Think about the kind of dog you want and let us know. grandpa and I will do everything to help you get what you want.

love grandma

have you thought about the kind of dog you want? All puppies are much the same—little roly-poly bundles of energy. However, remember that they grow up. Do you want a big dog or a little dog. Do you want a dog with long hair or short hair! It's important to think about these things. dogs are loads of fun, but they also need feeding and grooming That will be your responsibility. dear Shamari,

5219 Lakeside Drive

Publishing Share Writing

Address an envelope, and ask my parents to mail my letter.

My persuasive friendly letter is finished. I used this assignment to write about something that really mattered to me. When it came time to publish it, I decided to mail the letter to my grandparents! There are other ways to publish a friendly letter, too. Some of my classmates used their computers to send their letters through e-mail.

Before I put my letter in the envelope, I looked it over one last time. Here's the publishing checklist I used.

My Checklist

- ✔ My letter clearly states an opinion.
- ✔ The letter has an introduction, one or more body paragraphs, and a conclusion.
- ✔ I used a personal tone that shows respect for my reader.
- ✔ Facts provide support for my reasons.
- ✔ Signal words connect ideas.
- ✔ Spelling, grammar, and punctuation are all correct.
- ✔ My handwriting is neat, and the five parts of a friendly letter are written correctly.

Practice!

Make a checklist to check your friendly letter. Then make a final draft. Don't forget to use your best handwriting! Address an envelope to the person you are writing to, and then mail the letter.

1000 Martin St.
Raleigh, NC 27601
March 16, 20—

Dear Grandma and Grandpa,

I am very grateful that you are going to get a pet for our family. Mom and Dad said we could have either a puppy or a kitten. I think you should get us a puppy. Dogs are much more fun than cats. Dogs are also more useful than cats.

Dogs have always made better pets than cats because dogs are more fun. First, dogs go on walks with people and play games like fetch. Also, they can learn tricks like lying down and rolling over. A dog will wag its tail, bark, and jump around. In addition, dogs are very loving animals. A dog will put its head on your lap or nuzzle you to be petted. However, cats are very different. Cats do not go for walks. They don't play games or learn tricks very easily. They don't jump around and join in the fun. Cats can be loving, but a cat has to be in the mood to be stroked or petted.

Dogs also make better pets than cats because dogs are useful to people. Some dogs are trained to assist or guide people. Others have saved or rescued their owners. Many dogs will bark if a stranger comes into their homes. Cats don't do these helpful kinds of things for their owners.

When you make your decision, I hope you will consider my reasons for getting a puppy. It's important to have a pet we can have fun with. It's also good to have a pet that can help us.

Love,

Shamari

Think About It

Use the rubric to check my friendly letter. Are all the traits of a good persuasive friendly letter there? How does your friendly letter compare against the rubric?

Ways to Publish a Friendly Letter

Persuasive friendly letters are a great way to share ideas and information with family and friends. One way to publish this type of letter is to mail it to the person it was written to. Here are some other creative ways to publish a friendly letter.

✓ Use a computer to send your letter electronically as e-mail.

✓ Make an audiotape, CD, or video of yourself reading the letter. Send your recording.

✓ Use your letter as the basis of a story or article that explains why you wrote the letter and describes what happened after you sent it.

✓ Read your letter to a small group. Ask classmates to discuss why they feel your letter is or is not persuasive.

✓ Exchange persuasive friendly letters with a classmate. Read each other's letter and write a letter in response.

Writing Across the Content Areas
Friendly Letter

You can write a persuasive friendly letter on just about any subject. Here are some ideas based on the subjects you study in school.

Science

- Research an issue of scientific importance. Find out what citizens can do to bring about change. Persuade a friend or relative to take action.
- Persuade your teacher, principal, or the PTA to organize and fund a science fair for your class.

Social Studies

- Imagine that you are an immigrant to a state or region you are studying. Write a letter to persuade a family member who stayed behind to join you in your new home.
- Persuade your parents to take action on a current school or community issue.

Language Arts

- Persuade a friend to try out for a speaking part in a school play.
- Convince the librarian that a certain book should be added to the school library.

PERSUASIVE test writing

Read the Writing Prompt

When you begin a writing test, the first thing you will read is the writing prompt. Most writing prompts have three parts.

Setup This part of the writing prompt gives you the background information you need to get ready for writing.

Task This part of the writing prompt tells you exactly what you're supposed to write: a persuasive essay to convince your community to support, or not to support, a law that requires bicyclists to wear a safety helmet.

Scoring Guide This section tells how your writing will be scored. To do well on the test, you should include everything on the list.

Think about the rubrics you've been using in this book. When you take a writing test, you don't always have all the information that a rubric gives you. No problem! The scoring guide lists everything you need to think about to write a good paper. Many scoring guides will include the six important traits of writing that are in the rubrics we've looked at:

Information/Organization · Content/Ideas · Sentence Fluency · Voice/Audience · Word Choice/Clarity · Grammar/Mechanics

Many states in the United States have laws that require bike riders to wear safety helmets. Even so, there is a lot of debate over whether these laws are helpful. Some people believe that wearing a helmet prevents injury and death. Others believe that the dangers of bicycling have been exaggerated, and that helmets should not be required.

Write a persuasive essay to persuade your community to support, or not to support, a law that requires bicyclists to wear a safety helmet.

Be sure your persuasive essay

- states an opinion and reasons and is organized from the strongest reason to the weakest.

- states your position in the opening sentence and includes only information that supports that opinion.

- includes details that strengthen explanations and reasons.

- explains the meaning of any unfamiliar words.

- has question-and-answer sentence patterns.

- has correct grammar, spelling, capitalization, and punctuation.

Writing Traits in the Scoring Guide

The scoring guide in the writing prompt on page 353 has been made into this chart. How is the information on this chart similar to the writing traits in the rubrics you've been using? Test prompts won't always include all of the six writing traits, but this one does! They can help you write your best persuasive essay.

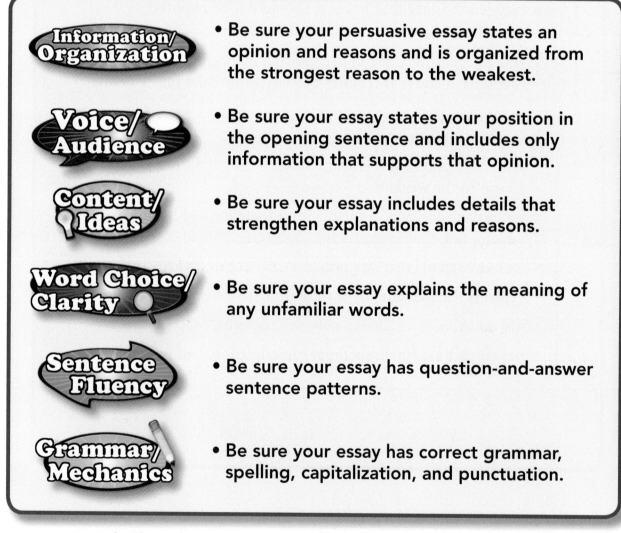

Information/Organization
- Be sure your persuasive essay states an opinion and reasons and is organized from the strongest reason to the weakest.

Voice/Audience
- Be sure your essay states your position in the opening sentence and includes only information that supports that opinion.

Content/Ideas
- Be sure your essay includes details that strengthen explanations and reasons.

Word Choice/Clarity
- Be sure your essay explains the meaning of any unfamiliar words.

Sentence Fluency
- Be sure your essay has question-and-answer sentence patterns.

Grammar/Mechanics
- Be sure your essay has correct grammar, spelling, capitalization, and punctuation.

Let's look at the persuasive essay by Jasmyn Hill on the next page. Did she follow the scoring guide?

Heads Up — We Need a Helmet Law

by Jasmyn Hill

We need a helmet law in this state, and we need it now. The law would require every bike rider under the age of 16 to wear a helmet. There are many reasons why this law is needed. The main reason is that a law would mean that more kids would wear helmets. This would save lives.

Let's take a look at a few facts. Every year bike accidents send about 500,000 children to the hospital or doctor's office. What's worse is that more than 600 of these children die. Up to four out of five of these deaths or serious injuries are caused by head injuries. The fact is that helmets protect the head. A bike helmet can cut the risk of head injury by up to 85 percent.

The sad truth is that very few children wear helmets while riding bikes. Studies show that only about 15 percent wear them all the time. Why do so few wear helmets? For some kids, one reason is fashion. They don't want to ruin their look with a helmet. Helmets, though, are far from unfashionable. Every official bike race requires riders to wear helmets. This means that all the very best bicycle riders wear helmets. Would anyone call Lance Armstrong unfashionable? I don't think so. He has won the Tour de France multiple times, and he always wears a helmet.

Another reason kids ride bareheaded—or without helmets—is that they say helmets are hot and uncomfortable. However, today's helmets are better than ever. They are lightweight, and they fit better. Many helmets are ventilated, which means they have holes in them to let in a cool breeze.

If kids would wear helmets voluntarily, or on their own, we wouldn't need a law. Studies have shown that helmet use increases greatly after a law is passed. In other words, helmet laws work. Today, at least 21 states have helmet laws. We need to follow the lead of these states and pass a helmet law here.

With all the dangers of daily life, it makes sense to do whatever we can to lessen the risk of injury. Wearing a helmet when riding a bike is one of the easiest ways to prevent serious injury and even death.

Using the Scoring Guide to Study the Model

Okay, let's use the scoring guide to check Jasmyn's writing test, "Heads Up—We Need a Helmet Law." See if you can find examples from her writing to show how well she did on each part of the scoring guide.

Information/Organization

- **The essay states an opinion and reasons and is organized from the strongest reason to the weakest.**

Jasmyn states her opinion very clearly in the first paragraph, the introduction of her essay. She believes a helmet law is needed right away. Each paragraph in the body of her essay supports her opinion with reasons. Take a look at her strongest reason.

> Let's take a look at a few facts. Every year bike accidents send about 500,000 children to the hospital or doctor's office.

Voice/Audience

- **The essay states a position in the opening sentence and includes only information that supports that opinion.**

Jasmyn's first sentence states her position. The reader knows immediately that she is in favor of a helmet law. The scoring guide also reminds you to keep all your reasons, facts, examples, and details focused on the opinion stated in the introduction. Jasmyn does a good job. Look at this example.

> The sad truth is that very few children wear helmets while riding bikes. Studies show that only about 15 percent wear them all the time. Why do so few wear helmets?

Content/Ideas

- The essay includes details that strengthen explanations and reasons.

The scoring guide tells you to include details that strengthen explanations and reasons. If you want to persuade the reader to accept your point of view, it's important to back up your statements with details. Jasmyn has included some really good facts to strengthen her claim that helmets are necessary for protection.

Every year bike accidents send about 500,000 children to the hospital or doctor's office. What's worse is that more than 600 of these children die. Up to four out of five of these deaths or serious injuries are caused by head injuries. The fact is that helmets protect the head. A bike helmet can cut the risk of head injury by up to 85 percent.

Word Choice/Clarity

- The essay explains the meaning of any unfamiliar words.

Words that are unfamiliar to the reader can cause confusion. The scoring guide reminds you that it's important to explain the meaning of unfamiliar words. In her essay, Jasmyn makes sure that she clarifies any words she thinks might be misunderstood by her reader.

Another reason kids ride bareheaded—or without helmets—is that they say helmets are hot and uncomfortable. However, today's helmets are better than ever. They are lightweight, and they fit better. Many helmets are ventilated, which means they have holes in them to let in a cool breeze.

Using the Scoring Guide to Study the Model

Sentence Fluency

• The essay has question-and-answer sentence patterns.

Your writing flows more smoothly for the reader when you use a variety of different sentence patterns. The scoring guide reminds you to use question-and-answer sentence patterns to add variety to your essay. In this example, Jasmyn uses a question-and-answer pattern to add variety and to highlight the point that wearing a helmet is not unfashionable.

Every official bike race requires riders to wear helmets. This means that all the very best bicycle riders wear helmets. Would anyone call Lance Armstrong unfashionable? I don't think so. He has won the Tour de France multiple times, and he always wears a helmet.

Grammar/Mechanics

• The essay has correct grammar, spelling, capitalization, and punctuation.

Looking back at the scoring guide, you can see the reminder to check your grammar, spelling, capitalization, and punctuation. Don't overlook this step! Check your essay for mistakes you made and correct them. Watch for errors that you make often. Jasmyn has done a good job in her essay. Her final draft is free from errors.

Planning My Time

Before giving us the writing prompt, my teacher always tells us how much time we have to complete the test. Since I know how much time I have, I can plan how to use it. First, I think about how much time I have. Then, I divide the time into the different parts of the writing process. In my plan, I always give myself some time to study the writing prompt. Here's how I divide my time into four steps.

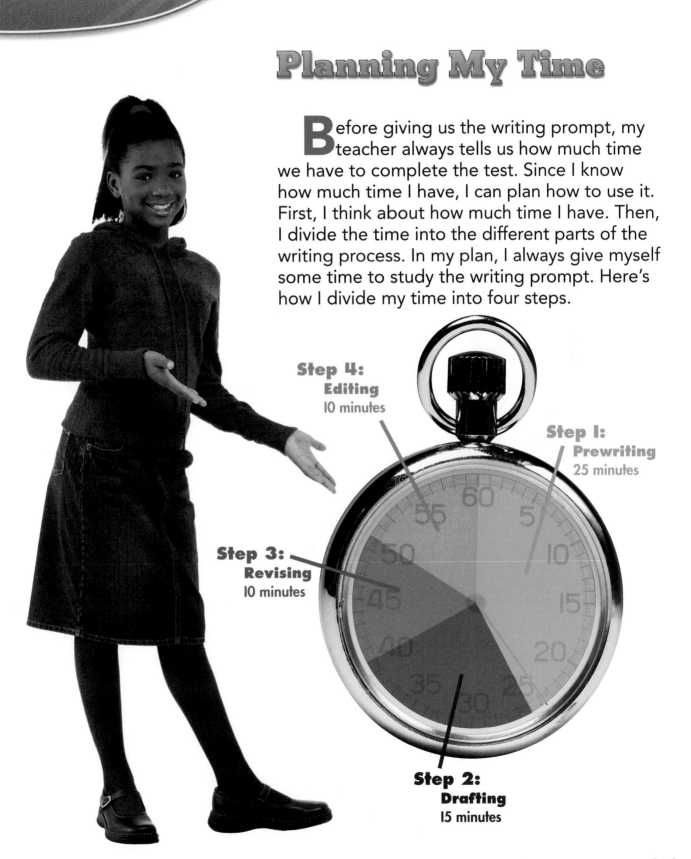

Step 4:
Editing
10 minutes

Step 1:
Prewriting
25 minutes

Step 3:
Revising
10 minutes

Step 2:
Drafting
15 minutes

Prewriting Study the Writing Prompt

Information/Organization

Writing Strategy Study the writing prompt to be sure I know what to do.

Once my teacher has given me the writing prompt, I study it to make sure I know exactly what I'm supposed to do. Remember that most writing prompts have three parts. You should find each part and label it: the setup, the task, and the scoring guide. Then, you can circle key parts in the writing prompt that tell you what kind of writing to do and what to write about. Look below to see how I did this.

My Writing Test Prompt

Setup — Many people believe that music lessons provide benefits for children beyond musical knowledge or skill. Moreover, they believe all children should have some kind of musical training.

Task — Write a persuasive essay to convince parents in your school that all children (or not all children) should take music lessons.

Scoring Guide — Be sure your persuasive essay

- states an opinion and reasons and is organized from the strongest reason to the weakest.
- states your position in the opening sentence and includes only information that supports that opinion.
- includes details that strengthen explanations and reasons.
- explains the meaning of any unfamiliar words.
- has question-and-answer sentence patterns.
- has correct grammar, spelling, capitalization, and punctuation.

Now that I've studied the prompt, I'll think about how the scoring guide relates to the six writing traits I've studied in the rubrics. All the writing traits might not be included in every scoring guide, but I need to remember them all in order to write a good essay.

- Be sure your essay states an opinion and reasons and is organized from the strongest reason to the weakest.

I'll use a graphic organizer to help me organize my reasons from the strongest to the weakest.

- Be sure your essay states your position in the opening sentence and includes only information that supports that opinion.

I'll let my reader know what my position is. I'll keep all of my information focused on that opinion.

- Be sure your essay includes details that strengthen explanations and reasons.

I'll need to present strong explanations and reasons. Details like facts and examples will help.

- Be sure your essay explains the meaning of any unfamiliar words.

I'll clarify any words my reader might not know.

- Be sure your essay has question-and-answer sentence patterns.

I can use questions and answers to highlight important points and get the reader thinking about them.

- Be sure your essay has correct grammar, spelling, capitalization, and punctuation.

Whenever I write anything, I always check grammar, spelling, capitalization, and punctuation.

Prewriting Gather Information

Information/Organization

Writing Strategy Respond to the task.

Writers gather information to help them write. This is a key step when you write for a test. You can gather a lot of information from the writing prompt. Take another look at the task in the writing prompt. The task explains what you are supposed to write.

From my writing prompt, I know I'm supposed to write a persuasive essay. I also know the topic. First, I'll decide on my opinion, and then I'll quickly jot down some of my reasons for it.

Task — Write a persuasive essay to convince parents in your school that all children (or not all children) should take music lessons.

My Opinion: Yes, all children should take music lessons!
Reasons to Support My Opinion:

It's great to learn how to make music—music is forever.

Kids have less time for video games & television.

Music lessons make children smarter in math and language.

Kids learn to concentrate and keep trying.

When you get better, you have interesting opportunities.

Remember! Take time to think about how you'll respond to the task part of the writing prompt before you write. To gather information, decide on your opinion, and then quickly jot down some reasons that support your position.

Prewriting Organize Ideas

Information/Organization

Writing Strategy Choose a graphic organizer.

I need to start organizing my ideas. A good graphic organizer for a persuasive essay is an Order-of-Importance Organizer. It will help me put my list of reasons in order from most important to least important.

Most Important: Music lessons make children smarter in math and language.

Next in Importance: Kids learn to concentrate and keep trying.

Next in Importance: Kids have less time for video games & television.

Next in Importance: It's great to learn how to make music—music is forever.

Least Important: When you get better, you have interesting opportunities.

Think About It

Look at my graphic organizer. Does it include the reasons I'll need to write a good persuasive essay?

Remember! Choose the best graphic organizer for the assignment. Use it to organize the reasons that support your opinion from the strongest to the weakest.

Prewriting Check the Scoring Guide

Information/Organization

Writing Strategy Check my graphic organizer against the scoring guide.

In a writing test, you don't always have much time to revise. That's why prewriting is so important! So, before I start drafting, I'll check my Order-of-Importance Organizer against the scoring guide in the writing prompt.

Most Important: Music lessons make children smarter in math and language.

Next in Importance: Kids learn to concentrate and keep trying.

Next in Importance: Kids have less time for video games & television.

Next in Importance: It's great to learn how to make music—music is forever.

Least Important: When you get better, you have interesting opportunities.

Information/Organization

• states an opinion and reasons and is organized from the strongest reason to the weakest.

I'll state my opinion in the introduction of my essay. Since my graphic organizer arranges my reasons from strongest to weakest, I'll use it as a guide while I write.

Voice/Audience

• states your position in the opening sentence and includes only information that supports that opinion.

I'll be sure to start off by clearly stating my position. I'll keep all the information focused on that opinion.

Content/Ideas

• includes details that strengthen explanations and reasons.

My notes and organizer don't have a lot of details, but I can add these as I write my draft.

Word Choice/Clarity

• explains the meaning of any unfamiliar words.

As I write and edit my draft, I'll look for words that might need explaining.

Sentence Fluency

• has question-and-answer sentence patterns.

There are no questions in my organizer, so I will have to remember to use questions and answers to highlight important points.

Grammar/Mechanics

• has correct grammar, spelling, capitalization, and punctuation.

I need to check my grammar, spelling, capitalization, and punctuation when I edit my draft.

Remember! Before you begin drafting, look back at the scoring guide in the writing prompt. Be sure that you understand everything you need to do.

Think About It

Does my graphic organizer cover all the points in the scoring guide? What else do I need to include?

Drafting **Write a Draft**

Voice/Audience

Writing Strategy State my position in the opening sentence. Make sure everything in my essay supports my opinion.

A good persuasive essay lets the reader know right away what point of view the writer has on the issue. So, I'll state my position. Next I'll use my Order-of-Importance Organizer as a guide for writing the body of my essay. It reminds me of the reasons that support my opinion.

[DRAFT]

Music Lessons: Good for Your Child, Now and Forever
by Shamari

my position

All parents should consider haveing their kids take music lessons. Many kids will be glad they took the lessons when they get older. They'll find that taking music lessons has had many positive effects on them, helping them in many ways.

Studys by scientists have shown that taking music lessons can make children smarter. Music students are learning more than how to play notes. They are learning how to concentrate and to

Proofreading Marks

⌐ Indent	ℓ Take out something
≡ Make a capital	⊙ Add a period
/ Make a small letter	⨍ New paragraph
∧ Add something	ⓢ Spelling error

keep trying until they reach their goals. Learning music also helps children get better at math and at language That means that kids who take music lessons are more likely to be able to learn other subjects faster and easier, too.

Another good thing about taking music lessons is that kids will use less of their leisure time playing video games or watching television. Not only do music students have to spend some time taking the lessons, they also have to practice.

Finally, as kids get better at playing the instruments of their choice, they will have other opportunities.

Playing a musical instrument is a talent that kids can carry with them into adulthood. That's why it's important for them to at least try taking music lessons with their parents' incouragement and support.

Think About It

Read my draft. Does my essay begin with a clear statement of my position? Does all the information that follows support my opinion?

Remember! Every persuasive essay needs a clear opinion and strong reasons. Your essay should begin with a sentence that clearly states your position. Then, all the information that follows should support the opinion.

Revising Extend Writing

Content/ Ideas

Writing Strategy Strengthen any explanations or reasons that seem weak.

Now that I've written my draft, I'll check it against the scoring guide. I want to be sure I've included all the points I'll be graded on.

I've clearly stated my position in the opening sentence. All of the information I've included supports that opinion. But I do see where one of my reasons seems weak because I don't have any details to support it. If I'm going to persuade the reader to accept my opinion, I'd better add more details to strengthen that reason.

[DRAFT]

Finally, as kids get better at playing the instruments of their

choice, they will have other opportunities.
∧

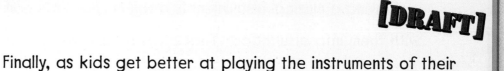
They might choose to join the school band, for example. When they get older, they may even consider a career as a musician or a teacher. ← added details

Remember! Read your draft. Do some of your reasons or explanations seem weak? Add details that will strengthen them.

Revising Clarify Writing

Word Choice/ Clarity

Writing Strategy Explain the meaning of any unfamiliar words.

The scoring guide reminds me to explain the meaning of any words that may be unfamiliar to my reader. This will make my essay easier to read and understand. I'll read my draft again. If I find any words that might be unclear or confusing, I'll add an explanation.

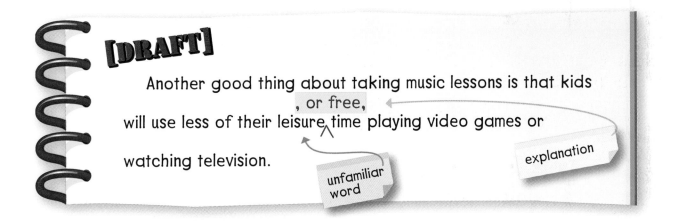

[DRAFT]

Another good thing about taking music lessons is that kids

, or free,

will use less of their leisure time playing video games or

watching television.

unfamiliar word

explanation

Remember! Read your draft. Explain any words that may be unfamiliar to your reader.

Think About It

Look at my revisions. Did I add details to strengthen my reason? Did I clarify the meaning of unfamiliar words?

Editing Check Sentences

Sentence Fluency

Writing Strategy Use question-and-answer sentence patterns.

As I read through my draft again, I noticed a spot where a question-and-answer sentence pattern would make my writing more interesting and would highlight the point I'm trying to make as well.

[DRAFT]

Another good thing about taking music lessons is that kids
, or free,
will use less of their leisure time playing video games or

watching television. Not only do music students have to spend

some time taking the lessons, they also have to practice.

question-and-answer sentence pattern

After all, how many of those games or TV shows will they be able to use or enjoy when they grow up? Probably none, and music is forever.

Remember! Include question-and-answer sentence patterns to make your writing more interesting and to call attention to an important point you're trying to make.

Editing Proofread Writing

Grammar/Mechanics

Writing Strategy Check the grammar, spelling, capitalization, and punctuation.

The scoring guide reminds me to check and correct my grammar and spelling. I also need to make sure that I've used capitalization and punctuation correctly. It's a good thing that I planned how to use my time. Now I have time to check for errors.

Music Lessons: Good for Your Child, Now and Forever
by Shamari

[FINAL DRAFT]

All parents should consider ~~haveing~~ having their kids take music

lessons. Many kids will be glad they took the lessons when they

get older. They'll find that taking music lessons has had many

positive effects on them, helping them in many ways.

~~Studys~~ Studies by scientists have shown that taking music lessons can

make children smarter. Music students are learning more than

how to play notes. They are learning how to concentrate and to

keep trying until they reach their goals. Learning music also

helps children get better at math and at language. That means

Remember! Every time you write for a test, you need to check your grammar, spelling, capitalization, and punctuation.

[FINAL DRAFT]

that kids who take music lessons are more likely to be able to learn other subjects faster and easier, too.

Another good thing about taking music lessons is that kids
, or free,
will use less of their leisure time playing video games or watching television. Not only do music students have to spend some time taking the lessons, they also have to practice. After all, how many of those games or TV shows will they be able to use or enjoy when they grow up? Probably none, and music is forever.

Finally, as kids get better at playing the instruments of their choice, they will have other opportunities. They might choose to join the school band, for example. When they get older, they may even consider a career as a musician or a teacher.

Playing a musical instrument is a talent that kids can carry with them into adulthood. That's why it's important for them to at least try taking music lessons with their parents' encouragement ~~incouragement~~ and support.

Think About It

Use the scoring guide to check my persuasive essay. Did I include everything I will be graded on?

Wow! We're done! We used information in the writing prompt and the six writing traits to complete a persuasive essay. Remember these important tips when you write for a test.

TEST TIPS

1. **Study the writing prompt before you begin to write.** Most writing prompts have three parts: the setup, the task, and the scoring guide. Remember, they won't be labeled. You'll have to figure them out for yourself.

2. **Make sure you understand the task before you begin to write.**
   - Find and label the three parts of the writing prompt. Then read them carefully.
   - Circle key words in the task. These tell you what kind of writing you need to do.
   - Read the scoring guide. Make sure you know how you'll be graded.

3. **Plan your time. Then keep an eye on the clock.** Be sure you know exactly how much time you will have to write. Then decide how much time you'll spend on each part of the writing process. Stick to your plan as closely as possible. Give yourself time to revise and edit your draft.

4. **Use the scoring guide to check your draft.** A scoring guide on a writing test is like a rubric, and it's a valuable writing tool. Like the rubrics you've used on other papers, it reminds you of what is important. Reread your draft at least twice, and compare it to the scoring guide. Make sure that it does what the scoring guide says it should do.

5. **Plan and use your time carefully.** Leave yourself time to carefully read your draft a final time and make any necessary corrections.

6. **Write neatly.** Remember, the people who score your test must be able to read it!

WRITER'S HANDBOOK

The Writer's Handbook will give you more help and some great hints for making your writing the best it can be. Use the Writer's Handbook any time you have more questions or just need a little extra help.

Table of Contents

Writer's Terms

Appositive is a restatement or definition of a term. It is set off by commas.

Argument is a set of reasons to support an opinion.

Attribute is a quality or characteristic of something.

Attribute Chart is a chart that organizes information about how two things are alike or different.

Audience is the person or people who will read or hear what you write.

Body is the main part of a writing piece.

Character Chart is a chart that lists specific details about a character, such as looks, thoughts, and actions.

Characters are people in a story, play, movie, or show.

Choppy Sentences are sentences that are all short and simple. Too many choppy sentences in a row cause writing not to flow well.

Cliché is an expression used so often that it became stale, such as **white as snow**.

Climax is the most exciting or important moment in a story.

Comparison is writing or thinking about how two things are the same.

Conclusion is the last paragraph of a long paper that ties up loose ends and summarizes all the main points.

Conflict is the problem in a story that has to be solved.

Contrast is writing or thinking about how two things are different.

Detail is a fact, example, or other information that supports a main idea.

Detail Sentence is a sentence that gives details to support the topic sentence.

Dialogue is the talking that goes on between characters in a story.

Dictionary is a reference book which contains the definitions and parts of speech of words.

Direct Quotation is the exact words of a person from a story. Direct quotations are set off with quotation marks.

Encyclopedia is a reference book, or set of books, with information about many different topics.

Example is an idea or occurrence that illustrates the main idea of a paper.

Fact is a statement that can be proven to be true.

Figurative Language is language that creates a picture in the reader's mind, usually through comparison.

First Person is telling a story from the point of view of the author, by using words such as **I, me,** and **we.**

Introduction is the first paragraph of a paper that states the main idea.

Lead is the first sentence of a piece of writing, which should grab the reader's attention.

Lead Character is the most important character in a story.

Loaded Words are words with added meanings that may cause the reader to have strong feelings about the topic.

Metaphor is a way of comparing two different things by calling one thing another. **Example: Amelia** was a graceful **butterfly,** floating across the dance floor.

Writer's Terms continued

Narrator is the person that tells a story.

Network Tree is a graphic organizer used to organize opinions, reasons, and facts. The writer's opinion goes at the top of the tree. Reasons for the opinion go on the next level. Facts and other details go on the lowest level.

Neutral Words are unbiased words that do not have added meanings that cause feelings in a reader.

Main Idea is the most important thought about a topic that is supported by details.

Main Idea Table is a chart that shows how a main idea is supported by details. The details "hold up" or support the main ideas.

Network Tree is a chart that organizes information about a topic. The topic or opinion goes at the top, with the main ideas or reasons on the next level. The bottom level contains facts to support the main ideas or reasons.

Opinion is a belief that cannot be proven true.

Order-of-Importance Organizer is a chart that shows reasons in order of their importance. The most important reason goes first, and the least important reason goes last.

Paragraph is a group of sentences that focus on one main idea or thought.

Parts of a Friendly Letter are the **heading,** the **greeting,** the **body,** the **closing,** and the **signature**.

Personal Tone is a warm and friendly way of writing.

Point of View is how the reader knows who is telling the story.

Plot is the combination of events that happen in a story.

Problem is a difficult situation that a character in a story or a person in real life must overcome.

Resolution is the way a character in a story overcomes a difficult situation.

Run-on Sentence is a sentence made up of two other sentences without the correct conjunction and punctuation.

Sentence Fragment is an incomplete thought. It is missing a subject, a predicate, or both.

Sentence Pattern is the use of sentences to add impact to writing. For example, the question-and-answer sentence pattern is often used in persuasive essays.

Sequence Chain is a chart that shows steps or events in the order in which they happen.

Setting is the time and place in which a story happens.

Signal Words are words that help tie ideas together and show that the writing is moving from one idea to another.

Simile is a way of comparing two different things using the words **like** or **as**. Example: Gabe is as clever as a fox.

Sincere Voice is when a person writes in a clear and honest way.

Spider Map is a graphic organizer that organizes information about a topic. The topic goes in the center. Categories about the topic go on the spiders "legs." Then specific details about the categories can be attached to the spider's "legs".

Story Map is a chart that organizes the setting, characters, problem, events, and ending of a story.

Suspense is a feeling of excitement that comes from not knowing what will happen.

Thesaurus is a reference book, similar to a dictionary, which lists **synonyms,** or words with similar meanings, and **antonyms,** or words with opposite meanings.

Third Person is telling a story in a way that shows that the writer is watching it happen but is not personally involved, by using words such as **he, she,** and **they**.

Time Line is a graph that shows events in the order in which they happened.

Time-Order Words are words that tell when something happened, such as **after, first, then,** or **finally**.

Topic Sentence is a sentence that states the main idea of a whole paragraph.

Tone is how the writing sounds to the reader. It may be funny, serious, or suspenseful. The tone of writing often depends on the purpose of the writing.

Voice is the unique way each writer expresses his or her ideas.

Word Picture is a descriptive device to help readers "see" the character or event as they read.

Web is a graphic organizer that organizes information about one main topic. The main topic goes in the center circle. Related details go in the outside circles.

Prewriting

Brainstorming

Brainstorming is a great way to generate many ideas in a short amount of time. You can brainstorm alone or with a group of people. Here's how it works: Think of the initial assignment. Write down words related to the assignment as they come to mind. Eventually, you will find the one word or phrase that will become the topic for your essay.

Journaling

A journal is similar to a diary. However, diaries are usually used to record daily events and feelings and we generally use journals to record thoughts, impressions, and responses to events. A journal is a great way to generate ideas for writing.

Freewriting

Freewriting is very unusual because it has no form. Write down everything that comes to mind during a specific period of time. When time is up, stop writing and look at what you've got. Read it over a couple of times. You'll be amazed at what you might find. Some of the best ideas for writing show up in the middle of freewriting.

Reading

Sometimes the easiest way to get ideas for writing is to read. How can you write about something you don't know about? Talk to your school librarian or go to the public library and ask for help at the information desk. As you read, take notes on things that interest you. The more you know, the more ideas for writing you will have.

Interviewing

An interview is the process of asking questions of another person and listening to and recording that person's answers. Interviews make good sources for writing projects, especially if the person you interview is an expert about your topic. Interviews can also be good ways to generate ideas for writing.

Note Taking

As you are doing research for your writing project, you will want to take notes. That way you will have the most important information in small pieces that you can use easily. However, taking notes can be tricky, especially for the beginner. Here are some things to keep in mind:

✓ Keep your notes short. You don't have to use complete sentences, as long as you include the important information.

✓ Make sure your handwriting is legible. If you scribble, you may not be able to read your own notes later.

✓ Use note cards. That way you can arrange your notes without having to rewrite them. Try using different colors of note cards to help you organize your notes.

✓ When listening to a speaker and taking notes, don't try to write down what the speaker is saying "word for word." Just make sure you get the important stuff.

✓ When you are interviewing, however, you will want to get the exact words down on paper. In this case, ask the speaker to repeat what he or she said, so you can write the quote. If it's possible, use a tape recorder during the interview, so you can listen to the quote as often as you need to. Just make sure you get the speaker's permission to record the interview.

✓ It's important to write down the source of your information on your note cards as you are taking notes. That way you can cite or credit your sources easily.

Research

When you look for information about a topic, you are doing research. It is important to use good sources.

Source

A source is anything or anyone with information.

Primary Source

Diaries, journals, and other writings of people who lived during the described events are considered primary sources.

Secondary Sources

Books or people who use other books or people to get information are called secondary sources.

How to Cite Sources

(Use punctuation and capitalization as shown.)

- Books: Author's Last Name, First Name. Book Title. City: Publishing Company, year.
- Magazine Articles: Author's Last Name, First Name. "Title of Article."

  Title of Magazine, volume number (if there is one), date, month, or season, and year of publication: page number. (If the article is longer than one page, state the first page and the last page of the article with a dash between them.)
- Encyclopedias/Dictionaries: Title of Encyclopedia or Dictionary, edition number (ed. __), s.v. "item." (If you looked up Olympic Games, it would be s.v. "Olympic Games.")
- Letters/Diaries/Journals: Mention them in the text as you are writing, rather than citing them later.
- Internet: State the Web address of the Web sites you used. Most Web addresses will begin with **http://** and end with **.com, .net, .org,** or **.edu**.
- Films/Videos: Title of Film or Video. City where the production company is located: Production Company Name, year.

Outlining

An outline helps you put your information in the order it will appear in your writing. It can be divided into the introduction, the body, and the conclusion. Every letter and number in the outline stands for something in your essay. Words or phrases that are shown with Roman numerals represent entire chunks of an essay. Words or phrases that are shown with capital letters represent paragraphs, which support a main statement or idea. Here's a basic outline.

I. Introduction
   A. Lead
   B. Related statement
   C. Transitional statement

II. Body
   A. First main idea
      1. First supporting detail
      2. Second supporting detail
      3. Third supporting detail
   B. Second main idea
      1. First supporting detail
      2. Second supporting detail
      3. Third supporting detail
   C. Third main idea
      1. First supporting detail
      2. Second supporting detail
      3. Third supporting detail

III. Conclusion
   A. Brief summary of main ideas
   B. Other related statement
   C. Closing statement

Grammar/Mechanics

Capitalization

Capitalize
- the first word in a sentence.
- people's names and the names of particular places.
- titles of respect and titles that are part of names.
- initials of names.
- place names and words formed from them.
- the months of the year and the days of the week.
- important words in the names of groups.
- important words in the names of holidays.
- the first word in the greeting or closing of a letter.
- the word **I**.
- the most important words in a title.
- the first word in a direct quotation.

Sentences

A sentence is a group of words that tells a complete thought.
A sentence has two parts: a **subject** and a **predicate**.

- The complete subject tells who or what the sentence is about.
    Example: The runners are ready.
- The complete predicate tells what happened.
    Example: The people in the stands **watched excitedly**.

A **compound sentence** is made of two simple sentences connected by a comma and a conjunction.

Subject-Verb Agreement

A subject and its verb must agree in number. Add **-s** or **-es** to a verb in the present tense when the subject is a singular noun or **he, she,** or **it**. Do not add **-s** if the subject is a plural noun or if the subject is **I, you, we,** or **they**.

Examples: My **sister reads** about urban wildlife in her social studies class.

The **students read** about how to protect the animals.

I like stories about wildlife, too.

Abbreviations and Initials

Abbreviations are shortened forms of words. Many abbreviations begin with a capital letter and end with a period. An initial is the first letter of a name. An initial is written as a capital letter and a period.

Abbreviate

- titles of address.

  Mister (Mr. Fred K. Mitchel); Mistress (Mrs. Janet Noda); Doctor (Dr. L. M. Roberto); Junior (Greg Ward, Jr.)

  Note: Ms. is a title of address used for women. It is not an abbreviation, but it requires a period. (Ms. Lynn Murphy)

- words used in addresses.

  Street (St.); Avenue (Ave.); Route (Rte.); Boulevard (Blvd.); Road (Rd.)

- days of the week.

  Sunday (Sun.); Monday (Mon.); Tuesday (Tues.); Wednesday (Wed.); Thursday (Thurs.); Friday (Fri.); Saturday (Sat.)

- months of the year.

  January (Jan.); February (Feb.); March (Mar.); April (Apr.); August (Aug.); September (Sept.); October (Oct.); November (Nov.); December (Dec.); (May, June, and July are not usually abbreviated.)

- directions.

  North (N); East (E); South (S); West (W)

Quotation Marks

Quotation marks are used to separate a speaker's exact words from the rest of the sentence. Begin a **direct quotation** with a capital letter. Use a comma to separate the direct quotation from the speaker's name. When a direct quotation comes at the end of a sentence, put the end mark inside the last quotation mark. When writing a conversation, begin a new paragraph with each change of speaker.

Example:

> Elise said, "I'm going to adopt a kitten from the shelter."
>
> Elise had wanted a pet for a long time. Her parents thought she was ready to help take care of a pet.
>
> "I'll go with you," said Jason. "I might find a cat or dog that I might like to adopt, too!"

End Marks

Every sentence must end with a **period,** an **exclamation point,** or a **question mark**.

- Use a **period** at the end of a statement or a command.
  Statement: My favorite colors are blue and green.
  Command: Please put on your life jacket before going in the lake.
- Use an **exclamation point** at the end of a firm command or at the end of a sentence that shows strong feeling or excitement.
  Command: Watch out for the jellyfish!
  Exclamation: What a beautiful sunrise!
- Use a **question mark** at the end of an asking sentence.
  Question: How many colors are in a rainbow?

Commas

Commas in Sentences

Use a comma

- after an introductory word in a sentence.

  Example: Yes, Rebecca and Todd's wedding was beautiful!

- to separate items in a series.

  Example: She carried white, yellow, and pink flowers.

- when speaking directly to a person.

  Example: "Laura, would you sing another song?"

- to separate a direct quotation from the speaker's name.

  Example: "I hope they take a lot of pictures," said Scott.

- with **and, or,** or **but** when combining sentences.

  Example: Lynda liked spice cake best, but Chris preferred chocolate.

Commas in Letters

Use a comma:

- after the greeting and closing of a friendly letter.

  Examples: Dear Taylor,

  Yours truly, Hayley

- after the city and before the state in the heading of a letter.

  Example: Columbus, OH

- after the day of the month and before the year in the heading of a letter.

  Example: September 7, 2003

Parts of Speech

Nouns

- A **singular noun** names one person, place, or thing.
  Examples: boy   hillside   book
- A **plural noun** names more than one person, place, or thing.
  To make most singular nouns plural, add **-s**.
  Examples: boys   hillsides   books
- For nouns ending in **sh, ch, x,** or **z,** add **-es** to make the noun plural.
  Examples: brush/brushes   bunch/bunches   fox/foxes
- For nouns ending in a consonant and **y,** change the **y** to **i** and add **-es**.
  Example: family/families
- For most nouns that end in **f** or **fe,** replace **f** or **fe** with **ves** to make the noun plural.
  Example: wolf/wolves
- Some words change spelling when the plural is formed.
  Examples: man/men   child/children   person/people
  woman/women   mouse/mice   goose/geese
- Some words have the same singular and plural form.
  Examples: deer/deer   sheep/sheep   moose/moose

Verbs

- An **action verb** shows action in a sentence.

    Example: We **study** many subjects in school.

- Sometimes a **helping verb** is needed to help the main verb show action. A helping verb comes before a main verb.

    Example: We **will study** many new things this year.

- Verbs can tell about the present, the past, or the future.

    Examples: We **learn** about how to protect the environment.

    Last week, we **learned** about the rain forests.

    Next week, we **will learn** about protecting our oceans.

To show past action, **-ed** is added to most verbs. Verbs that do not add **-ed** are called **irregular verbs**.

Some common irregular verbs are:

Present	Past	With *have, has,* or *had*
bring	brought	brought
eat	ate	eaten
give	gave	given
go	went	gone
ring	rang	rung
take	took	taken

- A **linking verb** connects the subject of a sentence to a word or words in the predicate that tell about the subject. Linking verbs include **am, is, are, was,** and **were**. **Seem** and **become** are linking verbs, too.

Pronouns

A **pronoun** can replace a noun naming a person, place, or thing. Pronouns include **I, me, you, we, us, he, she, it, they,** and **them**.

- A pronoun may take the place of the subject of a sentence.

    Example: Daryn likes to run, hike, and lift weights.

    He likes to run, hike, and lift weights.

- A pronoun may replace a noun that is the object of a preposition.

    Example: Hanna threw the ball to **Lakesha**.

    Hanna threw the ball to **her**.

- A **demonstrative pronoun** talks about things that are either nearby or far away. Use **this** and **these** to talk about one or more things that are nearby.

    Examples: This is my favorite tennis racket.

    These are good shoes for running.

    Use **that** and **those** to talk about things that are far away.

    Example: That is a good place to watch the race.

    Those are new bleachers.

Adjectives

- An **adjective** describes a noun or a pronoun.

    Examples: The mountains are **huge**.

    They are also **beautiful**.

Adverbs

- An **adverb** is usually used to describe a verb. Many adverbs end in **-ly**.

    Example: The family spoke **excitedly** of their vacation.

- **Very** is an adverb meaning "to a high degree" or "extremely." Never use **real** in place of **very**.

    Incorrect: Tori was **real** excited about the boat ride.

    Correct: Tori was **very** excited about the boat ride.

Comparisons

- To compare two people, places, or things, add **-er** to most adjectives and adverbs.

    Example: The chocolate milkshake is **thick**. That vanilla milkshake is even **thicker**.

- To compare three or more items, add **-est** to most adjectives and adverbs.

    Example: The strawberry milkshake is the **thickest**.

- The words **more** and **most** can also be used to compare two or more persons, places, or things.

    Example: Rico is excited about helping with the project.

    Francis is **more excited** about helping with the project.

    Samantha is the **most excited** of all.

- Sometimes the words **good** and **bad** are used to compare. These words change forms in comparisons.

    Examples: This apple tastes **good**. The orange tastes **better**. The peaches are the **best**.

    The weather is **bad** today. It is going to be **worse** tomorrow. It is supposed to be the **worst** on Monday.

    Note: Use **better** or **worse** to compare two things. Use **best** or **worst** to compare three or more things.

Prepositions

- A **preposition** helps tell **when, where,** or **how**. Prepositions include the words **in, at, under,** and **over**.

  Example: Miguel looked **at** the map.

Common Prepositions

about	beneath	inside	under
above	beside	near	underneath
across	between	of	until
after	beyond	off	unto
against	by	on	up
along	down	out	of
upon	amid	during	outside
with	among	except	over
within	around	except for	through
without	before	for	till
behind	from	to	below
in	toward		

Conjunctions

The words **and, or,** and **but** are **conjunctions**.

- Conjunctions may be used to join words within a sentence.

  Examples: Miguel wanted to go to the mountains **and** the ocean.

  His father said they could go to the mountains **or** the ocean.

  The mountains are beautiful **but** far away.

- Conjunctions can be used to join two or more sentences. When using a conjunction to join sentences, put a comma before the conjunction.

  Examples: We can go for a jog on the beach, **or** we can play ball.

  Miguel wanted to jog, **but** Cynthia wanted to play ball.

  Miguel jogged, **and** Cynthia played ball.

Homophones

Some words sound alike but have different spellings and meanings. These words are called **homophones**.

Here is a list of some homophones often confused in writing:

- **are** — is a form of the verb **be**.
- **our** — is a possessive noun.
- **hour** — is sixty minutes.
- **its** — is a possessive pronoun.
- **it's** — is a contraction of the words **it is**.
- **there** — means "in that place."
- **their** — is a possessive pronoun. It shows something belongs to more than one person or thing.
- **they're** — is a contraction made from the words **they are**.
- **two** — is a number.
- **to** — means "toward."
- **too** — means "also." It can also mean "more than enough."
- **your** — is a possessive pronoun.
- **you're** — is a contraction made from the words **you are**.

Signal Words

Signal words help writers move from one idea to another. Here is a list of some common signal words.

Time-Order Signal Words

after	first	later	next
before	meanwhile	immediately	when
during	until	finally	then

Comparison/Contrast Signal Words

in the same way	like	as well	also
but	however	otherwise	yet
still	even though	although	on the other hand

Concluding or Summarizing Signal Words

as a result	finally	in conclusion	to sum up
therefore	lastly	in summary	all in all

Listening, Speaking, and Thinking

Listening

These tips will help you be a good listener:

- Listen carefully when others are speaking.
- Keep in mind your reason for listening. Are you listening to learn about a topic? To be entertained? To get directions? Decide what you should get out of the listening experience.
- Look directly at the speaker. Doing this will help you concentrate on what he or she has to say.
- Do not interrupt the speaker or talk to others while the speaker is talking.
- Ask questions when the speaker is finished talking if there is anything you did not understand.

Speaking

These guidelines can help you become an effective speaker.

Giving Oral Reports

- Be prepared. Know exactly what you are going to talk about and how long you will speak. Have your notes in front of you.
- Speak slowly and clearly. Speak loudly enough so everyone can hear you.
- Look at your audience.

Taking Part in Discussions

- Listen to what others have to say.
- Disagree politely. Let others in the group know you respect their points of view.
- Try not to interrupt others. Everyone should have a chance to speak.

Thinking

Writers use a variety of thinking skills as they work through the writing process. These skills include logic, analyzing, setting goals, creativity, and problem solving. As you write, keep these skills in mind and try to put them to use as much as possible.

Logic

Writers use logic to support a point of view by using reasoning, facts, and examples.

Analyzing

Analyzing is a thinking skill that requires the writer to think about and examine the information learned about a topic. Once the information is examined, a general conclusion or more meaningful understanding can be made about the topic.

Setting Goals

When setting goals, writers must think about deadlines (when the assignment is due; how much time there is for prewriting, drafting, revising, editing, and publishing), the objective of the writing assignment, and the amount of research required.

Creativity

Using creativity means using the imagination. Writers let their minds wonder about many different ways to tackle an assignment before finally settling on one. It is often necessary to start an assignment, stop, try it a different way, stop again, and maybe even go back to the original idea. Thinking creatively and openly allows the writer to examine many options.

Problem Solving

Learning to problem solve helps writers make decisions about the writing assignment and helps them use facts and opinions correctly. Strategies for problem solving include naming the problem; thinking of everything about the problem; thinking of ways to solve the problem; choosing the best plan to solve the problem and trying it out; and analyzing the result.